DISTANT REPLAY

DISTANT REPLAY

Jerry Kramer

—— with ——

Dick Schaap

G. P. PUTNAM'S SONS
NEW YORK

G. P. Putnam's Sons
Publishers Since 1838
200 Madison Avenue
New York, NY 10016

Design by Levavi & Levavi

Library of Congress Cataloging-in-Publication Data

Kramer, Jerry, date.
  Distant replay.

  1. Green Bay Packers (Football team)—History.
I. Schaap, Dick, date.   II. Title.
GV956.G7K72   1985   796.332′64′0977561   85-16902
ISBN 0-399-13106-X

Printed in the United States of America

1   2   3   4   5   6   7   8   9   10

This book is for my own team: For Charlie, my dad, who is gone, who was the anchor of the family, and for Myrtle, my mother, who is the glue; for Wink, my wife, who is my anchor; and for all my children, Tony and Diane and Danny and Alicia and Matt and Jordan, with the hope that they will know the friendship and love that I've known, in union and reunion.

The Green Bay Packers of 1965, 1966 and 1967, coached by Vince Lombardi, won three straight National Football League championship games, a feat no other team has ever performed, and also won the first two Super Bowl games. The 1966 team, which won Super Bowl I on January 15, 1967, may have been the most gifted. Six of the starting players, plus the head coach, were elected to the Professional Football Hall of Fame, and four other members of the team are still viable candidates. Eight of the Packers who won Super Bowl I were named All-Pro that season.

In October 1984, twenty-nine of the men who played on that team, including every Hall of Famer and all the All-Pros, returned to Green Bay for their first full-scale reunion in almost eighteen years. They were in their late forties and their early fifties, most of them, but for one weekend, at least, they were all young again.

GREEN BAY PACKER CHAPTER

August 22, 1984

TO ALL MEMBERS OF THE 1967 SUPER BOWL TEAM

Dear Teammate:

We have put together a Super Reunion for you. This gala weekend in conjunction with the NFL Alumni–Green Bay Packer Chapter, will include a Charity Golf Classic and a Celebrity Banquet. You will be the Honorees! The Committee has worked very hard in organizing this affair and the fans of Green Bay and the State of Wisconsin are looking forward to your return. Your airfare, for you and your wife, and your lodging for (3) nights—Saturday, Sunday and Monday—will be paid for by the Green Bay Packers.

All of the proceeds from the above events will go to the Boys and Girls Club of Green Bay. It's going to be a First Class Affair. We hope you can make it back!

Best Regards,

Fred "Fuzzy" Thurston

Contents

The Green Bay Packers
of
Super Bowl I

January 15, 1967

NO.	NAME	POS.	HT.	WT.	AGE	COLLEGE
26	Adderley, Herb	DB	6-0	200	27	Michigan State
82	Aldridge, Lionel	DE	6-4	245	25	Utah State
88	Anderson, Bill	TE	6-3	225	30	Tennessee
44	Anderson, Donny*	HB	6-3	220	23	Texas Tech
57	Bowman, Ken	C	6-3	230	24	Wisconsin
12	Bratkowski, Zeke	QB	6-3	200	35	Georgia
78	Brown, Bob*	DE	6-6	265	26	Arkansas AM&N
40	Brown, Tom	DB	6-1	195	26	Maryland
60	Caffey, Lee Roy	LB	6-3	250	25	Texas A&M
34	Chandler, Don	K	6-2	210	32	Florida
56	Crutcher, Tommy Joe	LB	6-3	230	25	Texas Christian
50	Curry, Bill	C	6-2	235	24	Georgia Tech
84	Dale, Carroll	WR	6-2	200	28	Virginia Tech
87	Davis, Willie	DE	6-3	245	32	Grambling
86	Dowler, Boyd	WR	6-5	225	29	Colorado
81	Fleming, Marv	TE	6-4	235	25	Utah
68	Gillingham, Gale*	G	6-3	250	22	Minnesota
33	Grabowski, Jim*	FB	6-2	225	22	Illinois
75	Gregg, Forrest	OT	6-4	250	33	Southern Methodist
43	Hart, Doug	DB	6-0	190	27	Texas-Arlington
45	Hathcock, Dave*	DB	6-0	190	23	Memphis State
5	Hornung, Paul	HB	6-3	215	31	Notre Dame
21	Jeter, Bob	DB	6-1	205	29	Iowa
74	Jordan, Henry	DT	6-3	250	31	Virginia
77	Kostelnik, Ron	DT	6-2	260	27	Cincinnati
64	Kramer, Jerry	G	6-3	245	30	Idaho

*Rookies

80	Long, Bob	WR	6-3	190	25	Wichita State
27	Mack, Red	WR	5-10	180	29	Notre Dame
85	McGee, Max	WR	6-3	205	34	Tulane
66	Nitschke, Ray	LB	6-3	240	30	Illinois
22	Pitts, Elijah	HB	6-1	205	27	Philander Smith
89	Robinson, Dave	LB	6-3	245	25	Penn State
76	Skoronski, Bob	OT	6-3	250	32	Indiana
15	Starr, Bart	QB	6-1	200	33	Alabama
31	Taylor, Jim	FB	6-0	215	31	Louisiana State
63	Thurston, Fuzzy	G	6-1	245	33	Valparaiso
37	Vandersea, Phil*	LB	6-3	225	23	Massachusetts
73	Weatherwax, Jim*	DT	6-7	275	24	Los Angeles State
24	Wood, Willie	DB	5-10	190	30	Southern California
72	Wright, Steve	OT	6-6	250	24	Alabama

*Rookies

Introduction

More than a quarter of a century has passed since I first arrived in Green Bay, a raw and totally unsophisticated kid from a small town in Idaho, a rookie in the National Football League. A quarter of a century. Twenty-six years, to be exact. That's hard for me to believe. Aren't I still a flat-bellied, whippy-wristed college kid? No, I'm not. I still feel the same inside, but more and more this shell they've given me is showing signs of wear. Gray at the sideburns and maybe even a little higher. Too much stomach where part of my chest must have slipped. Wrinkles around my eyes. Aches and pains I never felt before. Amazing process, this living and dying. What the hell is going on?

I used to think I would live forever, which is funny, considering how many times I came so close to dying. As a kid, I shot myself, accidentally, with a ten-gauge shotgun and severed the nerves in my right arm, which left me with a permanent scar and a fist I could never quite close. Then, chasing a calf, I ran full speed into a splintered plank, and the jagged end ripped into my groin, sending me to the hospital for a few operations then and several more a dozen years later when doctors, fearing I was dying of cancer, cut me open and found four forgotten slivers of wood lodged in my intestines, gradually causing tumors and internal bleeding. I broke my neck and my leg and just about all my ribs playing football, and I suffered brain concussions and a detached retina, and by the time I was thirty, I had undergone a couple of dozen operations, most of them major. And yet I was positive I couldn't die. Perhaps because I had survived so many near-death experiences, death didn't seem like a threat. It wasn't something to worry about. But lately I've been worrying, maybe because I've got more to lose now.

I'm coming up fast on fifty, just a little more than a year away. I've been married twice, and I've got six kids, ranging in age from under five to over twenty-five. I've found out how it feels to make a million dollars in a single business deal, and I've found out how it feels to lose a million dollars in a single business deal, and believe me, Lombardi was right about winning. It is the only thing—as long as you do it, as he said, fairly, squarely and decently, within the rules, the written ones and the unwritten. Lombardi's been dead now for fourteen years. That's scary. I *knew* he would live forever.

I think a lot about death these days, which is funny, too, because I've never been healthier. I've had only one serious illness in the past ten years, only one near-death experience. I haven't broken a bone, not even a finger, since I stopped playing football sixteen years ago. My weight's not bad, about 240, twenty pounds less than when I stopped playing, and most of the time I feel awfully good. And yet now, more than ever, I sense that I'm mortal.

A year ago, I lost my father to cancer, and I don't think I'll ever get over his death. In some ways, I think it was more difficult for the family than it was for him. Dad was a very religious man and he was ready to go. He had his faith and he said he was locked in the arms of the Lord. Sometimes I wish I had that kind of faith. But I don't. I just have questions.

Which is one of the reasons I'm looking forward so much to the reunion of the team that won Super Bowl I, to seeing once again so many of the people I wrote about, when we were all young, in a book called *Instant Replay*. I want to take a fresh look at a group of men who are linked yet separated, aging, perhaps maturing, maybe sadder, maybe wiser, maybe not. I want to find out what they wonder about, and what they remember, what they worry about, and what they enjoy, how they're reacting to life and age and death. I want something to help me measure my own thoughts and memories, fears and pleasures, just as I used *Instant Replay* for therapy, for self-analysis, to explain to myself why I played professional football, what I put into the game and what I got out of it. Football was easy. Now I get so tangled up trying to figure out life—why am I playing it, how am I playing it— and I wonder if anybody else has answers. Or even clues.

I couldn't have gone looking for this kind of help a few years ago. The first ten or twelve years I was out of football, I wouldn't listen to anybody, I was just so full of how bright I was, how wonderful. It's nice to have self-confidence, but I was ridiculous.

I'll tell you how cocky I was. I had dinner in Los Angeles one night with Rod McKuen, the poet, who was a friend of mine, and Rod said, "Hey, Sinatra's recording some of my songs tonight over at this studio. You want to go?"

I said, "Hell, yes." Who wouldn't want to? We walked into the studio as Sinatra was recording a song called "Two Can Dream a Dream Together." He finished the song and came over and said hello to Rod, and Rod introduced me, and I said, "Hi, Frank, I've been a fan of yours for a long time, but, boy, you were beating the hell out of that song."

He said, "What?"

And I said, "You're beating the hell out of that song. That's a beautiful thought—two can dream a dream together—but you're just beating on it. It ought to be a little softer."

Sinatra looked at me like I had an asshole right in the middle of my forehead. He turned to McKuen and never said another word to me. I ceased to exist. Would you believe it still took a few years before I realized that I'd better stop listening to the wonderful sound of my own voice?

Now I want to listen to my old teammates, to other voices, loud or soft, either way, whatever they want to say.

—JERRY KRAMER
October 1, 1984

1. Don't Cry for Fuzzy

Fuzzy Thurston and
Tommy Joe Crutcher

Fuzzy Thurston, my old teammate, a gutsy and gusty barrel of a man, greeted me as if I had scored a game-winning touchdown. He wrapped his arms around me and buried me in his chest. We looked like a pair of big old hogs hugging.

We were in Shenanigans, Fuzzy's latest saloon. It was nothing fancy, a battered barn that had been sitting forever near the banks of the Fox River in Green Bay. A pool table and a couple of dart boards and a bunch of fading football pictures on the wall. It was Fuzzy's kind of place: It had people on one side of the bar and bottles on the other.

Fuzzy always lived his life as if it might end tomorrow. He jammed everything into it, relished every minute. He was always charging, always up. How are things, Fuzz? Fantastic! Sensational! Terrific! Every day, he was like a little boy at Christmas.

Now Fuzzy was fifty. He wore a piece to cover his bald head, a gray toupee that blended with the surviving hairs, and he spoke through an artificial voice box, a souvenir of cancer. In 1980, the doctors gave him radiation treatment. The next year, they took out one of his vocal cords. Two years later, they removed his larynx.

When I called his wife, Sue, a few days after the laryngectomy, to find out how he was feeling, Fuzzy handed her a note that said, "Tell Jerry I'm doing fantastic." She read me the message, and then Fuzzy handed her another note. "And that's bullshit," he wrote. Then he added, "Tell him I love him."

Fuzzy had to learn to talk all over again, to take a breath before he spoke, to exert pressure on the artificial voice box to produce sounds. He had to learn, painfully, to say one letter at a time. He learned. We played golf about five months after the operation, and as we loosened up on the first tee, lying about our handicaps, Fuzzy's words came out hoarsely, but clearly. "You got to give me three strokes a side for cancer," he said.

He wanted strokes, but he didn't want sympathy. Not Fuzzy. Fuzzy wanted some laughs and drinks and hugs and, every now and then, maybe a cheer or two, a reminder of the hero he, and I, and all the others, used to be.

Someone else might have used cancer as a crutch. Fuzz used it as a prop. Three holes into our golf match, he sliced a shot into the woods. He turned to me, calmly, and rasped, "Before my operation, that shot would have pissed me off. But now I have a much better perspective on life. That shot doesn't bother me at all." Then he calmly heaved his club into the woods.

He made one concession to his condition. He didn't drink so many vodka-and-tonics any more. He drank vodka-and-diet-tonics instead.

I saw Fuzzy really down only once, sometime between his operations, when the pain was so bad, so visible, I just looked at him and felt like I was being hit with a baseball bat. We started talking about depressing things, about growing old and being forgotten, and Fuzzy said something I'll always remember. "You know, Jerry," he said, "nobody wants to be Fuzzy anymore."

Nobody wants to be Fuzzy anymore.

When we were young, when we were champions, everyone envied us. Everyone wanted to know us. Everyone wanted to be us. It wasn't just the kids in the schoolyard shouting, "I'm Paul Hornung!" "I'm Bart Starr!" "I'm Fuzzy Thurston!" It was the school teachers, too, and the lawyers, and the stockbrokers, and the salesmen. Professional football was a soaring sport, and we were its soaring stars. We were everybody's heroes, and we knew it would never end.

Nobody wants to be Fuzzy anymore.

It cut right through me. It captured in six words the sadness of being an ex-athlete, the loss, the void. You grew accustomed to applause. You grew accustomed to being fussed over. All of us missed it. Some of us missed it more than others. Fuzzy missed it more because Fuzzy needed it more. Fuzzy always needed people, a crowd, an audience. He liked people. I got tired of people coming up to me and slapping me on the back and putting their arms around me, and I got tired of hearing myself say the same silly falsely modest things, but Fuzzy never tired of it. He loved it. Then, one day, or one night, not in his own saloon, but in a strange bar, in a strange town, the people didn't know who Fuzzy was, didn't know he was an ex–Green Bay Packer great, or didn't care. All they saw was an aging man with a gray toupee who drank a little too much and got a little too loud. They didn't see the history of the man, the courage, the skill, the zest. They didn't see the little boy.

Nobody wants to be Fuzzy anymore.

The next time I saw Fuzzy, he was up again. Everything was great. Everything was fabulous. He had survived bankruptcy, and he was going to survive cancer, and he didn't have any time, or use, for self-pity. "I've got beautiful friends and I've got a beautiful family," he said, "and if you've got that, you've got success." He puffed up his chest and sucked in his belly. He started strutting just thinking about his friends and about Sue and their three children, the daughter in college, the sons out of school and working and doing well and one of them married. "I got a granddaughter," Fuzzy said. "Unbelievable! She looks just like me when I was a baby." Fuzzy showed me a picture of her, and he drew in a breath and primed his voice box and said, "I wouldn't trade my life for anybody's, that's the way I feel about it."

Fuzzy's life had had more than its share of ups and downs. He was raised in western Wisconsin, in Altoona, a town so small the high school didn't even have a football team. "We only had twenty-eight boys in the whole school," Fuzzy once told me. He loved sports. "My dream was to become a high school coach," he said. "I thought if I could ever do that, I would really be happy."

He won a basketball scholarship to Valparaiso University in Indiana, and in his junior year, when he found himself growing wider, instead of taller, he tried out for football for the first time. One year later, he was good enough to be drafted by the Philadelphia Eagles. He was almost good enough to make the team. The Eagles kept him through their final exhibition game in 1956, then cut him from the squad.

Fuzzy went into the army, and when he got out in 1958, he tried pro football again. He signed with the Chicago Bears. During training camp, the Bears traded him back to Philadelphia, and this time he survived the cut after the last exhibition game, traditionally the final cut. Fuzzy found an apartment and told Sue to pack up and come to Philadelphia. But two days before the season began, the Eagles picked up a new player and dropped Fuzzy. He could have given up then, gone home and become a high school coach.

But Fuzzy wouldn't quit. He signed with Winnipeg, spent two weeks in the Canadian Football League, then got a phone call from the Baltimore Colts. He switched to his fourth team in three months and ended up playing in the National Football League championship game, the famous sudden-death game in which the Colts defeated the New York Giants. But the next year, as soon as Fuzzy showed up in training camp, the champion Colts discarded him, traded him to the last-place Green Bay Packers.

Fuzzy never shed any tears over being traded so often. "I was used to it," he said. "When I was five years old, my father put me in a wheelbarrow and tried to trade me for a bottle of whiskey." He paused. "My mother never forgave him," Fuzzy said. He paused again. "'Cause he couldn't make the trade," he said.

In Green Bay, finally, Fuzzy found a home.

He played for the Packers for the next nine seasons, and during those nine seasons, the Packers won the National Football League championship five times. That team had more success than any team that ever played the game. "That team had more love than any team that ever played the game," Fuzzy said.

The reunion was Fuzzy's idea, Fuzzy's dream, a party to celebrate the Green Bay Packers who, on January 15, 1967, in the Los Angeles Memorial Coliseum, defeated the Kansas City Chiefs in the first Super Bowl game. "They'll always remember that one," Fuzzy said. "They'll always remember the first one, and the last one."

Fuzzy always loved a party, a celebration. When we won our first National Football League championship, beating the New York Giants, 37–0, in Green Bay, on Sunday, December 31, 1961, we put on some New Year's Eve party. I may have still been a little hung over Wednesday morning when I packed up my family to go home to Idaho for the winter. We stopped by Fuzzy's house to say goodbye, and he hadn't gotten home yet. From Sunday. He never held back, never saved anything, on the field or off.

Fuzzy persuaded the Green Bay chapter of the National Football League Alumni to host the reunion and persuaded the Packers to put up $20,000 toward the expenses. Then he sent invitations to his former teammates, to each one he could find among the thirty-nine men who played with him in Super Bowl I. Seven, like Fuzzy, were already in their fifties; the rest of us were in our forties, mostly our late forties. Fuzzy wanted us all to come back to Green Bay and act like kids again.

The Packers of Super Bowl I had never had a formal reunion. We had gathered only in small groups, sporadically, for golf tournaments and for funerals. We tried to keep track of each other, but some of us dropped out of sight. I stayed in touch with Fuzzy because I went to

Green Bay three or four times a year to visit my children from my first marriage. But I had not seen several of the guys since 1968, since I played my last game, and I had not seen some since 1970, since I went to Vince Lombardi's funeral.

Coach Lombardi was coming to the reunion, of course. He was coming in each player's mind and in each player's heart.

"I always felt I could play," Fuzzy said, "but by the time I got to Green Bay, I was beginning to lose a little confidence. Then I saw you, Jerry, and I knew I could make it."

Fuzzy's first season in Green Bay, 1959, was also Vince Lombardi's first, and my second. Fuzzy and I became Lombardi's starting guards, and for the next eight seasons, except when I was licking my various wounds, we remained in the starting lineup. Fuzzy was the left guard, I was the right guard and our blocking was the most visible part of the power sweep, the play that became the heart and the symbol of the offense Vince Lombardi created. Fuzzy and I opened the holes and led Jimmy Taylor, the fullback, and Paul Hornung, the Golden Boy, old goat shoulders, to glory.

We were a perfect blend, each proud of his own skills, each proud of the other. As offensive guards, each of us was always concerned that the guard on the other side would pull the wrong way and we'd meet behind the center in a great embarrassing collision. In nine years in Green Bay, I think we collided once. "There are two good reasons the Packers are world champions," Fuzzy used to say when he spoke at banquets. "Jerry Kramer is one of them, and you're looking at the other."

Fuzzy and I were typical Lombardi Packers, neither of us an All-American in college, neither highly publicized at schools, Idaho and Valparaiso, that hardly had rich football traditions. If we had the natural ability to become great players, only Lombardi saw it, not anyone else, certainly not us.

Lombardi forced us to be better than we thought we could possibly be. Fuzzy was listed on the roster at six-foot-one, but he had to step on his tiptoes to reach six feet. He stretched himself to his limits in every way. He never had great strength, but he had a huge heart and fire and pride. Lombardi screamed at both of us unmercifully, perhaps because he had been a guard himself. His words stung. They hurt Fuzzy more than they hurt me. "He embarrassed me, he ridiculed me, he made me feel worse than a bug on the wall," Fuzzy said. "I hated that, and I hated him then. But I love him so much today, it's unbelievable."

The last time I went to Green Bay before the reunion, Fuzzy and I visited the Packer Hall of Fame. We went with a videotape camera crew that was shooting a story on the first Super Bowl game for *20/20*, the ABC News magazine show. I had never been to the Hall before, not even when I was inducted, in 1975, along with Fuzzy and six other Packers who played in Super Bowl I. Twenty of us from that team, half the squad, were eventually inducted. Our names dominated the Hall, and so did re-creations of our locker room and our meeting room.

The television crew wanted shots of us strolling among the memorabilia, reacting, reflecting, remembering. I walked into the familiar locker room and saw my old helmet. I winced. I used to hate that helmet. I saw Jimmy Taylor's locker next to mine. I winced again. I used to love Jimmy Taylor. "Be great to have the whole gang back here," Fuzzy said.

We entered the meeting room and I turned to Fuzzy and, spontaneously, surprising even myself, I said, "Fuzz, let's pretend for a minute that I'm a rookie, on the opening day of training camp, and you're Vince Lombardi. You stand up there and—"

Fuzzy understood. It didn't seem right to be in the room without Lombardi lecturing. "Won't be easy," Fuzzy said.

"I know it's not going to be easy," I said. "But give me just a little indoctrination into the Packer legend, the Packer way of life, the Packer attitude."

I settled into one of the chairs, and Fuzzy, responding to the challenge, threw back his shoulders, moved to the podium, studied the room and transformed himself into Vince Lombardi. "Gentlemen,"

Fuzzy growled, "welcome to Green Bay. This is what football is all about—the Green Bay Packers. You are the privileged few that have been chosen, maybe, to wear the greatest colors in football—the green and gold of the Green Bay Packers."

Fuzzy captured the words and the cadence perfectly. He saw an invisible audience, saw himself, young and eager, and I saw Vince Lombardi, alive and prodding. "We will expect from you one hundred percent total dedication," Fuzzy said, "and, gentlemen, I will not only expect it. I will demand it. I will get it."

I closed my eyes, felt a chill. Because of the cancer, Fuzzy, breathing his words through the voice box, sounded just like Coach Lombardi. "If you are going to make this team," Fuzzy said, "you will have to be very, very good. I welcome all of you. Now let's get to work."

"Let's go, let's go!" I shouted.

I applauded Fuzzy, and the tension eased, and I laughed. "You remember the first one?" I said. "The first time you heard him? The excitement in the room, the electricity, the emotion?"

"He was the most emotional man I ever knew," Fuzzy said. "He could stand up there and laugh. And he could cry."

Later, when the scene was shown on television, when Fuzzy's cracking, crackling voice echoed through the meeting room, people who watched told me they cried.

I did, too. Coach Lombardi died, at the age of fifty-seven, of cancer.

Fuzzy went into the restaurant business soon after he moved to Green Bay and, eventually, owned a share of eleven thriving establishments in Wisconsin and Minnesota. Most of them were called The Left Guard, one The Left End, after Fuzzy's teammate and partner, Max McGee. Fuzzy loved to hang out in one of the restaurants because it had a piano bar, and he could sit by the piano and sing. The year we won the first Super Bowl game, Fuzzy was in charge of getting the rookies to sing in training camp for the amusement of the veterans. Some of the rookies had god-awful voices and hated to sing. Fuzzy had a voice worse than any of them and loved to sing. His big number was,

"He's Got the Whole World in His Hands," and in Fuzzy's version, the "he" was Lombardi, and the lyrics changed almost every day. My favorite was, "He's got the greatest guards in his hands."

Despite Fuzzy's singing, the restaurants he and Max owned, with a third partner, were grossing between ten and fifteen million dollars a year by the early 1970s. Fuzzy owned a big house in Neenah, Wisconsin, and so many cars he lost count. If Fuzzy wasn't a millionaire, he certainly lived like one.

But he and Max had expanded too quickly, too precariously, and when the economy slipped in the mid-1970s, their restaurants slipped, too. McGee managed to get out safely, to retain one restaurant, change its direction and turn it into a gold mine—Max always had a terrific sense of timing—but Fuzzy stayed in too long, took too many chances and listened to too much bad advice. He went bankrupt.

Then the cancer struck, and even Fuzzy, with all his natural optimism and vigor, couldn't keep his spirits from sinking. He didn't know how long he would live. He gave up his dreams, his drive. He said he just wanted to get a little neighborhood bar and just get by, just exist.

Sue helped him through the crisis with encouragement and with hard work. She seemed stronger than I ever remembered her. They got rid of the cars they didn't need. They moved to a smaller house in Green Bay. Slowly, Fuzzy revived, regained his energy and his attitude. He took over Shenanigans and started talking about how he had doubled the gross and was going to double the double. He talked about endorsing a hairpiece and about setting up gambling junkets to Atlantic City. He began to dream again. "There's a circle of winners," Fuzzy told me years ago, "and once you get in the circle, you'll never be happy outside it."

He was fighting his way back into the circle. He put up the football pictures in Shenanigans and looked forward to the reunion. "Lombardi taught me never to quit," Fuzzy said, "and I never will. I can't quit. I won't accept quitting."

As soon as I got my invitation, I called Fuzzy and said, "Count me in." I was as excited as he was. I couldn't wait to see everybody. On

Friday, the day before the reunion was supposed to begin, I flew from my home in Idaho, near Boise, to Minneapolis and picked up my son Danny, a sophomore at the University of Minnesota, and drove down to Green Bay with him. I hadn't seen Dan in about eight or nine months, and I wanted some one-on-one time with him. I was surprised by the way he had beefed up. He had put on twenty or thirty pounds, and all of a sudden he looked like I thought I looked when I was in college. Except for the earring in his left ear. I never had an earring in college. Or afterward. I had a little trouble with Danny's earring, but during the ride, I didn't say anything. I didn't bring it up. I just ignored it.

We talked about hunting and about school—Danny said he might want to study photography, but he didn't sound committed yet—and when we weren't talking, I kept stealing looks at him, studying him. He sat like I sat. He moved like I moved. He was doing me. It got awful spooky, like watching my own reflection.

Of all my children, three from each marriage, Danny was the one closest to me, and farthest from me, the hardest for me to get through to. A few years ago, he had a serious automobile accident when he'd been drinking and he ended up spending a little time in jail. I felt for him. I saw him living life on the edge the way I'd lived it for so long, and it scared the hell out of me because I came very close to going over the edge more than a few times. Just blind luck, providence, saved me. I hoped Danny would be as lucky.

I thought of Fuzzy as I drove toward Green Bay, good thoughts, of pleasant times, of victories savored in locker rooms and on Monday nights, traditionally the boys' night out, when we would toast our skills and drown our pains, when we would end up, usually, in the arms of the whiskey man. I thought of our party at The Left Guard in Appleton after we won our fifth NFL title, our third in a row, when the temperature tumbled to twenty-two degrees below zero outside, and the pipes froze so there was no heat in the restaurant. We all wore our overcoats to dinner, except one player's date. She was a *Playboy* Playmate, and she wore a sweater, her concession to the cold, and a miniskirt. Fuzzy toasted her as well as the two greatest guards in the history of the National Football League.

When Danny and I got to Shenanigans, Fuzzy gave me my hug, and a kiss on the cheek, and then turned to Danny and gripped his arms, testing his muscles. "Getting big," Fuzzy said. Danny said he'd been doing some wrestling. "I'll take the old man on soon," he said.

Fuzzy reached out, a fifty-year-old man who had battled cancer, and, with a sudden burst of remembered strength, picked up my two-hundred-pound twenty-year-old son as if he were a doll and dropped him on a bar stool. "It'll be a while, son," Fuzzy said.

My other children from my first marriage met us in Shenanigans, Tony, the oldest, and his wife Darlene, and Diane, my daughter. My divorce probably hurt Diane more than anyone. She got married very young, and her husband once told me that she had a very idealized image of me, an image he was expected to live up to. The marriage didn't last long. But after her divorce Diane went back to college and started working toward a degree as a dietician. We were getting close again. She was beginning to trust me again, and trust herself. She was opening up, starting to be herself with me, instead of being what she thought I wanted her to be.

Tony was the child his mother and I worried about the most. He had a speech impediment, and we feared he'd have problems communicating and getting along in the world. But, perhaps motivated by his impediment, perhaps because he learned early that life demanded work, Tony, more than any of my other children, developed an ability to work. He pushed himself harder in school than either his brother or his sister. He has a degree in accounting and a good job with a whole-sale lumber company and a wonderful wife.

Fuzzy let out a whoop when Tommy Joe Crutcher ambled into Shenanigans. Tommy Joe was our fourth linebacker in Super Bowl I, a solid reserve. He was a good old boy from McKinney, Texas, who came to the Packers wearing a pair of boots that had to be forty years old and a pair of jeans to match. Tommy Joe spoke his own special language. Once, when he was playing cribbage, his opponent moaned, "If I could only get a cut," and Tommy Joe snapped back, "If a frog had wings, he wouldn't whomp his ass every time he jumped." When he lost the cribbage game, Tommy Joe admitted, "I ain't seen nothing like that since Cecil Barlow's cow got caught in the brush." Tommy Joe was country.

Fuzzy threw his arms around Tommy Joe, and I thought both of them were going to start crying. "One of my favorite people in the whole world," Fuzzy said of Tommy Joe. "A helluva man," Tommy Joe said of Fuzzy. "I'd trust him with my last dollar." The funny thing was that they both meant it, even though they hadn't seen each other in twelve years, not since Tommy Joe ended his second tour of duty with the Packers. They toasted each of the years they'd been apart and most of the months, too. Tommy Joe had heard about the cancer. "Same old Fuzzy," Tommy Joe said.

"You don't look any different to me," Fuzzy said. "You look good. But you got to understand, when you get cancer, your eyesight and just about everything else goes a little to hell. Except your sex life gets better."

Actually, Tommy Joe did look good. At the age of forty-three, he weighed a few pounds less than he did in his playing days, and he had all of his old hair, plus more, long and gray. I hadn't seen Tommy Joe in about fifteen years, but I could see a difference. He still looked country, but now it was a different kind of country. He looked like a character out of *Dallas*, not one of the younger characters, on the make, but one of the older ones, who had made it. His boots were costly, probably snakeskin or lizard, and new. His belt buckle was expensive. His jeans were just right, a little bit of wear, but creased and clean, the studied casual look. Everything struck me as tasteful, fitted, carefully selected. Tommy Joe looked like a wealthy Texas rancher.

Tommy Joe was a wealthy Texas farmer. He had a farm not far from the Mexican border. He invited a bunch of us down there after the reunion, for a long weekend of poker and golf and quail hunting, and he drove me around and showed me his spread. He showed me part of it, anyway. His farm was bigger than the island of Manhattan, about twenty-five thousand acres, and he was raising grain sorghum, livestock feed, much of which he exported, most of it to Mexico, but some to the Soviet Union and its satellites, some to Japan. He had started buying the land with the $15,000 he collected as a winner's share from Super Bowl I (in 1985, for winning Super Bowl XIX, the San Francisco 49ers got $36,000 apiece, not much of an improvement, compared to the way salaries have shot up). Tommy Joe had several partners, most of them not involved in the management, including a few ex–football players—Maxie Baughan and Claude Crabb from the Los Angeles Rams and Pete Retzlaff from the Philadelphia Eagles. They not only owned twenty-five thousand acres; they also owned four grain elevators. Tommy Joe ran the farm, and he worked hard at it. He was a very wealthy Texas farmer.

He wore his ring from Super Bowl I to the reunion, a single diamond in the center, with his name and number and the score of the game engraved on the ring, plus the words Harmony, Courage and Valor, three of the virtues Lombardi treasured. Fuzzy and I chose to wear our rings from Super Bowl II, the largest of all Super Bowl rings, topped by three diamonds, commemorating three straight NFL championships, within an emerald football. On one side, a Green Bay helmet sat within an NFL shield, and five flags flew above the shield, symbolizing five NFL titles in seven years. Above the flags were the scores of the NFL championship game, against Dallas, and Super Bowl II, against Oakland. Under the shield was the word Challenge; Lombardi had told us from the start of the season that winning a third title in a row would be our greatest challenge. On the other side of the ring was a globe capped by a crown, with our names above the crown and our numbers inside a football within the crown. Beneath the globe were the words Run to Win, a quotation from Saint Paul's Epistles that inspired a Lombardi pregame speech. The Super Bowl II rings cost $1,900 apiece, and are now worth close to $20,000.

Tommy Joe told us he would have worn his Super Bowl II ring to the reunion, but the diamonds fell out and he had to get it fixed. Most of the time, he said, he didn't wear any ring. Tommy Joe was one of the few guys on the team who had remained a bachelor. But he had a girl friend named Sandy Cole, whom he brought to the reunion. He didn't bring her to Shenanigans Friday night, though. They had had a long trip from Texas, and Tommy Joe wasn't sure Sandy was ready for Shenanigans. He left her at the motel to catch up on her rest while he tried to keep up with Fuzzy.

The more Tommy Joe and Fuzzy drank, the less I understood either of them. Tommy Joe was delivering sentences in slow motion, and Fuzzy wasn't going to waste his breath forming words carefully while there were still so many vodka-and-diet-tonics to be drunk.

As far as I could figure out, they were reminiscing about the famous mad dashes during training camp to get back to our dormitory at St. Norbert College in West De Pere, Wisconsin, before Lombardi's 11:00 P.M. curfew. Fuzzy was the only man in Packer history who snuck out *before* curfew. He had so much beer to drink after practice one day that, at nine o'clock, he climbed out his dormitory window, tiptoed out to the parking lot, wandered around in a daze for an hour and then, at ten o'clock, still an hour before curfew, snuck back in. The next day, he was bragging that he didn't get caught.

Customarily, Fuzzy followed a more dramatic routine. Thirty minutes before curfew, he'd be sitting in a saloon within ten minutes of St. Norbert. But his head would be down on the bar, his eyes shut; he was, apparently, unconscious. Five minutes later, he would lift his head, open his eyes, smile, say, "I'll have another vodka," gulp it down and then collapse again, dead to the world. But at precisely 10:45, he would rise like Lazarus and head toward the door. He always made it back to St. Norbert before curfew. Almost always. And usually under his own power.

"C'mon, c'mon," Fuzzy said to Tommy Joe. "We got to get back to camp. We got to get back before curfew. C'mon, the old man's waiting for us."

They both knew they weren't going back to St. Norbert, they weren't football players anymore, Lombardi was dead for almost fifteen years and nobody, except maybe Sue Thurston and Sandy Cole, really cared if they stayed out past curfew. But they went through the motions, giggling and hollering, and they walked out the front door of Shenanigans, with their arms around each other, and, suddenly, Tommy Joe slipped and his legs shot out from under him and he tumbled down the steps.

He wasn't hurt bad, but he scraped the skin on his chin and on his cheek, and puffed up his lips, and for the next few days, whenever anyone asked what happened to Tommy Joe, Fuzzy looked at him and said, "I kissed him too hard."

2. Same Time Next Season

We could say goodbye to each other at the end of each season, lead separate lives for six or seven months, pursue different interests, age and change and on rare occasions even mature, and yet the next season, as soon as we saw each other, the old feelings returned, of warmth and affection, respect and admiration. We were like the lovers in the play *Same Time Next Year*. Ours was an affair that endured, a bond stronger, in so many ways, than marriage.

Several years after my last football game—and my first marriage—ended, I was in Milwaukee for a golf tournament, a Lombardi memorial, and I was sitting in a bar and I thought I spotted, across the hazy room, a former Green Bay teammate. *Hey, that looks like Herb Adderley.* Then I said to myself, *Nah, can't be*, and I turned to talk to somebody. In a few seconds, I felt a tap on my shoulder and I spun around, and he said, "J. K.," and it was Herbie. We hugged.

"It's still there, isn't it?" he said.

It was. It always will be. It was as if we had never been apart.

Yet I hadn't seen Herb in almost ten years, and we were never *that* close. I mean, we didn't room together. We didn't party together. We didn't hunt together. We didn't play poker together. We didn't even go to the same football meetings. Herb met with the defense. I met with the offense. Separate rooms. Separate philosophies.

Still, the bond persisted.

Why?

The answer, the first answer, has to be Lombardi. He united us, initially, in our fear of him, our hatred for him. He was, deliberately, the common enemy, the focus of all our frustrations. If our muscles ached, it was Lombardi's fault. If our nerves were frayed, it was Lombardi's fault. If our minds reeled, it was Lombardi's fault. The fierceness of Lombardi—combined with the smallness of the city in which we played—forced upon us a camaraderie and a closeness that, nurtured by victory, grew into love.

Victory was important because victory was our measure of success, and for most of Lombardi's Packers, success on a grand scale was a wonderful new experience. The twenty-three men who lined up for Green Bay at the start of the first Super Bowl—eleven on offense, eleven on defense and one kicker—represented twenty-three different colleges, and not one of us had played on a team that won the national collegiate championship. Only one of us, Dave Robinson, was a first-string All-American in college. Only two, Robinson from Penn State and Adderley from Michigan State, were first-round draft choices, blue-chip professional prospects. Only three, Bart Starr at Alabama and Boyd Dowler at Colorado and Bob Jeter at Iowa, knew the satisfaction of winning a major bowl game in college.

Many of the rest of us had football credentials that had to be exaggerated to be considered modest. Elijah Pitts came from Philander Smith, a college not one of his teammates had ever heard of. Willie Davis was only the second man from Grambling College to play professional football. Fuzzy was the first from Valparaiso. Marv Fleming wasn't drafted till the eleventh round, Pitts till the thirteenth, Starr and Davis till the seventeenth, Bill Curry till the twentieth and Willie Wood wasn't drafted at all. Wood was a free agent. In other words, not one *expert* expected any of those six players to make it in pro football, and all six ended up in the starting lineup for the winning team in Super Bowl I. Two of them have already been elected to the Professional Football Hall of Fame.

Lombardi took the unsung and the unknown and made us famous, made us stars, made us winners. He made a miracle. The year before he came to Green Bay, our lineup included twelve men who eventually played in the all-star game, the Pro Bowl, five of whom wound up in the Pro Football Hall of Fame. With that nucleus, the 1958 Packers won one game, tied one and lost ten. We lacked a leader. We lacked discipline. Lombardi provided both. He transformed a country-club picnic into the Bataan death march. We marched to nine straight winning seasons and five NFL championships.

We liked each other before we won. We loved each other after we won. We loved Lombardi, too. We saw through him, and loved what we found. And yet our love for each other, and for our coach, was based on more than winning, for if it had been based only on winning—as athletic "love" so often is—it would have ended, or diminished, when the victories ended. We went beyond loving to caring, to caring about what happened to each of us, professionally, financially, emotionally. Even now, every Packer's triumph lifts each of us; every tragedy hurts each of us.

We cared because we respected each other, our differences and our similarities. We were so different, one-eyed jacks and straight arrows, street fighters and family men, churchgoers and barflies. The churchgoers must have prayed for the rest of us. We had Starr who wouldn't go to sleep at night till he had studied a dozen game films, and Hornung who wouldn't go to sleep at night. We had Ray Nitschke who loved to hit people, and Max McGee who hated to be hit. We had Marv Fleming, with his squeaky high-pitched voice, and Lionel Aldridge, with his soft, serious baritone. We never let our differences divide us, not differences in style, nor in race. In Super Bowl I, we had eight black players in the starting lineup, and fifteen of varying shades of white.

We judged each other, not on color or ancestry, not on what we did on Monday nights or Friday nights, but on what we did on Sunday afternoons, between one o'clock and four, the way each man played, the way he confronted violence, if he shrunk back or if he met and conquered it, with vigor and gusto, with intensity.

We respected each other's individuality, but for those three hours each Sunday, we stopped being individuals and we became a team, dependent on each other, confident that we could depend on each other. We blocked, tackled, ran, passed, caught passes, every man contributing, and we capitalized on our similarities. On the field, we were, to a man, intelligent, dedicated, honest. We gave a day's work for a day's wages. We were unspoiled, hungry for success, rising from backgrounds that were, at best, middle-class, but more often aspiring to be, from tenant farms and mining towns and inner-city ghettos.

Not long ago, I was watching television one night, and I heard a man named Ace Greenberg, the chief executive officer of Bear, Stearns and Co., the investment banking firm, talking about the kind of people he liked to hire. Greenberg said he liked people with PsD degrees: "Poor, smart and driven by a deep desire to be rich." It sounded like a description of the old Packers.

Whenever we won a big game, I always felt incredibly proud, proud of myself and of my teammates and of my coaches. I felt as if I were a part of something very special, but only a part. Our sense of togetherness was so ingrained I don't think any of us ever felt that *he* won the game, that *he* was the star. We always felt it was a group effort, and it always was. After our most dramatic victory, the last-second victory over Dallas that gave us our third straight NFL championship, I was one of the first men led in front of the cameras, presumably because it was my block that helped Bart Starr score the winning touchdown. But I didn't want to talk about what I had done. I wanted to talk about what

37

we had done. "There's a great deal of love for one another on this club," I said. "Perhaps we're living in Camelot."

I did not have an easy time then using the word "love" out loud. I worried that it didn't sound manly enough, that it was too gentle a word to describe so rousing a relationship. I still flinch a little when Fuzzy plants a kiss on my cheek, sparking old fears of displaying affection toward another man. But I know now that what I feel toward my Green Bay teammates is love, the same sort of love one would feel for a mother or a father, a sister or a brother, the sort of love that would survive disruptions, that would last forever.

On the eve of the reunion of the team that won the first Super Bowl, I lay awake in my room at the Thrifty Inn, unable to fall asleep even after all the toasts in Shenanigans. I was as curious as if I were going to meet an old lover, as excited as if I were about to revive an affair.

3. Bart Does the Right Thing

Bart Starr and Forrest Gregg

Nobody knew if Bart Starr was going to show up. Nobody knew if he was going to come back to Green Bay, to awaken the memories of his greatest victories and his most bitter defeat. Every time the door to the hospitality suite of the Thrifty Inn swung open and another teammate stepped in, to be embraced and cheered and heckled, I strained to see if it was Bart. I don't know if I would have come if I were he.

Less than ten months before the reunion, the week before Christmas, 1983, the board of directors of the Green Bay Packers fired Bart Starr. He had been head coach of the Packers for nine years, the longest reign of any Green Bay coach since Vince Lombardi. Bart had taken the job in 1974 with remarkably little experience, merely one season, two years earlier, as an assistant coach, tutoring quarterbacks for the Packers. As head coach, he was expected to do what he had done as our quarterback: lead Green Bay to glory.

But in Bart's first three seasons, his teams lost almost seventy percent of their games. In his last three, his teams won slightly more than fifty percent. "I wasn't qualified to be the coach when I got the job," Bart told me, "but I worked very hard for nine years, gave them every ounce of energy I had and was becoming a darned good coach when they fired me."

Bart was my teammate for eleven seasons. I crouched in front of him for perhaps a hundred games, almost touching every time he leaned forward to take the snap from the center. I saw him respond to pain with courage, and to pressure with poise, and I even heard Bart Starr swear, maybe once or twice in eleven years. And yet I never felt I really got to know Bart Starr. I never felt I got beneath the surface.

On the surface, Bart came as close to perfection as any man I ever met, perfection as a quarterback and as a human being. Bart never said he was perfect, but he did say he tried to be. "Coach Lombardi said that perfection is not attainable," Bart said, "but he said that if we chased perfection, we could catch excellence."

More than any of his teammates, Bart listened to Coach Lombardi, absorbed his endless lessons, buried himself in game films and in playbooks, studied, studied, studied. Some critics complained that Bart was merely an extension of Coach Lombardi, and Bart bristled, but only at the word *merely*. "I was proud to be called an extension of him," Bart said. "I owe my life to that man."

Bart was not being *merely* melodramatic. He did owe his football life to Lombardi. Before Coach came to Green Bay, Bart was a journeyman quarterback for three seasons, a sometime starter, an uninspiring presence on an uninspired team. After Lombardi took command, Bart became the best quarterback in football. "I wasn't mentally tough till I met Coach Lombardi," Bart said. "He taught me you had to have a flaming desire to win." Bart was rarely the best quarterback in the league on a statistical basis. But for three hours each

Sunday, he was, almost always, the best quarterback in the game in which he was playing.

Bart saved his finest performances for the most critical games. In six National Football League championship games, Bart threw 145 passes, completed fifty-eight percent and permitted, incredibly, only one interception. Bart got us into Super Bowl I. Two weeks earlier, in the NFL championship game against Dallas, he was magnificent. He threw twenty-eight passes, none for interceptions, and completed nineteen, sixty-eight percent, four for touchdowns. We won the game, 34–27, and Bart, naturally, gave the credit to Coach Lombardi. "He prepared us beautifully for every game, for every eventuality," Bart said, "but I don't think he ever did a better job than he did preparing us for that Dallas game. He cut all the fat out of our offense." Our game plan was built around only fourteen plays, eight running plays and six passing, executed to the brink of perfection.

Off the playing field, too, Bart pursued perfection. In 1968, the Junior Chamber of Commerce voted him one of the Ten Outstanding Young Men in the United States. Two years later, he was named to President Nixon's Council on Physical Fitness, then to the President's Advisory Committee on Environmental Protection. He was the first man to win the NFL's Byron "Whizzer" White Award, a citizenship award named after the former football player who became a Justice of the Supreme Court of the United States. Bart and his wife, Cherry, chaired the Wisconsin State Cancer Crusade in 1971 and 1972, the two years following Coach Lombardi's death. "The true measure of success," Bart said to me once, as we sat in the den of his home, surrounded by his trophies and mementoes and photographs, "is what you've contributed to your community and to your nation. I've tried to lead a life pleasing to my family and to my God." Bart's cool blue eyes never blinked.

Bart always said the right thing, always did the right thing. All the years we played together, I looked for a flaw, waited for a slip, an inconsistency, a contradiction in his nature. I never spotted one. I also never spotted great passion, never a feeling so strong he lost control. In this respect, if no other, I was more an extension of Coach Lombardi than Bart was. My emotions often ruled me. Bart ruled his. He was too good to be true, which made me uneasy. I couldn't help wondering if he always believed what he said, if he ever said what he believed. Sometimes I thought there was no *real* Bart Starr, only the Bart Starr he wanted you to see, the Bart Starr he felt the public expected.

He never let down the public until he stepped into Coach Lombardi's job, until he became coach of the Packers. Then, by the standards of winning and losing, he failed, and some members of the public that had once worshiped him turned against him. Bart was booed. Bart was criticized. Bart was fired. When he was fired, of course, he said the right thing. Even though he felt "extreme disappointment," he said, "I will be the Packers' number one fan. No one has more heart and soul in this organization than I do."

But several months later, after the reality, the pain, of the firing had sunk in, Bart reacted in a slightly less saintly, slightly more human way. "I'd never been fired from anything before," he told me, "and it really hurt. When you've coached your heart out, when you know you've given it your best shot, and you get fired, you'd be less than normal if you didn't resent that. You feel angry. You feel torn up inside."

Bart could bleed, could be bitter, just like us mortals. He might even be human enough to enjoy revenge. Bart had no pressing financial problems—he had long enjoyed a handsome income from an automobile agency he co-owned in Alabama—but he had, after his dismissal, associated himself with a group of Arizona businessmen who were trying to bring an NFL franchise to Phoenix. If they could acquire a team, Bart would become the general manager and the coach. Someday he might coach against the Green Bay Packers, the only team he had ever worked for. Someday he might beat the Green Bay Packers, perhaps in a Super Bowl game. Even a saint, I suspect, might enjoy that.

Bart was in Phoenix during the week leading up to the reunion, debating whether he should attend, whether he could bring himself to attend. "If it had been a few years later," he said, "it would have been much easier. But the pain was still fresh and, emotionally, I didn't know if I could handle it."

It did not make it any easier that Bart's successor as coach of the Packers was, ironically, a former teammate, Forrest Gregg, who, as a member of the team that won Super Bowl I, was also invited to the reunion. For fourteen years as an offensive lineman, Forrest had offered fierce protection to Bart, saving him from tacklers and from damage.

Forrest was named coach five days after Bart was fired, on the day before Christmas, 1983, nine years to the day after Bart was hired. "I didn't take this job to field a losing football team," Forrest said. "I took this job to field a winning team. That will happen."

Bart and Forrest had so much in common. They were born less than three months apart, first Forrest in Birthright, Texas, then Bart in Alabama, and neither of them answered to his given first name, neither Alvis Forrest Gregg nor Bryan Bartlett Starr. They both came out of college in 1956, Forrest from Southern Methodist University, Bart from Alabama, and both were drafted by the Green Bay Packers, Forrest fifteen rounds ahead of Bart. Both made the team in 1956 and played in the NFL through the 1971 season, Bart for sixteen years with the Packers, Forrest for fourteen with the Packers, one in the army and one, his final season, with the Dallas Cowboys. Both were chosen for the Pro Bowl for the first time in 1961, and Bart was named three more times, Forrest eight more. Lombardi loved both of them and called Forrest, who played in 187 consecutive games to set a Green Bay record, the finest football player he had ever coached. Both became head coaches in the NFL in 1975, and both were elected to the Professional Football Hall of Fame as soon as they were eligible, in 1977.

Both were serious, family-oriented men, Bart married to Cherry Starr, who always seemed to me to spring straight out of *Gone With the Wind*, and Forrest to Barbara Gregg, a sturdy and outspoken woman who might have been more at home in a less glamorous film, perhaps *Country* or *Places in the Heart*. Bart and Forrest each had two children. Bart Jr. was a nonpracticing attorney, in the commodities business in Memphis, and his brother Bret was in the pet supply business in Tampa. Forrest Jr. and his sister Karen were both students at SMU. Forrest Jr. played center on the football team. His father said he was not an exceptional player. "I told him the first time he lined up, 'If you enjoy it, play it,'" Forrest recalled. "'If you don't enjoy it, don't play it.'"

Forrest, at right tackle, and I played next to each other for most of my eleven seasons. In 1964, when I was hospitalized for internal bleeding that sparked rumors I was dying of cancer, Forrest moved into my position and made All-Pro both as a guard and a tackle. Forrest was big, but he didn't overpower opponents. He was a master of technique, of position. He would shield, slide, maneuver and almost always get the job done. We practiced and played together for so long, we could get inside each other's head. When we lined up for a play, and the defense suddenly shifted, we never had to discuss how we would adjust. I'd just say, "Forrest," and he would say, "Yeah," and I'd know exactly what he was going to do, and he'd know what I was going to do. He was so dependable. He was as committed to perfection as Bart was, but I never heard him say he was committed to perfection. Forrest was a hell of a player, a hell of a person. We never spent a lot of time together off the field—he was much more sensible than I—but I always felt I knew Forrest, knew him to the core. I trusted him absolutely.

I wasn't particularly surprised when Forrest and Bart both became coaches, because both were students of the game. But I was surprised by how quickly Forrest rose in the profession. After he retired, after winning his third Super Bowl game, as a Cowboy, he spent three seasons as an assistant coach, two in San Diego and one in Cleveland. Then he became head coach of the Browns. He turned a losing team into a winning team in his second season, but when the team slipped back the following year, he was pressured to resign. Three years later, he became head coach of the Cincinnati Bengals and again, in his second season, turned a losing team into a winning one, good enough to end its season in the Super Bowl. Forrest was the first man to play and to coach in the Super Bowl. "He's not phony," said one of his Bengal players, the punter from Harvard, Pat McInally. "He's genuine. He is what he is." Forrest put in two more seasons coaching Cincinnati, then resigned to accept the job in Green Bay, the challenge of following in the footsteps of Vince Lombardi. "This is home to me," he said. He was asked if he would be as tough as Lombardi. "That's impossible," Forrest said. "I can be demanding, but not *that* demanding."

Between coaching the Browns and the Bengals—and one season in Canada—Forrest beat cancer. In 1976, he developed a melanoma, a tumor, a serious form of skin cancer. One of every three patients with a melanoma does not survive for five years. Forrest spotted the tumor early, a darkening of a mole on his leg, reported it to his doctor, underwent surgery and in 1982, completely free of the disease, received the National Courage Award of the American Cancer Society: "The American Cancer Society salutes Forrest Gregg for his personal courage in his battle against cancer, and for the hope and inspiration he gives all Americans in the fight for life and health." President Reagan presented the award at the White House.

I lost touch with Forrest for a while. I didn't even know he had cancer. He probably never mentioned it to anyone. When he coached his way into the Super Bowl, I didn't want to bother him. "I heard Jerry Kramer still exists," Forrest told a friend of mine a few days before the game, "but I don't believe it. I think he's a ghost. But if you see him, tell him hello."

Of course Bart decided to come to the reunion. It was the right thing to do. "The overriding consideration was the players who were going to be there," Bart said. "We really did have something special, something that hasn't been approximated many times in football or in any other sport. Once I thought about the people I would be with, the decision was easy."

Bart flew to Green Bay the day of the reunion and went, first, to his home in nearby De Pere, a handsome sprawling ranch house. Bart moved into the house the year we won Super Bowl I. He said he would never forget the first time Lombardi came to visit. Vince toured the house, settled in the living room, facing the fire.

"You've got a beautiful house here," Coach said.

"Thank you," Bart said. "We owe it all to you."

Lombardi choked up, began to cry. Bart, remembering the moment, was very moved.

Bart and Cherry were always a team—once, while he was coaching the Packers, I sat across from them during a flight from Chicago to Green Bay, and he spent almost the whole trip diagramming plays that he and Cherry discussed—and together they came to the Thrifty Inn. When they entered the hospitality suite, everyone seemed to get a lift. I know I was glad to see them. It just felt good, and right, to see Bart. It always felt good to see Bart, to know that a person of that caliber existed. It was like seeing the Grand Canyon again, or Mount Rushmore, sturdy, unchanging, consistent. I still can't figure out precisely what motivates Bart to be the person he is, but maybe, in the long run, that doesn't really matter. What matters is just the person he is, the excellence he displays in so many aspects of his life.

Fuzzy Thurston, to no one's surprise, hugged Bart. "I love every one of my teammates," Fuzzy said later, "but none of them's higher on the list as a human being than Bart Starr. The man gave his entire life to the Green Bay Packers. I'll always cherish him for that. He's beautiful."

I shook Bart's hand and grabbed his arm, half hugged him. I'm not sure Bart needs to be loved. But I love him anyway, and I respect him.

Forrest did not get to the motel on Saturday. He was busy, preparing his Packers to face San Diego the next day. The Packers had lost four of their first five games, and Forrest was unhappy with his slow start. He would finish strongly, ending his first season in Green Bay with eight victories and eight defeats, exactly the same record Bart had achieved in his final season. Yet his .500 percentage made Forrest, after only one year, the third most successful of all Packer coaches, after Curly Lambeau, who created the team, and Lombardi, who perfected it.

I got a chance to watch Forrest coach a couple of months after the reunion, during the final week of the season. I joined him and the team in Chicago for their closing game against the Bears, and Forrest made me feel like I belonged. He invited me to the pregame meal, brought me into the coaches' meeting, introduced me to the players, let me sit in on his pregame talk. He spoke rationally, logically, firmly, not emotionally. He appealed to his players' pride, reminded them that a victory over the Bears, who were going on to the playoffs, would give them a .500 record and something to savor during the off-season, a reason to look forward to 1985. I couldn't gauge the impact Forrest had on the players, but he certainly affected me. I began getting nervous, kind of hyperventilating, pumped up in the stomach and short of breath. I was excited. I wanted to suit up. I wanted to play. I was smart enough not to.

I was stunned by how young the players looked, and how big they were. Their arms were massive, their shoulders huge. Two or three came over to say hello to me as they were dressing for the game, and I kept shaking their taped hands. My hands, large enough to handle a size-15½ ring, got lost in theirs. I felt like I was grabbing a basketball. I turned to Forrest and said, "Where's the valve? They've got to have a valve somewhere where you put the air in."

I'd wondered about the intensity of the kids playing the game, because of the high salaries, I suppose. I'd heard people say they weren't as tough or as dedicated as we had been. Bullshit. I saw some awful collisions on the field. I didn't see anybody backing up. I didn't see anybody trying to avoid contact. The hits were violent. They were whacking. The intensity seemed to me as great as when I played.

"There's a difference," Forrest said. "The players today ask for reasons. We didn't ask Vince, 'Why do you want us to do this?' He told us to do it, and we did it."

Bart and Forrest did not speak to each other or even see each other until Sunday afternoon, until a few minutes before the Packers who had played in Super Bowl I were reintroduced to the capacity crowd at Lambeau Field. We were standing in the tunnel leading from the locker room to the field, that special place where cleats and memories echo. We were waiting for our ceremony when the 1984 Packers finished their pregame warmups and trotted off the field, heading, through the tunnel, to their lockers. Forrest entered the tunnel with the team, and when he reached Bart, he stopped.

For fourteen years, they had been teammates, together at so many dramatic moments, contributing so much to each other's success. Now, each trim at the age of fifty, each still close to his playing weight, Bart at 190 pounds, Forrest at 250, they were facing in opposite directions. "Good luck," Bart said.

Forrest wanted to tell Bart he knew how he felt, that in 1978, after he had lost his coaching job in Cleveland, he went to a preseason game and sat in the stands feeling awkward, uncomfortable, unwanted. Forrest knew it had not been easy for Bart to come to Lambeau Field.

"Thanks," Forrest said, nothing more, and their hands touched, each wearing the ring with the three diamonds, the reward for glories they had shared.

4. The Game That Made History

Not long after dawn on January 15, 1967, a bright sunny morning in California, the paths of Bart Starr and Max McGee crossed for the first time that day, but not the last. Bart, blue eyes bright after a terrific night's sleep, was on his way out, to attend a devotional service. Max, brown eyes blurred after a terrific night, was on his way in, to recuperate. Each in his own way was getting himself ready for Super Bowl I, and because each was ready to produce one of the most brilliant performances of his career, we were able to get together almost eighteen years later and celebrate the outcome of a historic game. Between toasting and teasing, we remembered the game, exchanged details, recalled especially the very special parts Bart and Max played. They made our reunion possible.

The pressure in the first Super Bowl game was all on us, the Packers, not on our opponents, the Kansas City Chiefs. We were representing the establishment, the National Football League, in its forty-sixth season, against the upstart, the American Football League, in its seventh. We had just won our tenth NFL championship, more than any other team, our second in a row, our fourth in six years. The Chiefs hadn't even been in Kansas City for six years.

Rival NFL owners, coaches and players—men who cursed us, gouged us and kicked us during the regular season—suddenly became our allies, wished us well, urged us to uphold the honor of our league. Lombardi was flooded with phone calls and messages, stressing the importance of a decisive victory. Anything less would shame him, humiliate us. "If you didn't know it, I'll tell you now," Max McGee said. "Vince Lombardi hated the AFL. He would have liked to have won about eighty-eight to nothing."

Lombardi's stand was principled—and practical. He knew that the NFL meant order and tradition, values he respected. He also knew that the AFL, bidding against the NFL for players for seven seasons, meant higher salaries. Lombardi believed fervently in the tradition of modest salaries.

During the week leading up to the game, we studied films of the Kansas City Chiefs, and once we saw two of their defensive backs, covering a pass play, collide and fall down. Some of us laughed out loud. "Looks like Looney Tunes and Merrie Melodies," said McGee, a professional pass receiver since 1954.

Max did not expect to play against the Chiefs—"I was just basking in the California sun, getting ready to retire," he explained—but, still, just in case, he paid attention to the films. Max was an astute observer. Often, when the offensive team watched films, Max would mumble something unintelligible, and Lombardi would switch off the projector and say, "What'd you say?" And then Lombardi would rerun the play and make Max repeat his observation. Max was smarter than he pretended to be. "Better not let me into that game," he told Ray Scott, one of our broadcasters, after he viewed the Kansas City films. "I'd have a helluva day."

Fuzzy Thurston didn't like the films as much as Max did. "I was scared," Fuzzy said. "I had to play Buck Buchanan, and he was about six-eight, about 285 pounds. I wasn't laughing."

We went into every game thinking we were going to win. We went into this game positive. We didn't predict publicly we were going to win. That wasn't our style. We had enough pressure on us without that. Still Lombardi could see what we were thinking, and he didn't like it at all. He drove us as hard as he ever had, maybe harder.

"He let us know that under no circumstances were we going to lose this football game," Bart Starr recalled.

We spent the week before the game in Santa Barbara, shielded from the temptations of Los Angeles. "Every practice was almost like a game," said Ron Kostelnik, our defensive left tackle. "We got a pregame speech every day."

"I played the best game of my life on Wednesday of that week," said Bob Skoronski, our offensive left tackle. "In practice. I wish I had it on film to show my kids."

Most of the Kansas City players, like us, knew enough not to pop off, not to rile up the enemy. But, fortunately for us, one of the Chiefs couldn't keep his mouth shut. His name was Fred Williamson, a defensive back with an ego approximately the size of the Los Angeles Memorial Coliseum. When he wasn't bragging about his intellect, his charm and his good looks, Williamson announced he would attack us with the forearm weapon that had become his trademark and his nickname—The Hammer. "A blow struck perpendicular to the earth's latitude," Williamson defined it, "with sufficient force to crack a man's helmet." He suggested that the effect was the same as running full speed into a neck-high clothesline. He said The Hammer drove wide receivers into retirement.

We watched films of Williamson and found, more than once, that he delivered The Hammer illegally, headhunting, not tackling, after a play was over, leveling an opponent simply out of malice. Lombardi was furious. He hated dirty football. "I've never put in a bootsie play in my life," Lombardi told us, "but if he hits one of our receivers like that, Bart, I want you to call a sweep, and I want the ballcarrier to go for the sidelines, and I want the other ten men to go for The Hammer. And I don't want to see him get up." It was the only time in his nine seasons I heard Coach talk like that.

The night before Super Bowl I, we moved into a hotel in Los Angeles, closer to the Coliseum, and most of us figured we needed a good night's sleep. Max figured he didn't. He had had a good night's sleep Friday. "One good night's sleep carried me for two days," he said. Besides, Max still didn't suspect he'd play. After all, he had caught only four passes in the entire regular season, plus one in the NFL championship game against Dallas. All that catch did was win the game for us.

Boyd Dowler, the starting wide receiver against Dallas, hurt his right shoulder when he was hit after catching a touchdown pass at the end of the third quarter. Max replaced him and, midway through the fourth quarter, on third down and nineteen yards to go, caught a twenty-eight-yard pass from Bart for a touchdown. It was the difference in the game; if Max had not scored, Dallas could have kicked a field goal in the final minute and defeated us and gone on to play in the first Super Bowl in Los Angeles.

"Us country boys don't get to see Los Angeles too often," Max said, "so I go out the night before the Super Bowl and I meet this little girl from Chicago, a pretty little blonde, and we're getting on pretty good. I'm watching my watch, and it gets to about a quarter to eleven, and we've got an eleven o'clock curfew, and the fine for breaking curfew has been stepped up, as I recall, to five thousand dollars. I didn't think too much about it. I had a history of paying well for my nights out."

Lombardi had been trying for years to discourage Max's nocturnal habits by fining him ever-increasing amounts for violating curfew. When the price reached $500, Max managed to sneak out of our training camp dormitory safely but made one strategic mistake. He got caught speeding, the newspapers reported his ticket, and Lombardi exploded. "MAX!" Vince screamed at a team meeting. "That's five hundred dollars and"—Coach was shaking—"if you go again, it'll cost you a thousand." Then Lombardi grinned. "Max," he said, softly, "if you can find anything worth a thousand dollars, hell, call me, and I'll go with you."

In Los Angeles, apparently, Max found someone worth five thousand dollars. He did not, however, call Lombardi.

"So we drive back to the hotel," Max said, "and I tell the little girl, 'Just in case I can get back out, I'll meet you at the bar across the street, and we'll go out and have a few drinks.'

"I remember her saying, 'You're not supposed to go out.'

"'Don't worry about it,' I say. 'I'm not playing tomorrow. I'll be happy to come out, and we'll have a little fun.'

"I go upstairs and I get in bed, under the covers, with my coat and tie on, and Hawg Hanner, one of the coaches, sticks his head in the door, looks around, sees Hornung in his bed and me in mine and says, 'Okay, you're in there.'

"'Hawgy,' I say, 'are you gonna check late tonight?'

"Hawgy and I had played together for ten years. It wasn't like asking one of the other coaches. Hawgy and I used to sneak out together sometimes. He knew the feeling.

"'Yes, I am,' he says. 'Don't you dare go out of here.'

"He closes the door and, about two seconds later, opens it up, sticks his head in again and says, 'I ain't checking.'

"I almost run over him getting out of there."

"I watched the evening news, I guess, then turned off the light," Bart recalled. "I never had trouble going to sleep the night before a game."

"I go back to the pretty blonde from Chicago," Max continued, "and we go out and kind of do the town. A little dancing. A few beers . . ."

Max paused. "I get back relatively late," he said. "Something like close to breakfast time.

"I get cleaned up. I look like I just got out of bed and I go down and have the pregame meal."

Max missed the devotional service, but he did make the pregame meeting. We got out to the Los Angeles Coliseum long before noon, a few hours before the kickoff at 1:15 P.M. The sun was shining, the temperature was in the low seventies and more than sixty thousand people were in the stands. Another forty thousand seats were empty. The Super Bowl wasn't quite so super then. But sixty-five million people watched the game on television, on two networks simultaneously, CBS, which had the NFL rights, and NBC, which had the AFL. Frank Gifford, who was working for CBS, told me later he walked up to Lombardi, who had coached him in New York, and Lombardi was shaking, that's how much the game meant to him.

Of course Max wasn't too steady, either. "I was a hundred percent for every game I played," Max said. "I was a hundred proof for this one." He and Paul sat on the bench, discussing important things. Paul was about to get married, and while they were planning the bachelor party in Las Vegas, Kansas City kicked off to us. On the third play of the game, Lombardi let out a scream: "MAX!"

"It was that famous voice," Max said, "and I honestly didn't know he wanted me to play football. I thought for sure he was going to fine me in front of sixty-five million people for sneaking out the night before the game."

Boyd Dowler, hit by The Hammer, hard but clean, had reinjured his right shoulder. Lombardi wanted Max to play. Relieved, Max loped onto the field. He liked to get into the flow of the game right away. Bart immediately called a pass to Max.

"It was a little quick turnout," Max said, "and I turned, and the ball was on me so quick it hit me in the helmet. Went through my hands and—bong! I said to myself, 'Boy, this is gonna be a great day, right?'"

Max was half mocking himself, and half serious. "Max knew right away he could have a big day," Bart said.

Max knew that the Kansas City linebackers were moving in tight to try to stop Jimmy Taylor from running, leaving a cornerback, usually Willie Mitchell, to cover Max, one on one. Max didn't believe he could be effectively covered one on one, especially in important games. He was right.

Midway through the first quarter, the game scoreless, we were on the Kansas City thirty-seven-yard line, third down and three to go.

Bart called a pass to Max. Bart had already been sacked twice, once by big Buck Buchanan, and he was hit again just as he released the pass to Max. The ball sailed off course, two feet behind Max. "Let's face it, it was a rotten pass," Max remembered. "You pay a guy a hundred thousand dollars to throw to a twenty-five-thousand-dollar end, you expect him to throw better than that. I wasn't going to go back and get killed by some linebacker. I thought sure somebody was going to intercept the ball, so I reached back to knock it down, to break up the interception, and when I did, the ball stuck in my hand. Just like that. Stuck right in my hand."

Max grabbed the ball on the nineteen-yard line—Willie Mitchell lunged for him and fell down—and the oldest man on the field, at thirty-four, sprinted the rest of the way, untouched, for the first touchdown in Super Bowl history. "It was an accident," Max insisted. "I did not anticipate catching that ball."

Max did not anticipate catching six more passes either, or gaining a total of 138 yards, or scoring another touchdown, setting Super Bowl records for receptions, yardage and touchdowns that were not broken for two, nine and seventeen years. Max made the first touchdown look so easy, we probably let up, subconsciously certain of our superiority.

But the Chiefs were a better team than we had given them credit for. They were young, they didn't have our experience, but they had a lot of talent—Len Dawson, Jim Tyrer, Bobby Bell, Johnny Robinson, Buchanan, all guys who played in seven, eight or nine Pro Bowls. They tied us at 7–7, and at halftime, we were barely leading, 14–10; Fuzzy and I had escorted Jimmy Taylor on the Green Bay sweep to the second touchdown.

The Chiefs might have had a chance to upset us—if it hadn't been for The Hammer. We hated to see him get any satisfaction. He did catch up to Max once. "And he brought The Hammer with him," Max said. "He got me pretty good, kind of moved my helmet around a little bit. But we'd heard that he'd broken a lot of helmets, and far as I could tell, mine wasn't even dented. I just started laughing about this guy trying to knock my head off. I was having a heckuva day."

The contest ended, really, in the early minutes of the second half. They took the kickoff and moved to midfield, threatening us for the last time. Then Willie Wood, at safety, intercepted one of Dawson's passes and ran fifty yards to the Kansas City five. Elijah Pitts scored on the next play. The extra point gave the defensive tackle a perfect opportunity to take a free shot at my head, and most of them did, mean, but not dirty. But on this extra point, Kansas City's defensive tackle, instead of giving me his best shot, sort of leaned on me and said, "Ahhhhh," and I said to myself, "This game's over," and it was. They were satisfied with what they'd done. They hadn't embarrassed themselves. They'd played well. That was enough for them.

Later in the third quarter, Max scored his second touchdown. This time, Bart threw the ball perfectly, but as he released it, Max got knocked off stride, pounded in the chest by Johnny Robinson. "All at once the ball's there, and I'd just been hit, and I'm not ready," Max said. "So I juggled it, bounced it up in the air. Then I stuck up one hand and accidentally caught it. It wasn't that I was trying to make it look spectacular. It just happened that way."

The final score was 35–10, and in the closing minutes, on a running play, with our high-priced rookie, our bonus boy, Donny Anderson, carrying the ball, The Hammer got hammered, knocked unconscious. He had to be carried off the field. Our guys got all excited, jumping up and down on the sidelines, whooping and dancing.

"You know who got hurt?"

"Who?"

"It was The Hammer!"

"The Hammer! Way to go!"

"They nailed The Hammer!"

"The Hammer got it!"

Fuzzy Thurston was out of the lineup, getting a breather, and when the offensive team came trotting off, Fuzzy shouted, "Did you get him, Jerry? Did you get him?"

"No," I said. "I didn't touch him. I went outside."

Fuzzy turned to Gale Gillingham, his replacement. "You get him, Gilly? You get him?"

"No," Gillingham said. "I turned inside on the middle linebacker."

Fuzzy grinned. "Well then Andy must have hit him with his purse," Fuzz said. Donny did take a lot of abuse for his big bonus.

Actually, The Hammer nailed himself. He made a good tackle on Anderson, but as he did, Andy's knee came up, and Williamson stuck his face right into the knee. He knocked himself silly.

I must admit I didn't feel too sorry for him, not then, not eighteen years later, when we met again in the Coliseum, each of us being interviewed for ABC's *20/20* report on Super Bowl I. Williamson was in the movie business, producing, directing and starring, he confessed. His body was still trim. His ego was still vast. He said he was a creative genius. He also said he was a great golfer. I had seen his golf game. I didn't have to see his movies.

Super Bowl I ended for all of us nine plays after it ended for The Hammer. Bart's statistics were as impressive as Max's. He completed seventy percent of his passes, sixteen of twenty-three, for 250 yards, and both his percentage and his yardage remained Super Bowl records for more than a decade, proof that you didn't have to stay up all night to have a great Super Bowl.

"I had better days," Max said, "but I never timed one better."

He and Paul had a wonderful bachelor's party in Las Vegas, and at the reunion, Max said he had only one regret about Super Bowl I: He never did see the little blonde from Chicago again, and he still couldn't remember her name.

5. Max and Paul Don't Sleep Together Anymore

Max McGee and Paul Hornung

Max McGee and Paul Hornung were so close that in training camp they pushed their two single beds together, took off all their clothes, jumped into bed and wrapped their arms around each other.

Once.

They were protesting. They thought Vince Lombardi was unfair to single men because he let the married men sleep at home one night a week during training camp. Max and Paul, as bachelors, felt they should be allowed to sleep out one night a week, too. For their health. Their mental health.

They picked a night when they knew that Lombardi himself, not an assistant, would be checking the dorm rooms at curfew time, to stage their naked protest.

"Vince sticks his head in," Max recalled, "and if you ever wanted to see a look on somebody's face. Here's two of his so-called stars, buck naked. I'll tell you one thing, he gave us a couple of nights off."

Max shook his head. "The strange thing," he said, "was that Hornung enjoyed it so much, I had to move out."

The unexpected star of Super Bowl I was the star of the reunion, too, for a variety of reasons. Max had the funniest stories to tell. He had the most interesting memories of the Super Bowl game and of Super Bowl Eve. He was, at fifty-two, the oldest player to come back, and he was also the most recently married. Exactly one month before the reunion, after twenty years of the bachelor life, Max got married for the third time. He brought his bride, Denise, with him to Green Bay. He took her to Paris when they were single.

Max was in fairly good shape physically, perhaps twenty pounds heavier than he was in Super Bowl I, and he was in great shape financially. He may well have been the richest Packer at the reunion. He was, at least, a contender. When he converted part of The Left Guard in Minneapolis into ChiChi's, a Mexican restaurant, Max scored spectacularly. ChiChi's margaritas boomed, the concept was franchised and Max sold his stock, some of it, not all of it, for between ten and twenty million dollars. He reinvested some of his capital in golf and gin rummy, and some in more risky ventures, and his net worth kept growing. Max was building a multimillion-dollar home on a golf course in Phoenix. He probably would have been the star of the reunion even if his old roommate had shown up.

Paul didn't make it. He said he had to work. He had to do a football show Sunday and an interview Monday for the Turner Broadcasting System. He couldn't get to Green Bay. He probably didn't want to share Max with Denise.

Paul used to overshadow Max. Paul used to overshadow everybody. He was always the star of our team, even after he stopped being the best player. We all loved Paul. We thought he was the greatest thing that ever walked. Paul thought so, too. Which made it unanimous. I'm not kidding. Paul was my hero. He won the Heisman Trophy at

Notre Dame. He was everybody's All-American. I was a country boy from Idaho and just being on the same team with Paul Hornung was a thrill to me. Golden Boy. Golden Dome. Goldilocks. Paul was so pretty, and so good at playing football, and at getting publicity, a lot of people never realized how good Max was.

Max came from White Oak, Texas, the youngest of five brothers. The first four were outstanding athletes. Max was expected to be, too. "I wanted to be in the band," he said. "That's where the girls were." His brothers made him play football instead. He also played baseball and basketball and ran track. He was the state high jump champion and, at six-foot-two and 210 pounds, played fullback on the football team. In his final high school game, he rushed for more than four hundred yards. "The other team's left guard weighed 142 pounds," Max said. "Why would he want to tackle me?"

He was offered appointments to West Point and to Annapolis, and scholarships to Notre Dame, Texas, Michigan State and every other school that cared about its football team. He was heavily recruited. Once he saw a brand-new car parked in his driveway. "Whose is that?" he asked an alumnus of an important college.

"That's yours," Max was told.

"I didn't even own a pair of shoes," Max remembered, "but I had a new car. Got one for my father, too."

When Tulane gave his high school coach a job and Max a scholarship, he went to New Orleans, played football and discovered Bourbon Street. He never lost the address. He got out of Tulane in 1954 and wasn't sure what he'd do. "I never thought of pro football," Max said. "I figured I'd go back to White Oak, Texas, and start working in a gas station, like all my idols."

But Green Bay offered him $7500 a year to play in the National Football League. He turned down $12,000 from a team in the Canadian Football League and went to Green Bay for one year. Then he went into the air force and was a pilot for two years. On his first solo flight, he missed the country he was supposed to land in. He landed by mistake in Mexico. Max and the air force both survived his tour, and in 1957, he rejoined the Packers. His NFL career lasted eleven more seasons, and at the end, to Lombardi's amazement, he was running the forty-yard dash faster than he had at the beginning. "In the early years," Max explained, "I deliberately didn't run as fast as I could."

Max always seemed to operate on about a quarter of his remarkable athletic ability, always seemed to hold back extra talent, extra energy, for emergencies, for clutch situations. Under pressure, he could always produce the big play—in football, in golf, in pool, in anything. Max was a rare and versatile athlete.

Paul's career was relatively brief, but spectacular. He started as a quarterback, was shifted to fullback and floundered for his first two seasons as a Packer. Then Lombardi arrived and turned Paul into a halfback, and for the next three seasons, from 1959 through 1961, Paul led the league in scoring. In 1960, he ran for thirteen touchdowns, caught passes for two touchdowns, kicked fifteen field goals in seventeen attempts and kicked forty-one extra points, for a total of 176 points in twelve games, an NFL record that has not been seriously challenged. Paul also passed for two touchdowns in 1960. In 1961, he scored 146 points, then the second-highest total ever, including thirty-three in one game, against Baltimore. He was named the outstanding player in the NFL in 1960 and 1961.

Paul never played quite that brilliantly again. He missed half the 1962 season, because the army recalled him during the Berlin crisis, and all of the 1963 season, because the NFL suspended him for gambling, for betting on his own team with bookmakers. When he came back, he was golden again only once. In 1965, in a game against Baltimore, he scored five touchdowns. Then, after Super Bowl I, a neck injury forced him to retire. He deserved to be elected to the Professional Football Hall of Fame. He belonged there, next to his coach and six of his Super Bowl I teammates. He almost made it in the voting that took place a few months after our reunion. Paul was one of six finalists. Four of them—including Joe Namath and O. J. Simpson—made it. Paul missed.

I felt bad for him. And for myself. In the early 1970s, when the NFL put out a book commemorating its first fifty years, I was named the outstanding guard of the half century. I thought that made me a cinch for the Hall of Fame. I became eligible in 1975, and except for the first two years, when I finished among the top ten in the balloting, I never came close to getting elected. I felt slighted, but Paul said he had more important things to worry about.

"I'm vice president of a real estate firm in Louisville with fourteen million in equity," he said, "and a group of us just bought a soybean refinery that did a hundred million in sales last year. I've also got a manufacturing company, in the aluminum business, and I just got out of the coal business. Got out at just the right time."

He sounded like the same old Paul, still talking only in millions. Jimmy Breslin, the newspaper columnist, once wrote an article about Paul and said, "He makes a trip to the corner grocery sound like an Arctic expedition." I hoped Paul was doing as well as he said.

Paul and I had a falling-out in the early 1970s. George C. Scott, the actor, and I were hoping to produce a movie based on the life of Lombardi, using the material, essentially, from my three books, *Instant Replay, Farewell to Football* and *Lombardi*. We had signed a contract with Marie Lombardi, Vince's widow, and paid her some money, and then one day George called me and told me he'd heard that Universal Pictures and ABC were producing a Lombardi film and that we had to get an injunction to stop it.

I called Marie and told her we had to get an injunction. "Please don't fight, Jerry," she said. "Please don't get in a fight over it." How could I get in a fight with Mrs. Lombardi? I had spent about $50,000 out of my own pocket over three years, but I just wiped my hands and walked away from the project.

Paul was involved in the Universal/ABC picture. He was sort of the technical advisor and the liaison, the contact with the players and Marie Lombardi. I don't know exactly how much work Paul did, but I do know that the film starred Ernest Borgnine, which was what Scott and I had been planning, and much of the material was remarkably similar to the material in *Instant Replay*. The next time I saw Paul, I called him a whore, a son of a bitch, a bastard and then some bad names. We were not on good terms for several years.

Eventually, I forgave Paul. He never thought there was anything to forgive him for, never thought he had done anything wrong. "Hell, they only gave me ten thousand dollars," he said. "I didn't have to do anything." I accepted Paul's explanation because I wanted to. I loved him too much to keep on hating him. He may not have been perfect, but he was still my hero.

Paul was, really, the only player we had in Green Bay who came in a superstar and left a superstar, and I wanted him always to be a superstar. I wanted him to have a spectacular career in broadcasting, like Frank Gifford's, for instance. Gifford is trim, handsome, glib, distinguished, a model for retired athletes, at ease on a mountain top at the Olympics or hosting *Good Morning America*. Paul should be in that position. He's had his own show, and he's broadcast football, but I want more for him. I worry about him. He says he can't work out because he's got a running back's knees. They puff up and have to be drained about once a year. He says he weighs about 255 pounds, and for once, he's probably not exaggerating.

When I went to visit him in Louisville several months after the reunion, still excited to see him, Paul told me not to worry. He told me about all the golf tournaments he's invited to, all the dinners, all the parties. "Paul Hornung went through life on scholarship," he said. "That'll be on my grave. That'll be my epitaph. He went through life on scholarship."

I would have loved it if Paul and Max had been partners in ChiChi's, if they had both hit it big. That's the way it should have been. Wouldn't that have been a kick in the ass for both of them and for all of us? If Hornung and McGee had done it one more time, scored one more spectacular touchdown?

Paul said he could have gotten in on ChiChi's early, but he didn't because he knew Max was trying to get out. "Max wanted to sell his stock when it was a dollar a share," Paul said. "He couldn't wait. He said, 'I'll clear half a million after taxes.' But Max's stock was restricted. He wasn't allowed to sell it for two years. By then, the stock was up to eighteen dollars a share. Max cleared about nine million."

Max confessed that his success in ChiChi's, like his success in Los Angeles before and during Super Bowl I, was not calculated. "We just happened to hit the right formula at the right time," he said. "I was just plain lucky." Lucky—and shrewd enough to spot a niche in the market, smart enough to see that the cost of steak was becoming prohibitive, that the low cost of Mexican food could make ChiChi's work.

Max said everything he achieved was the result of luck—never brains or talent—but he also said that his greatest stroke of luck was to have come along at the same time Lombardi did. "I have great admiration for Shula, for Landry, for the other outstanding coaches," Max said, "but for some reason, whenever I draw the picture of a coach in my mind, it always seems to be Lombardi. You ever notice that? He had something different, you know."

McGee and Lombardi had a very strange relationship: It wasn't master-slave. Lombardi rarely criticized anything Max did on the football field, in a game or in practice. He seemed to know that Max's ego bruised easily. He also seemed to know that Max's body bruised easily. He allowed Max to avoid the nutcracker drill, our most violent exercise, a one-on-one test of courage. Max demonstrated his bravery in his own way: He talked back to Lombardi.

Max's most famous retort followed a tirade in which Lombardi suggested that he was a lousy teacher, we were lousy students and we were all going to start over from basics. Then Lombardi reached down, picked up a football and said, "Now this is a football."

"Hold on, Coach," Max shouted. "You're going too fast."

Another time, when a couple of NFL officials came to our training camp and gave us a test on the latest rule changes, Lombardi warned us it was a tough test. "I don't expect you to get all twenty answers right," Coach said. "I just took it and I missed two questions myself."

"Don't worry, Coach," Max shouted. "They'll change those two rules."

His teammates envied Max for his wit, his timing and his fearlessness, and Max took credit for two out of three. "I was terrified of Lombardi," he said. He hid his terror in humor, even in contract negotiations. "All I'd say was, 'Vince, what do you think?'" Max recalled. "'Let's get it as high as you can, but I'm not going to sit here and get on your list for asking for more.'"

Max thrived on fear, of Lombardi and of failure. "I did everything more from a fear of failure than anything else," Max said. He was afraid of being a failure in football, and he became a star. He was afraid of being a failure in business, and he became a millionaire. "I was also very nervous around girls," he said.

Max admitted one other fear haunted his playing days. "I was scared to death to go to bed at night because I was afraid I'd miss something," he said. He and Paul missed very little except curfews. They claimed they set an NFL record by sneaking out seventeen nights in a row. "Lombardi only caught us one time out of each ten," Max said. He and Paul did not rest up during the off-season, either. "If we went to a race track," Max said, "we didn't get home till four in the morning. Those night races on the Seventy-ninth Street Causeway in Miami lasted a long time."

Eighteen years after Super Bowl I, McGee and Hornung were enjoying new roommates and, not coincidentally, new life styles. Neither was a bachelor anymore. Paul, who separated from his first wife in 1968 after less than two years of marriage, married again in 1979. McGee held out for five more years. "Athletes don't grow up real quick," Max said, in one of the understatements of all time. "I was finally ready, and I finally found the right lady. We actually enjoy each other's company. I feel more comfortable with her than with anyone else. I can have fun with her without playing gin."

Denise McGee, who owns a pair of dress shops called E.S.P. and

Charizma in Minneapolis, turned thirty shortly before the wedding. She was born the year Max entered the National Football League. "Tried to get one half my age," Max said. "Almost made it."

Hornung chose an "older" woman. Angela was eleven years younger than he. The Hornungs lived in a lovely condo, filled with antiques and paintings. They were based in Louisville, Paul's home town, and the McGees in Minneapolis and in Phoenix. The two couples were as compatible as the two bachelors once had been. They held their own annual reunions at the Kentucky Derby, and in the summer of 1984, they took a three-week vacation together in Europe. They went to London, Paris, Venice and Nice. They traveled on the Orient Express. They had come a long way from Green Bay. Max and Paul went to sleep every night and never tried to sneak out. Neither complained. "I told Angela if she ever left me," Paul said, "if she ever put me back on the streets, I'd kill her."

"How in the hell did I ever do all those things we used to do?" Max wondered. "I don't miss them at all." Then Max volunteered a confession. "I hate bars now," he said. "I can't stand them. Fuzzy still can handle them. I can't."

Max, however, had not turned against golf links and card tables. "I've got to compete," he said. "I don't care if it's golf or gin rummy, or whatever, but I've got to compete. That keeps the blood running. I'm not one of those guys who absolutely hates to lose. I like winning, but I don't mind losing. I just like to compete."

Occasionally, Max and Paul still managed to get together without their wives, with the boys, sometimes at Paul's annual golf tournament at the Golden Nugget in Las Vegas. "We play golf, we have a martini, then about nine-thirty or ten, we have an ice cream and go home," Hornung said. "Nobody'd believe it. Lombardi wouldn't believe it. He'd have to give back some of the money he collected."

Their schedules had changed, and so had their hairlines, thinning, and their waistlines, thickening—although Max, after the reunion, shed fifteen pounds to try to get down close to his playing weight—

but, in so many ways, Paul and Max had not changed. Paul still seemed to be maneuvering, looking for an edge, trying to do everything, run and pass and kick and sell programs, too. He was settled down, and more than pleased with his marriage, but he couldn't really unwind. He was still hyper, antsy. Max, on the other hand, was obviously happy. He always was. "When I was a kid," he said, "I had to wear the old clothes of my older brothers. It never bothered me. I needed one clean shirt and one clean pair of pants to go to school, and I was happy."

His great wealth had not changed him greatly. "Max doesn't know how much money he's got," Paul said, "and it doesn't make any difference to him. If he's got four million dollars or four dollars, he's going to live the same."

"All my life," Max said, "I've done exactly what I've wanted to do. Even when I didn't have money, when I was broke, it didn't stop me from going places and doing things and having fun. I still have fun." He paused. "I just drive a faster car now," he said.

Neither Max nor Paul wore his Super Bowl ring. Max found that every morning, when he woke up, his fingers were too swollen for him to slip the ring on. By noon, the swelling would subside, but he didn't want the trouble of carrying the ring around all morning, waiting for it to fit. Paul's problem was less complicated. He was allergic to the ring.

Max loved the reunion, loved showing off his new wife and his old golf swing, loved drinking moderately and leaving the parties early. And he loved remembering. "We had something most people will never experience," he said. "Forty guys who all fit in together, who all loved each other. It was all created by winning and by Lombardi." Max smiled. "And I think," he said, "that experience was probably worth the other seventy years you live."

6. A Six-Hundred-Acre Guy

When I heard that Max had sold his ChiChi's stock for millions, I cheered. When I heard that Tommy Joe had built his farm up to the size of Manhattan, I applauded. I'm tickled to death every time I hear about one of the guys hitting a home run.

And I've always tried to keep track, partly because I'm curious, partly because I really care about how the guys are doing and partly because I need, still, to measure myself against my teammates. I used to do it on strength and speed and agility. Now I do it on assets and liabilities. How's this guy doing? How's that guy doing? How am I doing in the race? Sure I want to win. I used to want to get the highest grade Lombardi gave for blocking.

It has nothing to do with jealousy. I don't begrudge any of the guys his success, and I wouldn't want to change places with any of them or anybody else in the world. Not for a year. Not for a week. Not for a day. My life has been a hell of a trip, and I'd hate to give up any piece of it, the good or the bad.

If I have any envy at all, it would have to be of Max, not because he made such a big score, but because he handled it so well. He hasn't really changed. He seems so at peace. He's been able to control his money instead of the other way around.

I wish all of the guys could make the kind of score Max made. I wish I could make that kind of score, too. I'd love to make a score so big I'd never feel driven again. I don't think there is a score that big.

Several times in my life, I've had in my hands more money than I'd ever dreamed of, and three times I've tried to stop, to rest, to let up. The last time was in the spring of 1981. I was in a deal that produced a nice chunk of cash, what I'd call a pretty good lick. I decided to retire. I fished. I hunted. I visited. I worked on my backswing and my personality. I got in my wife's way in the kitchen. I drove her crazy and myself, too. After six months, I had to go back to work. I had to be busy. I had to be doing something that could pay off.

It's not that I have to have silk suits and champagne. I'm much more comfortable with jeans and a can of beer. But, like Max, I've got to compete, whether it's in golf or gin or business, and in business, you keep score with money. And I guess I need to win more than Max does. Maybe it's because I never scored a touchdown all the years I played football. I like the feeling of the big score. And, I must admit, I have nothing against champagne.

I can remember when I used to think in much more modest terms. Where I grew up, in northern Idaho, if you did well, you ended up working in the woods, maybe owning a truck or a jammer, a system of cables and pulleys that hauls logs out of the woods and stacks them on the road. That's what you might be able to do if you got lucky. But putting together any kind of money, putting together, say, ten thousand dollars, at one time, nobody did that.

When I was sixteen, I got a job working in the woods and one month I made $1,051. I'll never forget the amount. It was a ton of money. I went to the bank and cashed a $500 check, got it all in twenties, twenty-five twenties, the most money I'd ever held in my life. And I gave one of my sisters two bucks to iron the twenties for me, to take out all the wrinkles. I thought I was the richest kid in the world.

My frame of reference changed in the next twenty years. I never got rich playing football—even with a Super Bowl check, I barely earned $50,000 in my best season—but football led to so many other opportunities, so many good deals, chances to invest in real estate and in restaurants, chances, in my case, to write books, to deliver speeches, to broadcast football games, to produce motivational films. In the late sixties and the early seventies, everything seemed to click. *Instant Replay* was a hit. Petrolane bought out my off-shore diving company. My motivational film, *The Habit of Winning*, starring a handful of my teammates, was so well received companies like General Motors and IBM purchased hundreds of prints.

By the time I'd been out of football for five or six years, I owned a six-hundred-acre ranch outside of Boise, had cattle on the ranch, a little money in the bank and a lot on paper. I was meeting famous people, from Richard Nixon and Spiro Agnew to Norman Mailer and Gore Vidal to George C. Scott and Tiny Tim, and I was in a position where I could screen and even turn down some very flattering career opportunities. Roone Arledge and Howard Cosell tried to persuade me to come to New York and be a fulltime sportscaster, and they offered me far more money as a starting salary than Lombardi had ever given me in my prime. I was tempted, but decided I didn't want to live in New York. I also had a chance to move to Los Angeles, to get into the film business, as a producer, and I talked it over with my wife, Wink, and we decided Los Angeles was no place to raise a family. I would have loved to have been in a movie with John Wayne—that would have been one of the greatest thrills I could imagine—but, other than that, I didn't mind passing up Hollywood.

I was so self-satisfied in those days. I really thought I was a smart guy. I put myself way up on a pedestal.

Then I got knocked off. I lost a million dollars in six months. An apartment-house deal went bad, the cattle business took a dive and my

Petrolane stock dropped from 33 to 7. It knocked me on my ass. I was really down. I sat at home, sucking my thumb, feeling sorry for myself and angry with myself. How could I be so dumb? Just a big dumb jock in over his head. Thought he could play with the big boys. I couldn't get started. I couldn't do anything except mope.

I wondered about changing my life style, lowering my sights and my expectations. I had never lived on a truly lavish scale, but I hadn't exactly deprived myself, either. If I wanted a new shotgun or a new set of golf clubs, I didn't worry about it, I bought it. If I wanted to go fishing in Costa Rica, I went. I was comfortable. But all of a sudden, my cushion was gone. I didn't have stock I could sell off any time I pleased. I didn't have cash in the bank. I was close to being busted, and I was more than a little uncertain how it had all happened. I sat down with Wink, and I told her we could sell our six-hundred-acre ranch and buy a smaller place, maybe sixty acres, and live happily ever after. "How do you feel about it?" I said.

"Whatever you want," Wink said. "Whatever will make you happy."

I thought about it for a while, and then I told myself, *To hell with that. I'm not a sixty-acre guy. I'm a six-hundred-acre guy.* That's what I need to make me happy and comfortable, six hundred acres, not sixty and not six thousand. I was going to have to do whatever it took to keep me at the six-hundred-acre level. I stopped sucking my thumb, and I went back to work.

I got into the coal business in Kentucky in the mid-seventies, and I met some great people and some tough people. I sat in poker games in east Kentucky where I was the only one at the table who wasn't holding a gun. I did all right. In poker and in coal.

Lombardi helped me.

"Winning is not a sometime thing here," he once told us. "It is an all-the-time thing. You don't win once in a while. You don't do things right once in a while. You do them right all the time. There is no room for second place here. There's a second-place bowl game, and it's a hinky-dinky football game, held in a hinky-dinky town, played by hinky-dinky football players. That's all second place is: hinky-dinky."

You don't do things right once in a while. You do them right all the time.

Of all the lessons I learned from Lombardi, from all his sermons on commitment and integrity and the work ethic, that one hit home the hardest. I've found in business that only fifteen or twenty percent of the people do things right all the time. The other eighty or eighty-five percent are taking short cuts, looking for the easy way, either stealing from others or cheating themselves. I've got an edge, because whenever I'm tempted to screw off, to cut corners, I hear that raspy voice saying, "This is the right way to do it. Which way are you going to do it, mister?"

You get up early. You go to the office early. You answer letters. You answer phone calls. If you think you have to sit down with a guy, you go see him, you don't just call him on the phone. You follow up. You study your business. You make decisions based on hard facts and strong feelings. You try to do everything right.

Otherwise, you end up with a hinky-dinky business.

I worked at the coal business. A lot of times, when I would much rather have been in Idaho with my family, or on a golf course with Fuzzy, I was in Kentucky, in meetings, negotiating, bargaining, planning. I didn't make a big score in the coal business. But I turned myself around. Financially and psychologically.

I got out of the coal business at the end of the seventies, but I stayed in the energy field. I went into business with a fellow named Art Preston. Art is an oilman, honest, decent and extremely intelligent. He reminds me of the guys I played with.

Art and his brothers, Jack and Jim, have a company called Preston Oil. Jim is a landman, an expert on leases. Jack is a petroleum engineer who, when the oil business slumped in the sixties, went back to college, studied medicine and became a surgeon—for fifteen years. Then he returned to the oil business. Art is a geologist. In the oil business, a lot of people make money drilling, and a few make money finding. Art is one of the finders, one of the rare people who truly understand the mechanics of the oil business, the laws of nature.

On any deal, Art's overriding rule is to do what's fair. I've never seen him do anything else. I don't know too many people like that. Art's also very patient, very calm, very tolerant. He'll let you make mistakes, let you learn. He'll say, "That might not be a very good idea," as you're driving off a cliff. He doesn't say, "Hey, stupid, stop the car." I'm exaggerating, but you get the idea.

Our first major venture together was a heavy-oil project not far from Bowling Green, Kentucky, a situation I'd heard about when I was in the coal business. Art thought it was feasible, and we took leases on the land, originally a nineteen-thousand-acre mineral deed. We knew there was a lot of oil on the property because of some asphalt quarries that had been active half a century ago. We also learned that Shell Oil had considered the possibilities of the property in the early 1960s when the price of oil was considerably lower than it is today. We did some additional studies and, with the help of George Ward, a chemical engineer who came to us from Exxon, we decided to go ahead with a one-acre pilot program.

We drilled six wells in a hexagonal pattern, with an injection well in the center. Then we ignited an underground fire and pushed air and water through the fire to produce steam, which would reduce the viscosity of the heavy oil so that we could pump it out of the ground. At first, we got just a few barrels a day. Then we got it up to an average of fifty a day, sometimes a hundred.

We took core samples and calculated that there were approximately 450 million barrels of oil in place under the ground we had leases on. We knew the oil was there. We knew we had the technical know-how to move it. The question was could we move it economically.

Pittston Coal liked our chances enough to invest in the project, to put up enough money so that, after all our expenses were paid, after Art got his original investment back, my share of the profits came to a million and a quarter dollars. I put that in the bank in 1981 and tried, unsuccessfully, to retire.

After that, the price of oil went down, and Pittston pulled out of the project, sold us back their share. But we're still hopeful. George Ward, who runs the operation, is so convinced of the value of the project that he's brought his son into it. His son is a chemical engineer from Princeton with an MBA from Harvard, and if he thinks the heavy oil can pay off, an old football player from Idaho isn't about to tell him differently. If it works, if we can move the oil economically, the potential is enormous.

Art and I didn't do so well on another project, a geothermal well in Dixie Valley, Nevada. Our holdings had as much potential, our scientists said, as a hundred-million-barrel oil field. We drilled down more than ten thousand feet, came back up, diverted our well horizontally two thousand feet and went down below ten thousand feet again, searching for hot water and solid rock. For a month, we kept getting conflicting reports, looks good one day, looks bad the next. Finally, our engineers and geologists came to the conclusion that the well was a failure, that, as deep as we had gone, there wasn't enough heat, there wasn't enough water and the rock was incompetent, it was too soft. They said that drilling any deeper would be a waste. We had already spent three-and-a-half to four million dollars. I felt like shit. Art had never even come to the site. He had left it all up to me. I dreaded calling Art, telling him I'd failed. I got his brother Jack first. "Looks like we got a bad well," I said.

"Never did like that geothermal much, anyway," Jack said. "We need to get back into gas and oil in Oklahoma." He wasn't at all upset. Art reacted just as beautifully. I reached him in Kentucky—he was checking out some of his thoroughbreds—and I said, "We got a bummer."

"Now don't get down," Art said. "Keep your chin up." Our idea, when we started, was to take a shot, to aim at some big projects, some elephants, Art called them. "We've still got more elephants to go after," he said.

We do have other deals we're considering, and one of them, or the heavy-oil project in Kentucky, could be the big score I've been shooting for. What would I do then? Twenty years ago, I might have chartered a 747 and taken all the guys from the first Super Bowl team, and some of the guys from the earlier teams, like Ron Kramer and Dan Currie and Johnny Symank and Bill Quinlan, and flown them all around the world for about three months, with stops at all the best golf courses and the best fishing holes and the best saloons.

But now I'd like to think I'm a little more sensible, a little more interested in the welfare of my family than in a good time with the boys. I'd like to make certain everyone in the Kramer tribe has a chance to go to college. I'd love to set up an educational trust, named after Mom and Dad, to help my nieces and nephews, as well as my own children.

If I make the big score, will I stop trying to add to it? I'm afraid not. I guess I'm like Art. "If I was ninety-seven years old and on my death bed," he once said, "doped with medicine and filled with tubes, in the middle of surgery, and somebody came by with a deal that sounded good, somehow or other I'd get my hand up and say, 'I'm in.'"

I know I'll never retire again. It's not the money. It's that compulsion to be busy, to be productive. Where does it come from? It comes, first, from having had nothing, from growing up without, from hustling to find summer jobs; the phone never rang for so long that now, when it does, I have to answer it. It comes, too, from Lombardi, from the obligation I feel toward him, and to my teammates, the obligation to succeed. He showed me that I'm capable of doing anything I set my mind to, and if I don't use my ability, if I don't achieve, then I'm wasting my time, betraying him and cheating myself.

I'll always work, but someday, I hope, I won't put in so many hours as I do now, I won't travel so much. My dream is to strike a harmonious balance among work, family and my own personal quest. I don't know if it's spiritual or emotional or what, but I do know that I'm searching for some kind of answers that will bring me a certain measure of peace.

Maybe, eventually, I'll be able to temper my competitive instincts. I'll stop trying to hit the ball farther and run faster and earn more than anyone else. I realize that the only meaningful competition is against myself, against my potential and my limits, but I can't help it. I still like to go head-to-head against the people I know.

There's one thing I haven't mentioned that has always driven me and probably always will: the need to prove that there is more to me than the physical, that I'm intelligent, that I'm not just a dumb jock, that I have a head on this big scarred body. Ever since I was a kid, bigger and stronger than almost all the other kids, I've lived with the fear that people thought I was dumb, and, worse, with the fear that I really was dumb.

When I entered the seventh grade, my first day, I walked into the school and somebody said, "What class are you in?" I said, "The seventh grade," and he said, "Seven-one or seven-two or seven-three?" I said I didn't know, and he told me that seven-one was for the smart kids, seven-two for the average kids and seven-three for the dumb kids. I walked into seven-two, and when my name wasn't on the blackboard, I said to myself, *You big dummy, you ought to know better.* And I went to seven-three. When my name wasn't there, either, I finally went to seven-one, which was where I was supposed to go in the first place. I began to suspect that maybe I wasn't really stupid.

But the feeling or the fear that big meant dumb never really left me, and a couple of years ago, it came home to me in a striking way. I was eating dinner with Willie Davis in Los Angeles, and Wilt Chamberlain came into the restaurant and walked over to our table to say hello to Willie. I was introduced, and I stood up, and as I stared up at this incredible physical specimen, seven-foot-one, towering over me, the thought shot through my mind: *Boy, he must really be stupid!*

I almost couldn't believe it. I was guilty of the same prejudice that had haunted me all my life. And, of course, I found out that Wilt was large, living proof that the prejudice was false. Wilt is a very intelligent, sensitive and witty man. We ended up at his house, shooting pool and swapping stories till dawn.

And yet I still have those fears about big being dumb.

I also still have the six-hundred-acre ranch in Idaho.

7. A Pair of Big Businessmen

Willie Davis and Ron Kostelnik

Once they were the left side of the Green Bay Packers' defensive line, but when they showed up for the reunion of the team that won the first Super Bowl game, one of them, Willie Davis, owned five radio stations and a beer-and-wine distributorship and sat on the board of directors of MGM/United Artists, and the other, Ron Kostelnik, was the president of and sole stockholder in a company grossing eighteen million dollars a year. They had become big businessmen. Very big businessmen.

Someone coaxed Willie Davis onto a scale, and my old roommate, the president of All-Pro Broadcasting, weighed in at 284 pounds. The president of Mainline Industrial Distributors wouldn't even get close to the scale. Ron Kostelnik simply conceded that he outweighed Willie by a wide margin. "No contest," he admitted. The left side of our front four had turned into professional and personal conglomerates.

Willie and Kos came to extreme wealth from extreme poverty. The great-grandson of slaves, Willie was the son of a Louisiana laborer who was earning fifty cents a day when Willie was born in the heart of the Depression. Kos, whose grandparents came over from the Ukraine, was the son of a Pennsylvania coal miner.

"If it hadn't been for football," Willie said, "I'd probably be a laborer, too."

"I wouldn't be in the mines," Kos said. "I was always too big for the mines. I'd be in a steel mill."

Not long before our reunion, Willie sat in an MGM/United Artists board meeting with his fellow directors, including Alexander Haig and Cary Grant. He traveled to Africa to represent President Reagan. And he attended the Olympic Games as a member of the Los Angeles Olympic Organizing Committee. "I could never have dreamed any of this," Willie said. "If I had ever staked out a spot I wanted to reach, I'm way out beyond that."

Kos said he would have to leave the reunion a day early. He and his wife were going to Japan on a business trip. "A couple of years ago," Kos said, "I was at the world headquarters of B. F. Goodrich, one of the companies whose products I distribute, and I sat at a huge table in a big conference room thinking to myself, *What the hell am I doing here?* It was all I could do to keep from giggling. I'm the luckiest guy in the world."

In a way, Kos's success, while not quite on the vast scale of Willie's, was the more remarkable, because Kos, unlike Willie, never really was a football *star*. Willie played his way into the Professional Football Hall of Fame; Kos didn't even make the Green Bay Packers Hall of Fame. In fact, of all the Packers who started in Super Bowl I, Kos probably was the least known. His consolation was that he, like Johnny Weissmuller, was later named to the Cambria County (Pennsylvania) Hall of Fame.

Willie and Kos came to the reunion to see old friends and, even more than most of us, to celebrate a man who saw something special in them when no one else did. Willie was a substitute school teacher discarded by the Cleveland Browns when he met Vince Lombardi in 1960. Kos was a scared rookie out of the University of Cincinnati a year later. I watched Kos in training camp. I studied him. I hit against him. I could see he wasn't going to make our team. Lombardi had much better eyesight than I. He could see inside people.

Willie was born in Louisiana and raised in Texarkana, Arkansas, mostly by his mother, Nodie Bell, a sturdy woman with strong values. When Willie was named to the board of directors of MGM/United Artists, Nodie Bell had only one question. "Do they make pictures everyone can go see?" she asked. (Willie's mother and my mother would have gotten along perfectly. When *Instant Replay* was published, my mother said to me, "Now don't use any words in there that Roy Rogers wouldn't use.")

Nodie Bell died a few weeks before our reunion—we were all reaching the age where we were vulnerable to the pain of losing parents—and Willie was, for him, very subdued in Green Bay. He was feeling a great deal of pain.

His mother was the first person who inspired Willie. Nathan Jones was the second, a big man, perhaps six-foot-five, who coached football and taught science at Booker T. Washington High School in Texarkana. The most important thing Nathan Jones taught Willie was that a man could be big and strong and intelligent at the same time.

At Grambling, on a football scholarship that made him the first member of his family to attend college, Willie used both his brawn and his brain. He was a fierce football player, captain of the team in both his junior and senior years, and, as an industrial arts major, minoring in math and physical education, he was a fierce student, on the dean's list in both his junior and senior years. Once again, his football coach, this time Eddie Robinson, provided inspiration.

"Eddie Robinson sold America," Willie said, "better than most people who received much more from America. He truly believed that tomorrow was going to be better. 'If you think the right things, and do the right things, something good is going to happen,' he used to say, and I'd say, 'I believe, Coach, I believe.'"

Professional football scouts did not have much faith in Grambling football in the 1950s, and even though Willie was a black-college All-American, he was not drafted until the seventeenth round, by the Cleveland Browns, the NFL's dominant team in the fifties. The army drafted him, too, which took priority. Willie spent two years in the service, made the all-army football team, then reported to Cleveland in 1958. He thought the right things, did the right things and, against all odds, won a spot on the team Paul Brown, a Hall of Fame coach, was building around Jim Brown, a Hall of Fame fullback.

Remarkably, Willie broke into the Browns' starting lineup in his rookie season and, more remarkably, in three games he played the full sixty minutes, both ways, offense and defense. He was the last Cleveland Brown to do that. He still had enough energy in the off-season to take graduate courses in education at Western Reserve University and to teach math and industrial arts in secondary schools. He was probably the last Cleveland Brown to do that, too.

In 1959, Willie got married. His wife, Ann, was a graduate of the University of Cincinnati with a master's degree in education from Kent State. Then Willie got traded. Driving home from a day of substitute teaching, after his second Cleveland season, he heard on the car radio he had been traded to Green Bay. He felt wounded, unwanted, rejected. The lessons he had learned from Nathan Jones and Eddie Robinson suddenly seemed empty.

Then he met Vince Lombardi. "He was an extension of Nathan Jones and Eddie Robinson," Willie said, "and more." Willie had just signed a new contract with Cleveland for $8,500 a year. Lombardi tore it up and raised him to $9,500 a year. "There was never any doubt in my mind I wanted to play for the man," Willie said.

He played defensive end for Lombardi. He played with skill, with intelligence and, above all, with passion. He didn't miss playing offense. "The offensive man plays with an interior control system,"

Willie said. "My temperament was suited to defense, to challenge, to interrupt. My mentality is to get there, to attack."

Willie never forgot that Cleveland discarded him. Nor did Lombardi. Once, after the two had been together for a few years, in the privacy of his office, Lombardi said, "Willie, do you know that I applied for the coaching job at Notre Dame twice and never got as much as an acknowledgment to my letter?" Tears came to Lombardi's eyes. "When you came here, Willie," he said, "I saw what kind of guy you were. I understand why you play the way you do. I understand how much this game means to you."

"He didn't have to say another word," Willie said. "I would have done anything in the world for the man. If I would've gone to war, I would've wanted Lombardi to be my general."

Occasionally, Willie did go to war, with Lombardi, a war of words called contract negotiations. "I always came away thinking, *Why did I accept this?*" Willie said. *"Why didn't I stick to the number I went in with?"*

One year Willie elected to put his persuasive arguments for a sizable raise in writing. He walked into Lombardi's office during the spring and said, "Coach, I kind of had the opportunity to put everything down in a letter."

"A letter?" Lombardi said.

"Yes."

Willie handed the letter to Lombardi, who read a few lines and laughed, read a few more, down to the numbers, and frowned. He read three-quarters of the way through the letter, then, unable to contain himself, put it down. "Willie, I can't argue with one point in your letter," Lombardi said, "but we also have the Starrs and the Greggs and the Kramers to pay, and I don't want to have one guy really out of line."

"Yeah, Coach," Willie said, "but I was at the Pro Bowl and talking to guys like Merlin Olsen and Deacon Jones and I felt bad, because I thought I was in the same class with them, and the money just wasn't anything like the same."

"What'd they say they were making?" Lombardi demanded.

Willie told him the numbers. Lombardi pulled a notebook out of his desk and thumbed through it. "Not true," he said. "Not true."

They argued for a few minutes, then both fell silent. Finally, Willie said, "Coach, you know the difference between me driving back to Chicago today feeling enthusiastic, really looking forward to training camp, and me driving back thinking about pulling into the lane of oncoming traffic is the difference between what I want and what you're offering."

Lombardi perked up. "What are we talking about?" he said.

"Coach," Willie said, "we're talking about fifteen hundred dollars. Initially, we were talking about a lot more, but the number now is fifteen hundred dollars."

"Well, if it's fifteen hundred between you driving back feeling positive and driving back feeling negative," Lombardi said, "you've got it." He paused for a beat. "But," he said, "I want this damn letter because I want to make sure nobody else ever gets ahold of it."

"Lombardi never let me forget that time he gave in," Willie recalled. "'I'm flexible, I'm flexible,' he liked to say."

Willie played eight seasons for Lombardi, ten for Green Bay, and never missed a game, 138 straight regular-season games, six NFL championship games and two Super Bowls. He hated to sit out even a play. Once, I was standing on the sidelines when Willie came out of the game with a dislocated finger. As he turned his hand palm up for the trainer to examine, I saw the bone sticking through the skin. The trainer grabbed the finger, yanked the bone back in place, then taped the finger to the adjoining fingers. Willie ran back to the game.

He was our defensive captain and, among his teammates and the fans, our most popular player. His nickname was "Doctor Feelgood," a name he acquired after he told us that, in his youth, the girls all called him "Doctor," because "I made 'em feel so good."

Willie played in five Pro Bowls and was named All-Pro five times.

"To fail," Willie said, "would have been to let down Nathan Jones, Eddie Robinson and Vince Lombardi."

Ron Kostelnik grew up in football country, in the mill and mining towns of western Pennsylvania, near Johnstown. He played for Central Cambria High School and he was not heavily recruited. Shippensburg State Teachers College, less than an hour from home, offered him a half-scholarship. The University of Cincinnati, three hundred miles away, made the only other offer, a full scholarship. Kos had never been more than thirty miles from his hometown. He decided to see the world. He went to Cincinnati.

He was not exactly a big star at Cincinnati, either. Red-shirted his sophomore year, kept idle because of an injury, Kos played only two varsity seasons, and even though he made the All–Missouri Valley Conference team, hardly anyone noticed. The conference in general, and Cincinnati specifically, was far better known for basketball than football. The Big O, Oscar Robertson, was the center of attention at Cincinnati. The big Kos was drafted by the Buffalo Bills of the one-year-old American Football League. The Bills picked him in the fourteenth round. "I figured, going that low," Kos said, "I wouldn't be picked at all in the NFL draft."

But Lombardi chose Kos in the second round, right behind Herb Adderley and eleven rounds ahead of Elijah Pitts. "I was shocked," Kos said. He had one year of college eligibility left, but passed it up to join the Packers. To my amazement, The Rhino—later Cully, short for Culligan Man, because he was always looking for water—made the team. For eight years, we faced each other in practice, right guard against defensive left tackle.

The first three seasons Kos spent as a reserve. Then he moved into the starting lineup in 1964. He and Willie were the left side of the line, Henry Jordan and Lionel Aldridge the right side, a delicate and deliberate balance, one exceptionally quick man on either side, Willie and Henry, perfect for rushing the passer, the other two, Kos and Lionel, not quite so quick, perfect for containing the running game. "I had Willie Davis on one side of me, Henry Jordan on the other and a nut like Ray Nitschke behind me to cover my ass," Kos said. "How could I go wrong?"

Kos was a solid player, not spectacular. Of our twenty-two starters on offense and defense in Super Bowl I, Kos was one of only five who never made All-Pro or played in the Pro Bowl. "Who was Ron Kostelnik, if you really analyze it?" Kos said. "I was part of the Green Bay Packers football team. I was a good professional football player. We had good professional football players, and we had all-stars, like Jordan and Kramer and Thurston. And on top of that, we had super all-stars, like Starr and Hornung and Taylor. I was one of the supporting players, supporting a great cast."

Like Willie, Kos had the proper mentality to play defense. I used to kid him sometimes and say it was the proper lack of mentality. He struck back. "The offensive man," Kos pointed out, "knows exactly what he's supposed to do. He knows the play. The defensive man, he doesn't know the play. He has to react, to improvise. He has to be just a little sharper than the offensive folks."

"He can't remember the play," I told Kos. "That's why he's on defense."

One reason Kos preferred defense was that Lombardi, who ran the offensive meetings, did not get a chance to scream at you as often. Kos was one of several Packers, like McGee, who didn't respond well to harsh criticism. Lombardi always seemed to know who was sensitive, who was not. "He didn't get on me too much," Kos said, "'cause he knew I'd crack."

Negotiating contracts, of course, Lombardi attacked, but not harshly. "He had a book," Kos remembered, "and if you had a mediocre season, he'd take out the book and say, 'This is how many tackles you made last year. This is how many times you sacked the quarterback.' But if you had a hell of a year, you never saw the book."

Kos had a hell of a game to get us to Super Bowl I. Against Dallas, in the NFL championship game, he was in on fourteen tackles.

Like so many of us, when Lombardi left Green Bay in 1969, to spend the final year of his life coaching the Washington Redskins, Kos left, too, traded to the Baltimore Colts. A month after the trade, Green Bay played in Baltimore, and Kos, who was always one of the first players taped and dressed before a game, visited the locker room of his old teammates. In his Baltimore uniform, he felt like an intruder. At the end of the season, he retired.

Then, in 1970, he went to his first Green Bay game as a spectator. Again, he was uncomfortable. "People kept looking at me," Kos said, "and I didn't know if it was because they recognized and respected me, or because they thought I was a has-been."

Kos was not a has-been. He was just getting started. He had just bought Mainline Distributors. He was risking every cent he had saved from nine seasons of professional football.

Right before we played Super Bowl II, right before we won our third straight championship, Lombardi told us that if we won, "I'd be so proud, I just fill up with myself." That's the way I felt seeing Willie and Kos at the reunion. That's the way I felt when I visited them at work, Willie in his office in the heart of Watts, Kos in his factory in Appleton, Wisconsin, one of his nine branches.

At the end of 1964, Willie Davis, the classic overachiever, enrolled in the prestigious graduate school of the University of Chicago, to pursue a master's degree in business administration. His plan was to play football for the Green Bay Packers from July to December, and to go to classes from January to June. He was always tardy. Pro Bowls and Super Bowls kept preventing him from getting to school on time.

In 1966, in his second term at Chicago, Willie fell behind in his courses and in his grades; he was in danger of being placed on academic probation. At the same time, as a unanimous All-Pro and a member of the NFL championship team, as a hero in Green Bay and Wisconsin, he found new job opportunities opening up to him. Willie was very tempted to drop out of the University of Chicago, forget about the master's degree and take advantage of the new opportunities. He told Coach Lombardi what he was considering. "You know," Lombardi said, "I've never known Willie Davis to be a quitter."

The words stung. Willie didn't quit. He went back to Chicago, turned his intensity to the books, raised his grades and in 1968, the year he received his MBA, made the dean's list. "In whatever setting you place Willie Davis," said the dean of the Graduate School of Business, "he'll be a leader. People pay attention to him." The dean was George Shultz, later President Reagan's secretary of state.

Armed with his degree, Willie worked for the Schlitz Brewing Company while he played his final seasons in Green Bay. He also invested a few thousand dollars in a company called Valley School Supply. Ron Kostelnik invested, too. So did Bob Skoronski, who, after the 1968 season, retired from football and went to work full time at Valley School Supply.

Willie ended his football career in 1969, then put all of his savings into purchasing a Schlitz distributorship in Los Angeles, all of his energy into making the investment a success. Nathan Jones, Eddie Robinson and Vince Lombardi knew he couldn't miss. If this basically gentle, good-natured man had been able to turn himself into a fury to survive and flourish on the football field, imagine how he drove himself to endure and prosper in business. "I was willing to work hard," Willie said. "I was willing to pay the price. I was willing to do all the things that were necessary to become a winner."

He won. His distributorship thrived. So did Willie. He signed up the Forum, the home of the Los Angeles Lakers and Kings, to sell his products. He signed up United and other airlines. He expanded, added Inglenook wines, then Heublein liqueurs. He was named to the board of directors of Schlitz, one of the first blacks to hold such a position in a major American corporation. When Stroh's took over Schlitz, Willie gave up a directorship, but added the Stroh's line.

In 1977, he saw an opportunity to purchase a bankrupt radio station at a bargain price, considered the odds and the potential in the crowded Los Angeles market, and bought what became KACE-FM. He knew the beer business. He learned the radio business. "I was scared," he admitted. His fear spurred him. He turned the station around as dramatically as Lombardi had once turned the Packers around. Willie made it profitable, made it a responsible voice for and to the Watts community. He formed All-Pro Broadcasting and bought four more stations, two in Milwaukee, one in Seattle and one in Houston. He built an empire. He passed on Lombardi's principles to his people. "I reminded them," Willie said, "that success is planned, success is earned and that there's no laughter in losing. Losing should always be unexpected."

Willie's waistline swelled, but never his head. He never forgot his roots, never took his success for granted, never stopped appreciating what he had achieved. He hired his younger brother and his father. He became, by any reasonable measurement, one of the major black entrepreneurs in the United States, and one of the most influential. He advised and supported the mayor of Los Angeles, Tom Bradley. He added awards from the Boy Scouts of America and the NAACP to the Byron "Whizzer" White Award he had earned as a football player. He gave his time and talent to the Urban League and to the NCAA, to hospitals and charities, to an endless list of civic and educational institutions. His secretary, Edna Garnet, called him a slow learner. "He never learned to say no," she said.

He served, at various times, on the boards of Mattel, Fireman's Fund, Sarah Lee Foods, the Alliance Bank, then MGM/United Artists Entertainment. "Some people feared I would just be a token at MGM," he said, "that they were just responding to pressure from the NAACP. There was pressure. They could have picked Lena Horne or Sidney Poitier. But they wanted a businessman. And as long as I can be my own man, as long as I can advance my opinions on the basis of my beliefs, I have no problem. I bring a mixture of street sense and learned intelligence to the boards I sit on, and I feel good about that. I feel comfortable. I contribute."

At MGM, Willie added, sitting with Haig and Grant and Art Linkletter, among others, he would never have to worry about an ego problem. "I'm in the back of the line when they ask for autographs," he said. "I'm Willie Who?"

He was too modest. Willie and I went to dinner one night at Chasen's, a very expensive and exclusive restaurant, an institution in Beverly Hills. When you enter the front door of Chasen's, the first thing you see is a portrait of Jimmy Stewart, Gregory Peck and Fred MacMurray, three of the gods of Hollywood. The way they fawned over Willie in Chasen's, I thought that threesome had become a front four.

Willie just acted like Willie. He laughed, put away some chili and some roast chicken, and then strawberries with hot fudge on them.

In 1965, when Willie Davis started business school, Ron Kostelnik, who already had his master's, in physical education, went to work for Mainline Industrial Distributors. He was in public relations during the football season and in sales during the off-season. In 1970, his football days finished, Kos bought the company. Mainline was struggling, relatively small, grossing barely a million dollars a year.

Kos earned $30,000 for his final season as a football player. He paid himself $25,000 for his first year as a chief executive officer. He cut himself to $20,000 the next year and to $18,000 the third. "At one time," he said, "I was the third- or fourth-highest-paid employee of my own company." The following year, he sold his stock in Valley School Supply. He used up his savings to keep his family, and Mainline, going. "I had been force-fed so much of that drive, excel, win, I had to make the company work," Kos said. "I was very conscious of my public image. You know: *Here we go with this dumb football player who's bought this company and doesn't know what the hell he's doing.* I was very conscious of that feeling. I was afraid of the embarrassment of failure."

Kos built up the company steadily and skillfully, added and modified products and services, expanded so that, at the time of our reunion, Mainline was stocking fifteen thousand different items, from bearings and bushings to conveyors and couplings to gaskets and gears, in nine branches in two states, and representing such companies as Anaconda, Browning and B. F. Goodrich, grossing more than eighteen million dollars a year. Mainline celebrated its twentieth birthday, the fourteenth year of Kos's ownership, with a handsome brochure featuring photographs of the company's officers and branch managers. Kos had found the right people and had kept them. The turnover at Mainline was stunningly low. "I've hired talented, dedicated people," Kos said, "and I've treated them fairly. When I'm retired and lying on the beach at Hilton Head, I don't want to have to worry about how they're doing." Kos said he personally negotiated salaries each year with his nine branch managers. "They're so well paid," he said, "I've got to start using Lombardi tactics."

Mainline's twentieth-anniversary brochure began with a quotation: "For he wishes not to seem, but to be, the best." It was pure Lombardi, even if it did come from Aeschylus.

Obviously, neither Ron Kostelnik nor Willie Davis came to the reunion with any pressing financial problems. Both were and—more important—*felt* secure. Both were aware, however, of their own mortality. Willie, at fifty, said he no longer feared that his life would be cut short, only that his projects, his plans might be interrupted. At forty-four, Kos, one of the younger men at the reunion, shied away from the word "death." He worried, he said, about "longevity."

I worried for both of them about their weight. Willie laughed and shrugged me off. He had a gym in his condo at Marina del Rey and he worked out. Kos admitted he was frustrated, aware that the problem had gotten out of control. At his size, he feared exercising too strenuously. He no longer tried for every tennis ball. He did not jog. He took long walks. "I'd love to walk into a room suave and streamlined," he said, "but . . ." Perhaps the reunion inspired him. He went on a diet afterward, lost fifteen pounds and was proud he was headed down toward three hundred.

Both Willie and Kos were pleased with their children, but concerned, concerned that they might have given them too much.

Willie's son, Duane, and daughter, Lori, were both in their early twenties. "One of my fears is that my kids have it too easy," Willie said. "They don't have to dig, they don't have to deal with uncertainty. They assume. They expect. *Hey, it's gonna be there.* And, of course, one of the driving forces of my life was to make sure it was there. I constantly try to bring the possibility of uncertainty into their lives, but a manufactured fear is never the same as a real fear."

Duane Davis played football at the University of Missouri. He was a good football player, not a great one. "Terry Donahue, the coach at UCLA, told a friend of mine," Willie said, "that if Duane had been brought up in a ghetto, he would have been one of the best football players in the country. He didn't have to say anything else.

"It's not important whether Duane is a great football player or not. He's a good kid, a kid I'm proud of in every sense of the word. I just wish he *knew*, I wish he could *feel* all the reasons I had to make it playing football. I talk to him sometimes and I paint all the bleak pictures and say all of the things to upset him, to create fear and concern, and I look in his eyes, and he says, 'Dad, I know where you're coming from.' He doesn't have the slightest idea of where I'm coming from."

Duane was working at KACE-FM, learning the business. "One side of me says it's unfortunate he didn't grow up in a ghetto," Willie said, "and the other side says there's no way I would've wanted him to."

Willie, Kos, so many of us were living proof that deprivation was a great motivator. Which left us all with a conflict: We wanted to give our children so much that we didn't have, and we wanted to give them, too, something we did have, something that would carry them down the road. We wanted to put our fire in them.

Kos spoke of his son, Mike, who used to hang around our locker room, a quiet, polite, bashful boy, and of his three daughters. Mike was in his last year of college; the girls were younger, one in college, one in high school, one in junior high. "We have a statement around the house that they're only with us for a short time," Kos said. "I'm a soft touch. My wife would say that I spoil them terribly. My kids have been all over the country, and one of the girls went overseas on an exchange program. I wonder if we're taking away from them the joy of earning these things for themselves. Mike wanted a car when he was in high school. I didn't have a car till I left college to drive to Green Bay. Mike didn't get the car. But he did get the opportunity to work in our warehouse to earn the money for the car."

Ever since we roomed together my last season—the second pair of black-and-white roommates in the NFL, I guess, after Gale Sayers and Brian Piccolo—I've loved to listen to Willie talk, with his great pauses, for thinking, for choosing his words carefully, for making certain he has something to say. The last time we had a chance to have a long talk, in California, Willie, as usual, had so much to say.

On struggling against the odds: "You've spent a lifetime being a long shot, and you start wondering, *Who is this long shot that keeps coming in?* You know, sooner or later, you ought to be the favorite, but somehow you're always the long shot."

On slowing down: "I don't have the physical energy to work the hours I once worked, at least not consistently, but I am smarter and what used to take me fifteen hours to do, I can now do in nine."

On stopping: "When am I going to stop? When I'm incapable of working hard enough and well enough to be successful, and that's out of my hands."

On heroes: "Martin Luther King never wavered in the face of adversity. It took death to stop him. I can still hear him. Like I can hear Lombardi. You know, a lot of times, when good things happen, in the quiet of the night, I think, *Coach would be delighted. He would be so happy.*"

I've always enjoyed doing things with Kos, playing golf and poker, shooting quail, eating and drinking and laughing the way we did when our days were planned for us, when our worlds revolved around football. A few months after the reunion in Green Bay, Kos came to the mini-reunion of our old poker game at Tommy Joe's place in Texas.

There were six of us old football players there, and every time we turned around, Kos was clicking away with his camera, taking pictures, for his den, for his album, for his mind. "I'm not going to break down and cry," he said the last night we were in Texas, "but I don't want this weekend to end."

Kos's wife, Peggy, who teaches English in high school and coaches the boys' tennis team—coincidentally, Peggy and Ann Davis, both teachers, both went to the University of Cincinnati—sent me a note after ABC's *20/20* carried the story about the first Super Bowl team. She said it was "just the right combination of pathos, wit, courage and love." She also sent along a copy of a poem written by the Reverend Gordon Gilsdorf, a priest in Green Bay. He called it "On Being Fifty":

> Wines grow bitter with age
> or better.
> Fifty is a vintage year,
> the best:
> sunshine and rain enough,
> the perfect grape.
> One fear only now, the bottle
> going empty
> or the chance sudden spill
> of it all.
> So let us raise the glass
> while we can,
> feel the glow of the grape
> and love.

We did a good job at the reunion on both the grape and the love.

8. The Missing Half of the Defensive Line

Henry Jordan and
Lionel Aldridge

The right side of the defensive line did not attend the reunion of the team that won Super Bowl I. Henry Jordan, the right tackle, was dead. Lionel Aldridge, the right end, was still alive. Probably. Henry died of a heart attack at forty-two. Lionel disappeared at forty-three.

Henry was my neighbor. He was a year older than I, almost to the day. His house faced mine on Careful Drive in Green Bay. His wife, Olive, and my first wife, Barbara, were close friends. When Barbara wasn't home, Olive fed me. Henry's three children, Butch and Theresa and Suzanne, were about the same ages as my three. The Jordans and the Kramers did family things together.

Lionel was my teammate. He was five years younger than I. I never knew where he lived in Green Bay. I never spent much time with him away from the field. I thought of Lionel as bright and quick and elegant. I didn't realize how sensitive he was.

When Lionel joined the Packers in 1963, a rookie out of Utah State, we needed him badly. After the 1962 season, after we won a second straight NFL championship, Coach Lombardi had traded our starting defensive right end, Bill Quinlan. Lionel moved quickly into the starting lineup. But I sensed that he was still a little unsure of himself. For the team's sake, and his, I wanted him to succeed. I tried to help him. I offered him a little advice and a lot of encouragement. "Way to go, Lionel!" I'd yell. "Way to hustle! Way to play!" Before every game, I talked to Lionel, pumped him up, got him ready.

Lionel had a good season for a rookie, and from then on, I figured, with his size and strength and obvious talent, he'd get along fine without me. I stopped being his cheerleader.

Several years later, when both our football careers were over, when Lionel was working as a broadcaster, he said to me, "Why'd you dump me, J. K.?"

I said, "What?

"Why'd you dump me? Why'd you drop me after my first year?"

"Lionel, I didn't dump you," I said. "I just didn't think you needed me anymore."

Henry Jordan seemed to be the most relaxed man on our team. He was the only one who could sit in the locker room, in his little cubicle, before a game, and fall asleep. He sometimes slept almost until the opening kickoff.

Henry missed the most dramatic moment of the most dramatic game of our careers. On December 31, 1967, with the temperature in Green Bay thirteen degrees below zero, with sixteen seconds to play, with Dallas leading by three points, with the ball in our possession, third down and a foot to go for a touchdown, with the NFL championship at stake, we called a time-out. Henry, standing on the sidelines with the rest of the defensive line, turned to Ron Kostelnik and said, "C'mon, Ron, there's nothing we can do. Let's go sit in the dugout and try to get warm."

Everybody else in the stadium was standing and shivering and screaming. Bart Starr called a quarterback sneak. I drove into Jethro Pugh, the Dallas tackle, lifting him up, and Bart slithered through the hole for the touchdown that won the game and the NFL title. Neither Henry nor Kos saw the play. "Henry was my leader," Kos said. "I listened to everything he said."

Henry was worth listening to, especially when he talked about Lombardi. "He treats us all the same," Henry once said. "Like dogs." That was his most quoted line, but Henry had others almost as good. "I play for the love of the game, the love of the money and the fear of Lombardi," he said. "When he says, 'Sit down,' I don't look for a chair." Henry's second favorite target was himself. "I have to pay a barber to *find* my hair," he said.

I'll never forget the time in training camp, after we'd been locked in St. Norbert's for a few weeks, Henry stood on the practice field for ten minutes, staring at a pretty girl at the far end of the field, "Hey," he said, finally, "that's old Olive"—his own wife.

With his easygoing ways and his gentle humor, Henry appeared to be an unlikely candidate for an early heart attack. But Henry wasn't quite so relaxed as he seemed. He had his own demons.

He was born on a tenant farm in Virginia. His parents were, literally, dirt poor. As a child, he sat on the mule his father used to plow the cotton field. He always remembered the day he walked past the grocery store and couldn't go in and buy a piece of penny bubble gum because his mother didn't have a penny. "That chased him all his life," Olive said.

I used to try to persuade Henry to have fun. "Let's go skiing," I'd say.

"Don't have any skis," he'd say.

"I've got an extra pair. And I've got extra poles. And extra boots and an extra jacket and extra gloves."

Henry never bought any gear. Want to play golf? Use my extra set of clubs. Want to go fishing? I had an extra pole.

I knew that Henry studied the stock market, that he had invested, cautiously and wisely, a couple of hundred thousand dollars. "For Christ's sake, Henry," I'd say. "Loosen up. Spend some of your money."

"I can't do it, Jerry," he'd say. "I'd like to, I really would. But I can't. It just hurts me to spend money like that."

He owned a nice home and a nice car, and he took good care of his family, but Henry just wouldn't spend any money on foolishness. He hardly ever drank, just an occasional brandy. When he was buried, Olive told me, "Henry would be so proud of me. I got the whole funeral done for less than two thousand dollars."

I pieced Lionel's background together from people who worked and played with him. He was born in Louisiana. He never knew his father. He was raised by his mother, who sent him, when he was in his teens, to live with an aunt and uncle in California. He won a football scholarship to Utah State and, on that Mormon campus, began dating the woman he later married. "How come you're going out with a white girl?" someone asked him. "I don't see any black girls here," he said. Lionel majored in sociology. Lionel lived sociology.

Henry was a big kid, but until he turned fourteen, his father wouldn't let him play football. His father said he had "baby bones." In school, his classmates teased him, called him "Alice" and "Suzy." He finally told his father he was either going to play football or quit school. He played. He earned a scholarship to the University of Virginia in Charlottesville, captained the football team and, as a heavyweight wrestler, was the runner-up for the national collegiate championship. He also majored in business administration and made the dean's list. His wife grew up in Charlottesville, and when she heard people talk about Henry as if he were a big dumb jock, she wanted to scream at them. "He had an IQ of one hundred and seventy," Olive said.

He was drafted by Cleveland and, after two seasons, traded to Green Bay, in time to join Lombardi's first Packer team. Henry made All-Pro for five straight years. He also played in five Pro Bowls. "I faced him every day," Fuzzy Thurston said, "and I never played against anyone else that quick. He beat me every day. I'd say to him, 'Henry, take it easy. I'm having enough trouble with Lombardi, I don't need you whipping me every day.'"

Henry was another Packer who, by now, should have been elected to the Professional Football Hall of Fame. He had all the credentials. He also had all the credentials for his "PsD." He was poor, smart and driven.

Lionel Aldridge was not quite the football player Henry Jordan was, perhaps because he was not quite so driven. "I'm not sure Lionel ever played as well as we thought he could," said Bob Skoronski, who went up against him in practice for six years.

But Lionel was tough. Seven months after we won Super Bowl I, Lionel broke his leg in an exhibition game. He was supposed to be in a cast for six weeks. Two days after he broke his leg, he was working out on the weight machines. Ten days later, the doctors removed the cast. Four days later, Lombardi began yelling at him. "That bone," Coach told him, "is not a weight-bearing bone." Lionel missed only the first two games of the season.

Lionel never made any of the major All-Pro teams, but he did put in nine seasons in Green Bay, and while he played for the Packers, he started working part time for WTMJ radio and television in Milwaukee. He had a good voice, a pleasant manner, a bright future.

Then, in 1972, Lionel was traded to the San Diego Chargers, a team notorious for drug abuse. Some people who should know say Lionel got heavily into marijuana in San Diego. A Charger teammate insists he did not. Either way, the charged-up Chargers finished last both years Lionel played for them.

When I left football at the end of the 1968 season, social drugs were not yet a big thing. I never saw marijuana when I was playing, never saw cocaine, never saw heroin. Maybe the stuff didn't get to Green Bay. Maybe we didn't need it. We were Scotch and vodka and beer people. With Cutty Sark on the rocks, we could get just about as goofy as any human being could hope to get.

Early in my NFL career, we did take amphetamines, pep pills, most of us, even Coach Lombardi once in a while. We didn't know too much about them. They were the kind of things the wives were taking for dieting. Initially, our trainer carried a bottle of the pills, and you could go to him and get whatever you wanted. One of our guys always took too much of anything. He got so up before games, he had to take a big black felt-tipped pen and write numbers on his left hand and his right hand, so that he'd know which way to block on which plays. One of the wives used to take a pep pill at halftime so that she'd be ready to keep up with her husband at the parties after the game. At first, we had no knowledge of the downside effects of the drugs. Then, when the dangers became known, when society became concerned, the pills disappeared from the trainer's kit. Players still got them, if they wanted them badly enough, but not so easily, not so abundantly. We were much more into novocaine and codeine, painkillers, something to soothe our bumps and bruises, sprains and abrasions. We didn't have to feel high. We just didn't want to feel hurt.

Henry Jordan survived thirteen seasons in the NFL. When he retired, he became executive director of Summerfest, an annual non-profit civic carnival of food and entertainment staged near the shores of Lake Michigan. When Henry took over, Summerfest was in trouble, its image tarnished, its future uncertain. In seven years, Henry turned it into a resounding financial and public-relations success. He didn't waste a penny on foolishness. He provided better attractions, and attracted better crowds. "There's this myth about Henry the jock," said a member of the Summerfest board. "It's not true. He's learned the business. He's paid his dues."

The Jordans moved from Green Bay to Oconomowoc, a suburb of Milwaukee, and Olive Jordan liked to talk to Henry about "growing old together." Henry said they couldn't count on growing old together. He fretted every time he read about a former football player dying. Not long before his forty-second birthday, he had a complete physical exam, including a stress test. He breezed through the test. He had no symptoms of heart disease, no history.

On February 21, 1977, a month after his forty-second birthday, Henry worked out at the Milwaukee Athletic Club. He jogged for a while, then sat down and suffered a heart attack and died before he could be taken to a hospital.

Lionel Aldridge returned to Milwaukee at the end of 1973 and began working full time for WTMJ. He did daily sports reports on television and color commentary on the radio broadcasts of the Packer games. He was good at analysis, and NBC Sports hired him to work on NFL telecasts. "He was very soft-spoken, very gentle," recalled David Stern, who produced some of the NBC games. "But you could sense he had problems. He stared into space a lot."

"He was quiet and mysterious," said Michael Weisman, now the executive producer of NBC Sports. "He often had a vacant look."

Both Stern and Weisman heard rumors that Lionel had undergone surgery for a brain tumor. Neither asked him about it. Both found him easy, if a little disconcerting, to work with.

In 1977, Lionel's wife sued him for divorce, and during a fierce argument in front of their house, Lionel beat the family dog. He was taken to the psychiatric emergency ward at County General Hospital and treated for severe depression. Lionel knew he was mentally ill. He tried psychotherapy. He tried medication, prescribed to offset a chemical imbalance in his brain. Nothing seemed to help for more than a short time. By 1980, his job and his marriage destroyed, he began to drift, to Louisiana, to Utah, to Oregon, to California. He walked into Willie Davis's office in Los Angeles one day, barely recognizable, and asked for help. Willie tried to help him. So did other teammates. But Lionel quickly turned away. He worked on construction, maintenance, anything he could find, even a brief tour as an assistant coach at Utah State. He lived in the dormitory with the football players.

Less than a year before the reunion, Lionel reappeared in Wisconsin. He moved into the Milwaukee Rescue Mission, run by the Reverend Gabriel Varga, and signed up for a six-month spiritual rehabilitation program. He happened to see a Milwaukee newspaperman, who, with Lionel's reluctant approval, wrote a story about his travails, his mental illness. The Associated Press picked up the story, and when I read it, I phoned the Reverend Varga. He said Lionel was gone. He had fled as soon as the story appeared in the Milwaukee paper. "I'm sure he still has his pride," Ron Kostelnik said.

As soon as he saw the story, Kos drove from his home in Appleton to Milwaukee, roughly one hundred miles away, to try to find and help Lionel. "I felt close to Lionel, Kos said, "because we played together for six years, and neither of us was a star. When I got to the mission, he had moved on. I felt that a part of me had moved on, too. It was traumatic."

A couple of months before the reunion, Lionel surfaced again, in Green Bay. He went to the practice field, watched his old team coached by his old teammate, then had dinner with the Greggs. "He kept twitching," Forrest said. "He was disoriented."

Then Lionel vanished.

To a man, his old teammates wanted to help him, financially or emotionally or both. But he was not invited to the reunion because no one knew how to reach him. No one knew even if he were alive.

"I was in Appleton," Kos recalled, "and the manager of our office in Milwaukee called and said, 'Did you hear? Henry Jordan died.' I couldn't believe it. I called Henry's house, and no one was there, and I called the radio station and found out it was true and jumped in my car and . . ."

Kos stopped. He had tears in his eyes. "I can't talk about it," he said. "I still get too choked up. I spend ten seconds talking about Henry, and I start to cry. The shock of when he died was as religious an experience as I've had in my life. A piece of me was chopped out. It was like when Kennedy was shot."

"Ron was here that night," Olive remembered. "He wanted to know if we were okay financially. Henry had taken good care of everything, and had explained everything to me—he must have had a premonition—but if Henry hadn't, if we weren't okay, Ron wasn't going to let us go hungry. He was here for as long as we needed him."

I was in Costa Rica when Henry died. I'd been fishing for tarpon, and then I'd gone exploring in the jungle, and by the time I got the word, it was too late to get to the funeral. I was one of those few among Henry's teammates who didn't come to the church in Oconomowoc. Marie Lombardi, the widow, came from one coast. Willie Davis, the captain, came from the other. Lionel Aldridge, on the brink of his own sorrows, came as a friend, a teammate and a reporter. Max McGee came, too. He tried to sneak out of the church unseen at the end of the service. Max just didn't feel comfortable at a funeral. Olive saw him and was glad he had come. She realized how difficult it was for Max to handle sadness. As the crowd filed out of the church, a streak of lightning creased the sky, and a thunderclap boomed, signs Olive and the kids will never forget, as if the Lord were saying, "And that's that."

Olive and her children were not invited to the reunion of the team that won the first Super Bowl game, and Olive was very hurt. It was no one person's fault, but it was a mistake, senseless and unthinking.

In the weeks and months after Henry died, I thought about him often. Every year, the Green Bay Packers used to issue traveling jackets and traveling slacks, and every year Henry and I used to go to the tailor's together to get fitted. We didn't look much alike, but we had almost precisely the same dimensions, within a fraction of an inch. Height, neck, arms, waist, legs, biceps, we were just about identical. If we were that similar on the outside, what the hell were we like inside? Were we identical inside, too? Our lungs? Our hearts? It didn't exactly scare me. It just got me thinking.

I spoke to Henry Jordan a few months after the reunion. Henry Jordan, Jr. "This is Henry Jordan," he said over the phone. I couldn't call him Henry. I still called him Butch. His father would have been proud of him. He went to the University of North Dakota and, at six-foot-three and 220 pounds, played tight end on the football team. He also got his master's degree in business administration. Obviously, he was a smart kid. He played offense, didn't he?

Butch was living in Dallas, enjoying his work, involving economic analysis and forecasting. His sister Theresa was also in Dallas, working in public relations and advertising. Butch told me he watched Super Bowl XIX on television with an old friend, Griff Thurston, Fuzzy's son. Griff had just moved to Dallas. The last time they had seen each other was in a Wisconsin high school all-star game, Butch playing for the South, Griff for the North. Griff was a sensational running back, big and strong and swift, until he messed up his knees at the University of Wisconsin. Butch and Griff had their own little reunion. Coincidentally, their younger sisters, Suzanne and Tori, had become school-mates, at the Stevens Point branch of the University of Wisconsin.

Urban Henry died a year after Henry Jordan. Urban wasn't on either of the Super Bowl teams. He played with the Packers for only one year, in 1963, three years before the reunion team, and most fans forgot him long ago. He wasn't a great football player, but he made a great impression on me. He came to us from the Los Angeles Rams with a reputation as a headhunter. He was the kamikaze man on the kickoff team, a crazy man, completely without fear.

The first time Urban practiced with the Packers, or one of the first, Lombardi put us up against each other, one on one, me against him.

Urban was about six-foot-five, maybe 275 pounds, two inches taller than I and twenty pounds heavier. He came roaring into this nut-cracker drill. I mean, he just brought his hat and his lunch and everything with him, and I met him and met him and met him, some god-awful collisions. Neither one of us was about to back up. He wasn't a fancy footwork man, just powerful. Later, I saw him do semi-squats with so much weight on his shoulders that the bar would droop on the ends. I don't know how much he was lifting, but it must have been five or six hundred pounds. He was a hulk, and it was all-out war between us that day. We went bang, bang, bang, seemed like forever. One of the sportswriters watching wrote an article afterward that said the earth shook and the trees wiggled—that kind of stuff. There *were* some hellacious collisions. Urban decided right then and there that I had a little courage or a little insanity, maybe both. And I certainly knew that he wasn't bashful about physical contact. So right away, we had a fundamental basis for a relationship, some understanding and appreciation of each other, and that relationship just grew and grew.

Urban was raised in Morgan City, Louisiana, bayou country, and he was part Cajun, or all Cajun—a coonass, he called himself. His dad worked on the river boats. Urban and I started off hunting and fishing and drinking beer together, and our relationship developed into a long and deep friendship. It didn't have anything to do with families. Urban was a bachelor, never married, a man's kind of man, not a woman's. We were business partners, too, Urban and I and Jimmy Taylor, owners of the Packer Diving Company in Louisiana.

One time, after a hurricane, we got a contract to dive down and blow up a sunken barge that was blocking a channel, a danger to navigation. Urban knew the business better than Jimmy and I did, so I asked him, "Who the hell are we going to get to blow it up?"

"I'm going to blow it up," he said.

"You don't know anything about explosives," I said.

He said, "Yeah, man, I got a book. You use plastic explosives. It's all in the book. No problem." And he did it. He'd already taught himself how to dive, and he went down and blew up the barge himself. Urban was like that.

He was fearless, and he was bright, a quick learner, and he was different. Not long after he stopped playing football, he moved into an old slave's shack right on the edge of the swamp, paid something like $400 a year in rent. He loved the swamp. He lived there with Sally and George and Scrap Iron and a couple of other dogs. My wife, Wink, and I used to go down and visit him and stay in the shack and just love every minute of it. One time the three of us went to a bar nearby, and while I was in the phone booth, trying to make a call, Urban tipped it over and flattened the folding doors against the floor so I couldn't get out. He kept me there for half an hour, laughing his head off.

We did a lot of crazy things together. One night, about midnight, we decided we'd go into the swamp and go frog hunting. We each carried a gig, a little spear, and I had a light strapped to my head. We were half drunk and half crazy, two large men and one beer cooler in an old metal motorboat. It was darker than hell, and the tide was so high that the water hit the banks where the frogs usually sat and pushed them back into the bushes. There was no way we could catch them or even see them. We went a couple of hours without seeing a frog.

Then Urban turned to me and said, "Hold it, there's a gator. C'mon, we'll catch him." I could see two bright-red eyes, about the size of dimes, with maybe four inches between them. We shut our motor off and drifted toward the gator, and as we got close, it backed down into the water, leaving just a piece of its head exposed. "That's not a gator," I said. "That's a snake or a turtle or something."

Just then, Urban reached down and hauled whatever it was into the boat. It must have been about three or four feet long, and it spun around and began chewing on Urban's wrist, so he just sort of rolled out of the boat and threw it at me. The damn thing landed on my thigh, latched onto my leg, tore my pants and drew blood, and I still wasn't sure what it was. I tried to back up and get away from it, and I fell over the beer cooler. Urban was in the water, hanging on to the boat, laughing like crazy. I finally got my light aimed and saw that it was just a little gator. Urban dragged it out of the boat. Then he decided he wanted to catch some more. Not to keep them, just to catch them—for the fun of it.

The next gator we spotted had eyes the size of quarters, about six inches apart. We turned off the motor again, and as we drifted beside it, Urban did a dead fall into the water, grabbed the gator—about a six-footer—and began thrashing around till he had it pinned, under control. Then he just let it go.

He caught two or three more that way before we saw a pair of eyes the size of silver dollars, maybe ten or twelve inches apart. "Let's head toward him," Urban said, and I said, "No, you silly son of a bitch," but he got himself all set to jump. Then, about fifty feet away from this giant gator, a real granddaddy, Urban fell into the water, pretending he was trying to catch it. As he climbed back into the boat, he snapped his fingers and said, "Doggone, I missed him."

Urban was unbelievably talented. He supported himself for a while by painting scenes of the swamp, beautiful paintings, and selling them for as much as $2,000. Then one day he saw some porcelain birds that were selling for $7,000 and $8,000 apiece, and he said, "Hell, I can make a porcelain bird better than that."

He went and got a book and studied and built himself a kiln and started the long slow process of making birds from porcelain. He'd go out in the swamp and catch a bird and take it home and freeze it, and then study it, not just for minutes or hours, but for days at a time, making certain he memorized every detail. He had one book on bird's feet, and another real thick one on wing structure—that's how important detail was to him. When he made his first porcelain bird and painted it and built a lovely scene around it, he sold it for $2,000. He planned to do only four or five more, with a limited number of reproductions. But one evening, as he was cooking dinner, he had a heart attack and fell over, dead.

I was stunned. Urban was so full of life. He was forty-three years old. It was so hard to accept the fact that he was gone. I still get the urge every now and then to go to the swamp and drink and hunt and fish with him: *Hey, I think I'll go down to the swamp and spend a few days with Urban.* And when I realize that I can't, I get pissed off all over again. *Damn you, Urban, why'd you have to leave so early?*

I lost another good friend, a buddy, not long before the reunion. His name was Henry Kyle. I lost all my Henrys. Henry Kyle didn't play for the Green Bay Packers. He played college football at the University of Tennessee, and I don't know whether he was much of a college player or not, but I do know this: He reminded me of Max McGee in hand-and-eye coordination. I didn't think I'd ever see anyone as good as Max, but Henry Kyle may have been better. And he was a good ten years older than Max.

We were sitting in a country café in Tennessee once, and Henry reached out and caught a fly between his thumb and his forefinger. I think he did. I still find it hard to believe he did. He showed me the fly, and I said, "Bullshit, you had it in your hand." Henry let the fly go, then did it again. I think he caught the fly again the same way.

When he was in his middle fifties, and I was living down in Owensboro, Kentucky, in the coal country, Henry came to visit me with his two sons, both teenagers then, I guess. My older children were visiting, too, and we all went over to the river outside Owensboro. A big oak tree, with about a sixty-foot rope hanging from it, stood right on the edge of the river. We had an inner tube that we let float out to the middle of the river. Then the kids and I took turns trying to swing out over the water and drop feet first through the tube. None of us was able to do it. Henry watched us from the shore. "Hey, you old fart," I yelled at him. "You going to stand up there all day or you going to jump in the water and get wet?"

Henry grabbed the rope, swung out over the river, let go of the rope, did a perfect jackknife and went headfirst through the dead center of the tube without touching anything. It kind of irritated me. I went and tried to do the same thing and got halfway through the tube, my feet on one side, my head on the other. The tube and I sank down about twelve feet.

Henry was a tremendous athlete. He could whip me in pool, basketball, tennis, hitting the punching bag, shooting quail, just about anything. He took great pride in staying in shape, working out regularly, watching what he ate. He was bright, tough, hardworking, extremely successful in the apartment business. I met him through another friend, and Henry gave me some sound advice when I was getting into the apartment business, and we became good friends. We saw each other five or six times a year, and we talked every few weeks.

He grew up poor in eastern Tennessee. He came from hill people, and he was one of the few to escape to town. He was a fighter pilot in the Marines, and one of the original Blue Angels, the acrobatic flying team. He was a lawyer, too, and maybe even a CIA agent. Some people thought he was. Henry bought Four Star Productions, a television company in Hollywood, and moved into the old Clara Bow mansion in Bel Air just about a year before Ricky, one of his sons, shot him to death.

The prosecutor said it was premeditated murder, plotted by the two sons because they feared they would be disinherited. Ricky said it was self-defense. He said his father used to beat him. Ricky was in his early twenties, an ex-Marine, too, and he said he killed his father, who was in his sixties, in self-defense. The first trial ended in a hung jury; ten of twelve jurors thought Ricky was guilty.

There was no logic to Henry Kyle's death. Nor to Urban Henry's. Nor to Henry Jordan's. Why did they die? Why? You like the universe to be orderly, logical. You like God to be just, to be right. But you find as you travel down the road, the world isn't run exactly the way you'd like it to be. It doesn't make a hell of a lot of sense, and maybe it never will. Maybe it's not supposed to.

Am I afraid to die? I don't know. Certainly, I'm reluctant. I'm not ready. But I don't think I'm afraid. I know I'm not afraid of pain. I'm so familiar with pain, I can almost isolate it, remove it from me. I think the mind can overcome pain. Once, in Evansville, Indiana, I was in a bar with a couple of friends and we started talking about pain, and I held my hand over a flaming candle and said, "Pain is a funny thing. I can put my hand over this burning candle and I can feel heat. Then I can feel pain starting to move up my arm. The pain keeps getting stronger, but I can detach myself from it, feel it from a distance." I held my hand over the candle for a long time, and I was barely blistered. One of my friends tried to do the same thing, and he blistered his hand so badly we had to take him to the hospital.

I was once in terrible, constant pain for three straight weeks, in 1964, in the Mayo Clinic in Rochester, Minnesota. I had undergone an intestinal resection, and my large intestine burst, and I had to have an emergency colostomy, and when I woke up after surgery, my temperature was up to 104 and my intestine was sticking out my right side. I was a mess, physically and mentally. Often, I lay in my own waste. It was a horror show that I couldn't escape. I couldn't sleep for days at a time. I had to endure a series of operations, and one time they injected sodium pentathol in my arm, and usually, with sodium pentathol, if you start counting backward from ten, you fall asleep by five or four. I didn't fall asleep for a minute and a half. I thought sometimes of jumping out a window, to escape the horror, not the pain.

I lived through the colostomy and played football the following season with a gaping hole in my chest. They had put a piece of plastic in my sternum, to cover up a hernia, and the plastic had become infected, so they carved out a slit five or six inches long and two inches deep to allow the wound to drain. The cut ran from my chest to my belly button. My teammates would take a quick look and say, "We can see your lungs and everything," and then turn away. They couldn't see my lungs, but it really was ugly. Most of the time, after practice, I'd wait until everyone else had finished showering before I'd go in. Once, a rookie, practicing late, came into the shower with me and started staring at the gruesome wound. "This is a rough game, kid," I said.

Since I stopped playing football, I've been in awful pain only once, in the mid-seventies, in Bowling Green, Kentucky. I started getting stabbing cramps about ten o'clock one night and I lived with them till nine in the morning, then went to a doctor. He wanted to put me in the hospital. "Hell, no," I said, and got a shot, went home and stood the pain for about seven more hours till it got unbearable. I had a tangled intestine. Adhesions from old scar tissue had pinched off the intestine so that nothing could move through. The doctor said it was like going through labor pains for a full day. They put tubes down my nose, pumped out my stomach, kept me in the hospital for four or five days till they finally operated. As I was being wheeled into the operating room, the anesthesiologist leaned over me and said, in a cheerful drawl, "Hi there. You'll find out all of us boys from Kentucky ain't bad boys." The operation was a success; the surgeon did a super job.

I don't hurt much anymore. Even my neck doesn't remind me of my football days too often. My neck used to be nineteen and a half inches around when I was crunching it every day, blocking 270-pounders with my head. Now it's eighteen inches around. It never was very long. Lombardi didn't like people with long necks, which may have been his only prejudice. He had a chance to draft Paul Krause, who became an All-Pro defensive back for Minnesota, but he turned him down because he said Krause's neck was too long.

Some of the vertebrae in my neck are still jammed up a little, so I've got a traction device that usually travels with me. It's a plastic bag, which weighs about thirty pounds when I fill it up with water, and I attach it to a harness, then hang the bag over a door and put the harness around my head, under my chin, almost like I'm hanging myself. It sort of stretches my neck out, relieves some of the pressure on the vertebrae. I only use the harness when the pain gets real bad, when it comes down my arms and I can't even lift my fishing pole. But most of the time I just say the hell with the pain and ignore it.

I saw my father suffer through incredible pain when he was dying from cancer, and, of course, I wouldn't want to go through that. I wouldn't want anybody to go through that. But I don't dwell on it. I don't fear it. It wouldn't do any good to worry about it.

If I had my choice, I'd rather die a quick, clean death, go out fast, like Henry Jordan and Urban Henry and Henry Kyle. At least none of them lingered. To me, the most frightening thing would be to be paralyzed, to be inactive, to be unable to move. Being totally dependent is the worst nightmare I can imagine. I'd beg people to pull the plug.

In 1964, I went to my own funeral. My own wake, anyway. About the time I came back from the Mayo Clinic, pale and weak and fifty pounds under my playing weight, a former Green Bay Packer named Tom Hearden died, and when his death was reported on radio and television, some people got confused and thought I had died. Friends and neighbors began calling my house to express their condolences. Most of them were in tears.

I got into the spirit of the occasion. I called one of my neighbors and said, "Have you heard about Jerry?"

"Yes," he said. "My God, isn't that terrible?" He was practically sobbing. I almost couldn't convince him I was I.

I went to get my hair cut, and my barber looked at me as if I were a ghost. He thought I was already laid out, on display. "I couldn't go see you tonight," he said, "but I was definitely going to go tomorrow night."

I accepted his apology, and he cheered up. "You were one hell of a guy fifteen minutes ago," he said. "Now you're an SOB again."

I figured I'd never have a better excuse for a celebration. I got a few kegs of beer, and a former Packer named Gary Knafelc brought over a headstone, and several of the guys brought me wilted flowers. A lot of the guys who came to say goodbye to me in 1964 were saying hello to me at the reunion in 1984. I wish my Henrys could have been there.

9. What Have I Done with My Life?

I think about Henry Jordan, and I think about Urban Henry, and all the things the three of us had in common, and I wonder why I'm alive and they're not. And I wonder how much time I have left and what I'm going to do with it. I've had eight years already that Henry didn't have, and seven that Urban didn't. I've had the last of my three youngest children since those two died. I've watched the children spring up. I've had so much pleasure that Henry and Urban have missed. What have I done with the extra years? What have I done with my life?

I ask those questions, and I remember reading a book called *Life After Life*, by Raymond Moody, about people who were clinically dead and then came back to life. One of the people recalled floating up and encountering a being of light that somehow, nonverbally, asked, "What have you done with your life that you want to show me?" I remember putting the book down and asking myself the same question, then answering it by listing my possessions—my ranch in Idaho, my cars, my boat. Suddenly, I stopped and said to myself, "Oh, isn't that wonderful? The greatest thing you've done on earth is collect a pisspot full of toys. Isn't that neat?"

Then I started thinking about what I really wanted to do with my life. I wanted to contribute *something*, something positive, and I tried to think of what I could do of lasting value, something that meant a damn beyond this life experience. I began looking at my children and realizing that the best thing I could do on this planet would be to give them proper values, a set of guidelines that would help them survive in this world, and flourish. I realized that I hadn't done for them what my father had done for me.

I have no complaints with the values my father left me. I have faults, but I don't blame them on him. He was an extreme disciplinarian, very quick with the strap, and I think that both helped and hurt me when I was young, made me strong and brave and sometimes mean. When I was working in the woods, if I got through Friday and Saturday nights without having a good fight, I'd figure I'd wasted the whole week. I'm not so mean now. And I'm not so brave. But my father's values have stayed with me.

He had a store where he sold television sets, and once, when I was minding the store, I stole fifty cents out of the till. I jacked the handle back and forth about twenty-five times before I made up my mind to take the money. *What the hell?* I figured. *If he finds out, he'll just beat me, and he's doing that pretty regularly anyway.* He came home that night and confronted me: He was missing fifty cents. I was going to lie to him, tell him I hadn't taken it, but before I could, he just hung his head and said, "If I can't trust you, son, who can I trust?" And that cut a whole lot deeper than any beating.

Dad lived by a set of rules, fundamental principles. Once, during a college vacation, I spent two weeks trying to collect some of his bills for him. I went to some of the poorest homes in Idaho. Hardly any of the people could meet even the first payment on their television sets. It was a miracle they had scraped up enough for the down payment. I went back to my father and said, "How in the hell did you sell those people television sets? You could look at them and tell that they'd never be able to pay."

Dad had lived through hard times during the Depression. "Those are the people who need television sets," he said. "They don't have any other form of entertainment. They can't go to the movies."

"But what about all the cash they owe you?" I said.

"Well, I'll just see what I can do," he said.

I don't think he ever took a television set back from someone who couldn't afford to pay for it.

Dad's gone now, but his values, his principles are still alive. If I can pass them along, honesty and decency and a sense of fair play, if I can be certain that my children don't lie and cheat—I can't stand a sneak or a thief—that they think about other human beings and care about them and treat them politely, if I can do that and also nurture in each of them an ability and a desire to work, to be productive, then no matter what else happens, I won't be a failure.

I wasted a wonderful opportunity with my older children. When they were young, and I was playing football, I probably had more free time than I'll ever have the rest of my life. But I didn't spend enough of it with the kids. I thought the opportunity would be there forever, and the kids would be there forever, and I had other things on my mind. The world was on my mind. Having fun with the boys was on my mind. Ladies were on my mind. All kinds of things were on my mind, and my relationship with my children suffered. There were beautiful moments—I didn't leave them blank—but it was never what it could have been. I love them, and I'm pretty sure they love me, but I lost something along the way I'll never be able to regain.

I'm proud of the way they've grown up despite me. I'm especially proud of Tony, for what he's done, and Diane, for what she's doing. And Danny? I'm worried like hell about Danny. He's on my mind all the time. How in the hell am I going to communicate with him? We're talking more now, but I don't know if I'm getting through.

Where are you going? What are you going to do? How are you going to support yourself? I asked myself those questions all my life, but I don't think Danny ever asks them. He's a good worker, but work isn't important to him. I don't know what is. I don't know how to make him burn.

Danny could have been a pretty good football player in high school, but after the junior varsity, he stopped playing. It wasn't important to him. I wish I'd encouraged him more. I was so afraid of pushing him that I leaned over backwards and neglected him, and I'm sorry now. Danny could have had a lot of fun playing football, and he might have learned a few lessons about discipline and commitment. He did think about going back out for football in his senior year, but because of his automobile accident, he missed the first couple of weeks of practice, and the coach had a rule that you had to start from the beginning. I called the coach and asked if he'd make an exception, if he'd give Danny another chance, because I thought Danny needed football more than football needed him, but the coach said no, a rule was a rule. I can't help thinking Lombardi would have handled it differently.

My three youngest kids all have great promise. Alicia, the oldest, is almost a teenager. She's a sweetheart. She's going to be beautiful, like her mother, and I hope that doesn't get in the way of her being a good person. I tell the children, "I love your mother, and I like her, too, because she's a good person." Alicia takes school seriously, works at it—her mother's influence—and gets mostly A's. She's also a good little athlete, a one-girl track and field team. She just may destroy my old-fashioned prejudice against lady jocks. I always felt it was difficult for a woman to be both an athlete and a lady, and when Alicia was five and six, I didn't encourage her much to play any kind of sports. Then she came home one day with a picture of a girl up in Oregon who was playing quarterback on her high school freshman team, and Alicia said she wanted to start playing football. You should have seen how fast I got out on the tennis court with her. And on the golf course, and in the swimming pool. Anything but football.

Matt, at nine, isn't much interested in studying. He's bright, but he doesn't apply himself. He's a big kid. He's been off the growth charts for as long as I can remember. The doctor says I'll be able to look him in the eye when he grows up, but I'll have to stand on a box to do it. He'll probably be six-foot-six, or six-seven, maybe more.

I sat down with Matt one day and showed him how he had outgrown his coat. The sleeves came just a little more than halfway down his arm. "Matt," I said, "see how much you've grown. You're going to continue to grow for some time, till you're about twenty-one. Then you'll stop growing physically. Your body'll stop. But your mind should never stop growing." I gave him a pretty strong lecture. "You've got to help your mind grow," I said. "Do you understand in school? Are you learning?" I guess my old fears about a big kid being dumb still haunt me. I worry about Matt. Ideally, I'd like to see him balance athletics and academics. If he doesn't go to the University of Idaho, I'd love to see him go to a college like Stanford, where you can get an excellent education and play big-time college sports. He'll have to start applying himself for that, developing better work habits.

Jordan, my youngest, is my clone. Danny and Matthew and I started looking alike at about the age of eight. Jordan looked like me the day he was born. He just came right out and said hi, and it was me. It's like watching myself grow up. Sometimes I wonder if I'm loving him or loving myself. Jordy started out as a real roughneck, but now, at the age of five, he's getting very sensitive. He's a very sharing child. "This is for you, Daddy," he says, and he gives me flowers, toys, everything.

I hope I'm smart enough not to waste the opportunity to watch these three kids grow up, to help them, encourage them, love them. I'm on the road an awful lot of the time, three weeks some months, but when I'm home, I try to be with them, really be with them. Wink is a terrific mother, but I know they need a father, too. And I know this time that they're not going to be around forever. I like what Kos said: They're only with us for a short time.

It's difficult for me to judge whether I'm getting better with the children, but my former wife, Barbara, seems to think so. A few months after the reunion in Green Bay, not long after I took Danny with me to the get-together at Tommy Joe's in Texas, she wrote me a letter:

Jerry:

This is just sort of a strange note that I feel I want to write to you concerning your involvement with all three of the kids and [Tony's wife] Darlene. So often people only register complaints and I feel someone should tell you how much you have changed. There was a time when I felt everything was up to me, and that there was no output other than the support money from you. I felt you made no effort to guide or help the kids and were quick to blame them as well as me when things were not perfect. I don't really know if you were at fault—it was during the time in your life you were, as you said, "busy hearing your own voice"—or if I felt they were totally mine and you had no right to influence them and, therefore, shut you out.

To point out my reasoning, I will recall the horrible time at Tony's graduation when you and Dan were not even speaking. I tried to tell you to "hug him, he's still a little boy in a big body and he just never got much of you, he was too young when you left"— but you wouldn't listen to me. Such a wonderful opposite when I heard you brought him to Texas. He was quite discouraged and talking about quitting college next year—did you know this or sense this? At any rate, since his time with you, there has been no more mention of not going on and his spirits seem so happy again! You had to have *listened*, or read between the lines (as parents are supposed to be able to do).

Now I have to give an example with Diane. Did you know she was scared to death to give you the bill for the operation she had? I tried talking to her, but I could not convince her you would be worried, not mad. When you called and talked to her, she was almost pathetic. How could she possibly think you would be mad? Afterward, we talked for a long time, and she said she guessed she finally realized you were mellowing, but all her life she had been afraid of making you mad or upset or, even more important, of letting you down. I know it's hard to know when a child needs something when you aren't with that child day in and day out, but you seem to be reaching out and listening like you never have before. You offered to help Diane go see Theresa [Jordan] at Easter. She needs to get away for a few days. She has been going straight through with summer school and awfully hard courses and no breaks.

I have been wondering if it was Dan's wreck or your father's death that made you change. It seemed to start at the time of the wreck, but seems deeper now that your father is gone. At any rate, it surely is a nice feeling to know someone else is staying involved with the kids. I always felt you had so much to give your children, but you never seemed to know how to get the knowledge to them. Now it's happening, and I can see the difference in them. I hope you realize all of this is meant as a compliment. We always misunderstood each other one hundred percent, so I'm really trying to spell this out properly.

BARBARA

10. Run to Twilight

Jimmy Taylor and Elijah Pitts

While the old football players told war stories, the wives and, in a couple of instances, girl friends who attended the reunion sat down at a big table and played a little game. Each woman made up a question, wrote it down and put it in the middle of the table. Then each woman pulled out a question and answered it. Jimmy Taylor's second wife drew a very personal question: How old were you when your husband played in Super Bowl I?

Lisa Taylor thought for a few seconds.

"Five," she said.

That made Lisa twenty-three at the reunion. Jimmy was forty-nine. He had succeeded where Max McGee had failed. And Jimmy still had three years left of having a mate half his age.

Jimmy's running mate at running back in the first Super Bowl game, Elijah Pitts, did not get to the reunion. Elijah was busy in

Canada, working as an assistant coach for Hamilton in the Canadian Football League. He and his wife, Ruth, had been married for more than twenty years. "And I'm planning on keeping her for at least twenty more," Elijah said.

Jimmy's daughter, Jobeth, was older than his wife. That may have made Jimmy feel old.

Elijah's son, Ronnie, was old enough to be eligible for the National Football League draft. That definitely made me feel old.

I remembered Ronnie Pitts as an energetic four-year-old dashing around our locker room in 1967, a friendly little extrovert. Don Chandler, our place-kicker, once asked Ronnie what his favorite story was, and Ronnie said, "Snow White and the Three Pigs."

Another time, Jim Weatherwax, a reserve tackle, said to Ronnie, "Come on over here and say hello to Mike Kostelnik." Mike was about Ronnie's age, but not nearly so outgoing. Ronnie rushed right up to Mike and stuck out his hand, but Mike shyly turned away. Elijah yelled to Mike's daddy, "See, Kos, your kid won't shake hands with mine. You're prejudicing him at a real early age."

Little Ronnie Pitts, who grew up to be a hard-tackling defensive back at UCLA, was drafted several months after our reunion by the Buffalo Bills. He was the first choice in the seventh round of the 1985 NFL draft, which put him six rounds ahead of his father's position in the 1961 draft. Coincidentally, not long before the draft, Elijah joined the Bills as their offensive backfield coach, a job he had previously held in the late seventies. It was nice to see another of the Packer sons, like Duane Davis at KACE, go into the family business. "As long as you're coaching," Elijah said, "you're not going to get rich. But you can have a lot of fun."

Jimmy Taylor was rich. Since his playing days, he had dabbled, like many of us, in broadcasting and in public relations, but he had made most of his money from a thriving construction company and not a small amount from his partnership with me and Urban Henry, a partnership that ended, with a war over money, in bitterness and disappointment.

• • •

I shouldn't have been so disappointed in Jimmy. I should have known what to expect. Jimmy always did scramble for every penny. He had to as a child, growing up in Baton Rouge, Louisiana. His father was an invalid who died before Jimmy was ten. His mother worked in a laundry. At the age of ten, Jimmy took to the streets to support himself and to help his mother. He delivered newspapers in the morning, and again in the evening, and in between, he caddied and he hustled to survive. Jimmy was always street smart. He was never school smart.

Jimmy was a remarkable athlete. He was a scrawny kid who first made his mark in basketball, a short but scrappy guard, too small to play football until his junior year in high school. Then he became a third-string fullback. He grew to five-foot-ten and 170 pounds in his senior year, and he improved. He improved so much that he became the first athlete to play in both the high school All-American football game, in Memphis, Tennessee, and the high school All-American basketball game, in Murray, Kentucky. He was the Most Valuable Player in the football game.

Jimmy decided to concentrate on football in college, attended Louisiana State for one year, flunked out and went to a junior college in Mississippi where he met his first wife, Dixie. Then he returned to LSU and spent half his junior year sitting on the bench. Finally, in his senior year, he became a star, playing fullback, linebacker and place-kicker before the days of specialization. He was one of the country's leading rushers and scorers. He didn't make any of the major All-American teams, but he was named to the squad that was chosen to appear on Perry Como's television show. Each player had to state his name, his school and his position. "How am I going to remember all that stuff?" Jimmy supposedly said.

In 1958, the Packers made Jimmy their second choice in the draft. Dan Currie from Michigan State was first, Ray Nitschke from Illinois was third and I was fourth. In all modesty, it may have been the best draft any team ever made. All four of us became All-Pros; two of us are already in the Pro Football Hall of Fame, a third should be and the fourth, Currie, could have been the best of us all. Dapper Dan was my roommate for a while and one of my favorite people to party with. But he missed the best seasons in Green Bay. He spent seven seasons as a Packer, then was traded away just before we won the three straight championships. He was one of the few guys who never bought Lombardi's style or substance. Dan said it was all bullshit. The last time I saw him, he was working as a security guard at a hotel on the strip in Las Vegas.

Jimmy had two large problems his first year in Green Bay. He couldn't remember his teammates' names and he couldn't remember the plays. He called everybody "Reno" or "Roy" or "Rick." We called him "Doody Bird," or "Doody," for short. He didn't start at fullback until the final two games because he didn't learn the plays till then. He took a lot of abuse about his intellect. Paul Hornung used to double-talk him to death, string together meaningless words in meaningless sentences, and Jimmy would just nod and say, "That's right."

Like everyone else on the team, Jimmy was not overpaid. His rookie season, his salary was $9,500, and, as he always did, he was tithing, giving ten percent to his church. To save money, he and Dixie and the baby, Jobeth, lived behind a bar. I was earning even less, but once Jimmy borrowed twenty dollars from me. When he came to pay me back, he offered me ten. "What the hell is this?" I said.

"Better take it," Jimmy said. "Bird in the hand is worth two in the bush."

"You little shit," I said, for openers. I talked him into returning the entire twenty.

I should have learned then.

But I loved Jimmy. I loved Jimmy like a brother. In fact, he reminded me of my brother Russ, in size and in attitude. Russ was scrappy, too. Russ was a scrambler, too. I defended Jimmy, shielded him, kept people from making fun of him. We became roommates early in our careers and stayed roommates for five or six seasons. I even read poetry to him occasionally. It helped him fall asleep. Our wives went to games and parties together. Our children played together. Jimmy was a regular in the poker game in my basement.

On the football field, Jimmy just got better and better. He earned a reputation for being hard-nosed, which was one of his favorite words. He loved to run straight at people who wanted to tackle him, run straight over them. He liked us to open a hole for him, but once he got through the hole, once he got up to speed, he wanted to hit people, punish them, hurt them. He was mean. He was beautiful.

He had a tremendous rivalry with Cleveland's Jimmy Brown. Their careers overlapped for eight seasons, and in seven of the eight, Brown gained more yards rushing than Taylor did. But in 1962, the only year in Brown's career in which he did not lead the NFL in rushing, Taylor took away the title. And when they went head to head, our Jimmy beat their Jimmy decisively. The first time they met, in 1961, Taylor outgained Brown, 158 yards to 72, and outscored him, four touchdowns to none. The last time they met, in the 1965 NFL championship game, Taylor outrushed Brown, 94 yards to 50. We won both games.

Jimmy was a rock at 215 pounds and maybe an inch under the six-foot height he claimed. He was a fanatic about pumping iron, about doing isometric exercises, about hardening his body every day of the year. I'll tell you what kind of shape he was in.

One night during training camp, perhaps halfway through his career, Jimmy snuck out after curfew and got caught. He wasn't the first. He wasn't the last. But he may have been the most upset. He was upset because he got fined. I don't remember exactly what the fine was, probably fifty or one hundred dollars, but it didn't make any difference. If it was five dollars, Jimmy would have been upset. He hated to part with his cash.

Jimmy tried every way he could to get out of paying the fine, but Lombardi wouldn't relent. The next year, when Jimmy negotiated his contract, he tried to have a clause put in saying he couldn't be fined. Lombardi wouldn't accept that.

Jimmy was so angry he decided he wasn't going to sneak out anymore. Not at night, anyway. He started sneaking out at five o'clock in the morning. I didn't know where he was going, but I suppose he had some compelling reason to go somewhere at that hour. He left quietly. He didn't wake me up. And he always showed up on schedule for breakfast at seven-thirty, followed by two-a-days, a morning workout and an afternoon workout, either one brutal enough to exhaust mortal men. Most of us had no strength to do anything except eat and collapse for a quick nap between workouts. The idea of getting up any earlier than we had to would have terrified me. Jimmy did whatever he did from five to seven-thirty and still worked twice as hard at two-a-days as most of us. He never looked tired. That's how tough Jimmy was.

Elijah Pitts's father was a sharecropper in Mayflower, Arkansas. His mother was a housekeeper in, as he called it, "the big house," the house owned by the man who also owned the land Elijah's father farmed.

Mayflower had only a few hundred residents and a high school so small it didn't have a football team. Elijah rode a bus every day to Pine Street High School in Conway, twelve miles from Mayflower. He played so well at Pine Street High that schools as far away as the Big Ten heard about him and offered him scholarships.

Elijah had never been more than twenty or thirty miles from Mayflower and he was afraid to go any farther. "I was scared of tall buildings," he said. To Elijah, a tall building was any building more than one story high. He decided to go to Philander Smith College in Little Rock, seventeen miles from Mayflower. That was far enough away.

At Philander Smith, which had six hundred students, Elijah played well enough to be noticed by the Green Bay Packers, to be selected, as an afterthought, in the thirteenth round of the 1961 draft. He packed up all his possessions, which wasn't very much, said goodbye to Ruth, whom he was then dating, and told his friends that he wouldn't be back to Arkansas until after he finished his rookie season with the Green Bay Packers. Nobody told him how high the odds were against a thirteenth-round draft choice winning a place on the team that had just won the Western Conference championship, a team that already had, as running backs, Jimmy Taylor, Paul Hornung and Tom Moore, who had been chosen in the first round of the 1960 draft. "I went with the attitude that I was as good as anyone," Elijah said.

Elijah wasn't afraid—probably because Green Bay had very few tall buildings—till he met Lombardi. "Did he scare you the first time you heard him?" someone once asked Elijah.

"He scared me the last time I heard him, too," Elijah said.

But Lombardi, once again, saw something special. Elijah made the team. He played only sparingly on offense his first two seasons, but he was so fierce and fearless a tackler he was named captain of the special teams. He lived in an apartment in the back of an exterminating business owned by the family of Tony Canadeo, a former Packer running back who was elected to the Pro Football Hall of Fame and also to the board of directors of the Packers, the only civically owned team in the NFL.

Elijah shared his apartment with Willie Davis. Herb Adderley and Willie Wood, the defensive backs, shared another apartment in the same building. The four of them may have outnumbered the non–football-playing blacks in Green Bay at that time. Elijah got accustomed to the fumes from the exterminating business that wafted into his living quarters. He also got accustomed to doing most of the cooking for himself and Willie Davis. Willie said that Elijah would cook whatever dish he saw advertised on television that day. If he saw a spaghetti commercial, he would go out and buy spaghetti. If he saw a cheese commercial, he would go out and buy cheese. If he didn't see any commercial, he would go out and buy chicken wings. Elijah loved chicken wings.

In 1963, when Hornung was suspended, Elijah got to play behind Taylor and Moore and, sometimes, the latest first-round draft choice, Earl Gros. But by 1966, the season we went to the first Super Bowl game, Moore and Gros were gone, Paul was slowed down by an injury and Elijah teamed with Jimmy in our starting backfield. In the NFL championship game against Dallas, Elijah was our leading rusher. And in Super Bowl I, he, like Max, scored two touchdowns. Partly as a reward, the sharecropper's son from Mayflower, Arkansas, was pictured, running behind a Fuzzy Thurston block, on the cover of our 1967 team guide.

Even then, only four years from the end of his playing career, Elijah didn't suspect that he would become a coach. "I thought that was the last thing I would do," he said.

But in 1972, his playing days over, his knowledge of the game increased, Elijah became a scout for the Packers. Two years later, he became an assistant coach for the Los Angeles Rams. He worked with the running backs for four years in Los Angeles, three in Buffalo, then three in Houston before shifting to Canada for a season. "I apply some of Lombardi's teachings," he said. "Not the way he would, but in my own way. I couldn't do everything he did. I couldn't use all of his techniques. I don't believe in all of them. With today's players, Lombardi would have to make adjustments. But he'd figure out some way to succeed."

Of all Lombardi's tenets, "Fatigue makes cowards of us all" made the greatest impression on Elijah. "The first time I heard it," he recalled, "I said, 'What the hell does that mean?' But I learned, and I tell it to my players. If you're tired, you're a coward."

Elijah would like someday to be a head coach in the NFL, which has not had a black head coach in half a century, but, he said, "I won't be bitter if I'm not." One of his former housemates, Willie Wood, did become a head coach, but in the CFL, the Canadian league, and the WFL, the World Football League, not the NFL.

Elijah was disappointed to miss the reunion, the chance to share aromatic memories with Wood, Adderley and Davis. He still corresponded with Wood and, while his son was at UCLA, often saw Davis. "I'm happy as hell for Willie," Elijah said. "He's eating a lot better than chicken wings now."

He last saw his Super Bowl I running mate in New Orleans, a couple of years before the reunion. "Jimmy was carrying a tape recorder, doing an interview," Elijah said. "He was working. Or pretending to be."

• • •

When Urban Henry and I started the Packer Diving Company, we were the only two football players involved. We put up $5,000 apiece. At the beginning, most of our work was in Mexico. Then, as we began to get more and more jobs in Louisiana, I suggested that we bring in Jimmy Taylor as a partner. Jimmy was at the end of his playing days, but he was still a very big name in Louisiana. As a free agent after Super Bowl I, he had signed something like a twenty-year contract with the brand-new New Orleans Saints, and even though he played only one season for them, he was going to be doing public relations for them for a long time. I figured he'd be good for us, and I also figured we'd be good for him. Urban and I gave him ten percent of the company. Later, we gave him another eight percent. Then he bought twelve percent, so he ended up owning about a third of the company.

The diving business flourished and, eventually, we merged into a big outfit called Petrolane, and each of us received a large number of shares in Petrolane. Of course, there were expenses involved in the transaction. After the merger, after Urban and I paid most of the expenses, Jimmy owed Urban $1,700. He owed Urban the money for three or four years, and several times, when Urban needed money badly, he asked Jimmy to pay him. Jimmy always had an excuse, but never a good one. It was just Jimmy, squeezing every nickel and every dime.

One night, finally, we all got together at Urban's shack in the swamp to discuss the company's finances—and Jimmy's debt. Jimmy took a wad of money out of his pocket and, with a big show, like he was giving Urban a gift or something, he peeled off seventeen one-hundred-dollar bills. Like a real big shot. Urban reached over and slapped Jimmy in the face.

Jimmy, still in terrific shape, still working out every day, just sat there with his head bowed, and Urban slapped him again. Jimmy got up and Urban slapped him again. Jimmy walked to the door and Urban slapped him on the back of his head. Jimmy went out to his car and Urban reached in through the open window and slapped him again. Not once did Jimmy act like a man. He never faced up to Urban, never raised a hand to defend himself. I couldn't believe what I was seeing, this romping, stomping fullback, who had always shown such fire on the field, who had punished people as big as Urban, acting like a whipped dog with his tail between his legs. I heard later that he sold his Petrolane stock for close to one million dollars. He still owes me a few dollars, too.

Jimmy and I never said a word to each other at the reunion, not hello or goodbye or anything. We shared a room and all our secrets for more than five years, but now we can't even have a conversation. Three or four times in recent years, when we've both been playing in the same golf tournament, Jimmy has walked up to me and stuck out his hand, but it's always been empty—and it's always stayed empty.

Sometimes I'm tempted. Sometimes I want to say, "Jimmy, how could you act like that? How could you let us down? How could you screw your own friends? What's your side of the story?"

But I just can't do it. I'm just not a good enough person to be able to forgive and forget, to accept Jimmy on his own terms, with his flaws. It's sad.

If I can't trust you, who can I trust?

11. All Vince's Children

Bob Skoronski, Ken Bowman,
Bill Curry and Gale Gillingham

Bob Skoronski, left tackle and captain of the offensive team in Super Bowl I, felt as if he were about to play a game. Pumped up, perspiring, Ski could hear his heart pounding, could sense the adrenaline flowing. He couldn't help it, he said. He was just so excited to be coming to the reunion.

Not everyone shared his enthusiasm.

In Little Falls, Minnesota, Gale Gillingham, who played alongside Ski at left guard during much of the first Super Bowl game, tried to make up his mind whether to go to the reunion or to go goose-hunting. Gilly wanted to see his old teammates, but he knew he would be one of the youngest guys coming back. He also knew that he would be expected to play in the charity golf tournament. Golf was not Gilly's game, and he did not look forward to the embarrassment. Besides, he wasn't certain he had a sports jacket that would fit him well. Gilly weighed the pros and cons and decided to go goose-hunting.

The men who played on the right side of Gilly, the two who split the center's position in Super Bowl I, were also split on the reunion, one attending, one not. Ken Bowman, an attorney who lived and practiced in neighboring De Pere, was going to make the five-minute trip back to Green Bay. But Bill Curry, who was the head football coach at Georgia Tech, his alma mater, had to lead his team against North Carolina State the same weekend. Curry said he felt sick he couldn't go to the reunion, he wanted to be there so badly.

Curry's eagerness was a little surprising because, while each of the other three offensive linemen—Skoronski, Gillingham and Bowman—had spent his entire NFL career of a decade or more playing for the Packers, Curry had put in only two seasons in Green Bay and the bulk of his NFL career with the Baltimore Colts. But Curry brought a special zeal to the Green Bay experience, the zeal of a convert.

Once, during the training season preceding the 1966 season, Paul Hornung and Max McGee got into a philosophical debate over Paul's social habits. "You run around every night, Paul," Max said, "and then you go to church on Sunday. You're really a hypocrite."

Hornung demurred. "Max," he explained, "I go to church every Sunday in the hope that, sooner or later, the message will get through to me, and then I'll be able to overcome my weaknesses and become a better person."

Max refused to accept Paul's explanation. Paul refused to accept Max's premise. They argued back and forth for a while, and then Paul turned to Bill Curry, who was starting his second Green Bay season, and said, "Hey, theologian, come settle this."

Curry was studying theology at Emory University in his hometown of Atlanta. He listened carefully to Hornung's case, and to McGee's, and then said, "This isn't something between you and me, Paul, or between *you* and me, Max. This is something between Paul and—"

Curry lifted his eyes skyward, and McGee groaned. "Oh, no," Max said. "You're not going to bring that damned Lombardi into this."

Bill Curry was a very religious and a very frightened young man. Coach Lombardi intimidated him. "I'm scared to death," he once confessed. "I'm scared I'm going to do something wrong." Curry was, at twenty-four, our youngest starter in Super Bowl I, but several months after the game, he was placed by Lombardi on the expansion list, the list of players the newly created New Orleans Saints could claim. The Saints chose Curry, then traded him to Baltimore. He played in Super Bowl III for the Colts and told reporters that he preferred the Baltimore coach, Don Shula, to Lombardi because Shula didn't try to intimidate people. Curry said Coach Lombardi was too harsh.

The following year, 1970, Curry went to Super Bowl IV in New Orleans as a spectator. One evening, he visited a Bourbon Street saloon called the Absinthe House. The former theology student was then going through what he called his "wilderness phase." He said, "Nobody plays in the NFL without going through a wilderness phase."

In the Absinthe House, Curry happened to encounter Paul Hornung, who was still waiting for the message to get through. Paul greeted Curry with a pointed question. "What the hell are you doing, saying those things about the old man?" Paul demanded.

"They're true," Curry said.

"Like hell they are," Hornung said.

Curry insisted that Lombardi had been too fierce, too demanding, too impersonal. "If Coach Lombardi bumped into me now," Curry said, "he wouldn't know who I was."

"You're wrong," Paul said. "He'd greet you like a long-lost son."

A few months later, Curry went to the White House to attend a prayer breakfast hosted by President Nixon. As he climbed the White House stairs, Curry bumped into Coach Lombardi. "He greeted me," Curry said, "like a long-lost son."

Curry converted.

The next time he saw Lombardi, in the summer of 1970, Coach was in the hospital, dying. "I held his left hand," Bill said, "because all the tubes were on the right side. I told him 'You meant a lot to my life.'"

Lombardi looked up. "You can mean a lot to mine," he told Curry, "if you pray for me."

We were all Lombardi's sons, all his children, whether we played for him for two seasons, as Curry did, or for nine, as Bob Skoronski did, whether we were altered by him, as Gale Gillingham was, or annoyed, as Ken Bowman was. But of us all, Skoronski may have been his most devout disciple.

Bob Skoronski, the grandson of immigrants, believed in the American dream with a twist, a Lombardi twist. "All men are not created equal," Lombardi insisted. "The difference between success and failure is in energy."

Skoronski's formidable energy and enthusiasm carried him, like so many others who played for Lombardi, from an impoverished childhood to remarkable success on the football field to equal success in the business world. He also enjoyed remarkable success as a sire.

Ski was born and raised to be a Packer. His mother and father both worked in the B. F. Goodrich rubber mill near their home in Derby, Connecticut, and—another common strain among Lombardi's Packers (and one that helps explain why so many of us embraced Lombardi as a father figure)—his mother was the dominant parent. "She was a great leader," Bob said. "She had tremendous love for her children."

Her five children thrived on her love and leadership. Bob and his older brother, the first two members of the family to finish high school, went to Indiana University together on football scholarships. Bob could have chosen Notre Dame, but he would only go to a school that gave his brother a scholarship, too. Bob's two younger brothers went to Harvard, and his sister earned a doctorate. "I'm the least educated member of the family," said Bob, who got his BA in marketing.

Cocaptain and most valuable player at Indiana, Bob never missed a college game. Green Bay drafted him in the fifth round in 1956, the same year Forrest was selected in the second round and Bart in the seventeenth. Ski played right tackle as a rookie, then, after two years in the service, spent the next ten seasons at left tackle.

Bob wasn't one of my Monday-night buddies—he was more of a straight arrow, a family man—but he was one of my favorite people, earnest, intelligent, understanding. Above all, he was dependable, as a football player and as a human being. He never gave less than everything he had. "Football is not a natural game," Ski said. "To make contact, in spite of what people think, is not natural even for a 300-pound lineman." Bob was a 250-pound lineman. "It's something you've got to do from the heart and the soul," he said, "and pride will get you to do that."

Pride—and Lombardi. "When I think of him," Ski said, "I think of the conductor of an orchestra, getting all different kinds of instruments to play together, with a jab here, a slap there, a pat on the head somewhere else. He combined intimidation with an uncanny ability to feed people's egos. It was a sensational combination."

Ski's blocking grades were always among the best on the team, but, for some reason, he never got the recognition or the honors so many of us received. He never made All-Pro, never was chosen for the Pro Bowl until 1967, right after Super Bowl I capped his most successful season. Bob never complained, never whined, but still the lack of recognition must have gnawed at him. "Was my guy the only guy who ever got to the quarterback?" he asked long after he finished playing. "Did we always run to the right side? The captaincy of the Packers wasn't an elected position. Why did Lombardi select me?"

He answered his own questions quietly and confidently. "I've evaluated myself alongside the guys who were the greatest of all time," he said, "and I can sleep, I can sleep."

At the end of his playing days, Bob turned his energy to Valley

School Supply, the company he, Willie Davis, Ron Kostelnik and two other Wisconsin businessmen owned. Ski ran Valley. In 1969, when he took charge, the company employed seventeen people and grossed barely a million dollars a year. Fifteen years later, when Ski sold his interest at a handsome price, Valley employed more than one hundred people and grossed more than sixteen million dollars a year. "No one could have worked any harder than I did," Ski said, "but it was a labor of love. I can't think of a day I didn't look forward to going to work. I didn't think I could find anything nearly so exciting after football, but it was the thrill of victory all over again. To me, the greatest thrill was seeing people who worked for me start a family, buy a home and begin raising and educating their kids." He sounded paternal, like Kos, like Lombardi. "I loved watching people grow with the company," Ski said.

He loved watching his own family grow, too. Bob and his wife, Ruth Ann, raised four children. Their oldest, Bob Jr., went to Yale and was an All–Ivy League defensive tackle. Bob Sr. admired the way Yale kept athletics in perspective. The Yale coach, he said, wanted to win as much as any Big Ten coach, but football remained properly subordinate to academics. Bob believed that learning was winning, too. His second son, Steve, chose Indiana, became student manager of the basketball team Bobby Knight and Isiah Thomas led to the NCAA championship, then concentrated on earning his law degree. Ron won a football scholarship to Miami of Ohio, and Patty, the youngest, graduated from Indiana. "The kids always had chores, discipline and love," Bob said. "They're great kids."

Bob Jr., a stockbroker, gave his parents a great Christmas present a couple of months after our reunion: plane tickets, admission tickets and accommodations—a scarce set of items—for the 1985 Masters golf tournament.

During the 1970s, Bob was approached about becoming athletic director at his alma mater. The timing was poor; Valley School Supply was just beginning to flourish. Bob said he wasn't interested. He did, however, give a football clinic at Indiana that led to a meeting and friendship with Bobby Knight, who often asked Ski to talk to his basketball teams.

Coincidentally, the day before Knight slid a chair across the court and earned a brief suspension during the 1984–85 season, he and Ski ate lunch together. Skoronski could see how tense Knight was. Bobby had thrown a few chairs during practice the previous day, and he complained to Ski, "If this were the pros, I could trade these guys." Ski tried to calm Knight, but the coach, clearly, was going through a trying time. "I want the chair concession in the fieldhouse," Skoronski kidded him. The next afternoon, ironically, as Ski walked into the fieldhouse to watch Indiana play, he turned to a friend and said, "This is going to be a six-chair game." He was only off by five.

Ski appreciated Knight's honesty, his energy and his commitment to his game, to his players and to winning. Ski considered winning every bit as important as Lombardi did, and like Lombardi, he meant winning decently and fairly. And he valued striving to win even above winning. He subscribed totally to one of Lombardi's most memorable thoughts: "All the rings, all the color, all the money and all the display linger in the memory only a short time and are soon forgotten. But the will to win, the will to excel, these are the things that endure and are so much more important than any of the events that occasion them."

Skoronski's will to win, his will to excel, never diminished. He showed up at the reunion, at the age of fifty, in terrific shape, except for his hair, which was never his strong point. He weighed about 230, some twenty pounds below his playing weight. Five days a week, he got up at 5:00 A.M. and jogged between five and six miles. He also played racquetball two or three times a week.

Less than three months after the reunion, Ski attacked a new challenge with familiar fervor. On January 1, 1985, he bought Moe/Northern, an established electrical distributor, and promised, "Call me two years from now, and I think you'll find this has surpassed anything I've done before. Retire? Once you have the athletic spirit, it's difficult to retire to hunting and fishing. I love competition."

Bob also continued to be active in RAL Asset Management Group, an investment firm headed by a wide receiver in Super Bowl I, Bob Long, Robert A. Long. Through RAL, Ski had a financial stake in trailer parks and in a growing pizza chain called Rocky Rococo, which specialized in prepackaged pizza by the slice, swift service, or, as Ski put it, with his usual zest, "In and out, ba-boom, ba-boom, ba-boom, ba-boom."

He was always a super salesman, even when he was playing. He worked then for Josten's, a jewelry company, and he sold Lombardi both Super Bowl rings. In those days, the team, not the NFL, paid for the rings. "Lombardi never asked the price," Bob said. "He wanted the best." Bob was such a zealous salesman that, in the locker room, right after we won Super Bowl II, he walked over to Lombardi and showed him a design for the championship ring. "Coach," Ski said, "I want to show you what the guys just won."

Ski wore the Super Bowl II ring to the Super Bowl I reunion. He had given the Super Bowl I ring to his youngest son, Ron, who was, following in his father's footsteps, working for Josten's. Bob himself had not worn either ring for fifteen years before the reunion. "I got embarrassed," he explained, "because every time I wore one of the rings, people would notice it and just want to talk about the Packers. They seemed to think that was all I could talk about. They acted as if I were an athlete and nothing more. That always bothered me, the stigma of the athlete, the idea that he must have limited mental ability. People don't understand that intelligence had so much to do with our success. Our people were sensitive, gentle, real citizens of real worth. We combined excellence on the field and off."

Bob couldn't wait to get to the reunion. He wanted to see his old business partner, Willie Davis. "It never even entered my mind that Willie was black," Ski once said. "I never thought about it." He wanted to see his fellow tackle, his teammate and his rival, Forrest Gregg. "Forrest was the greatest tackle in the world," Ski said, "because of his downfield blocking. He was the premier downfield blocker in the game." He wanted to see everybody. "There may have been teams with more ability," he said, "but there was never one with more love. One of my few regrets in life is that we haven't spent enough time together since we stopped playing."

When Ski and Ruth Ann, after less than an hour's drive from their home in Appleton, entered the hospitality suite at the Thrifty Inn, the first person they spotted was Dave Robinson, the linebacker. "I'm usually not one for hugging," Ski said, "but—" Robby threw his arms around Ski, and Ski threw his arms around Robby. Almost around Robby. Not quite. "I recognized his face and his voice," Bob said, "but I didn't recognize the body." Dave Robinson was a beer distributor, and just like Ski, Robby found his work, obviously, a labor of love.

Ken Bowman's father decided to move his family out of the South Side of Chicago when their neighborhood deteriorated to the point that on payday he had to sprint home from the bus stop or risk losing his paycheck. He quit his factory job with International Harvester and used his life savings to buy a gas station in Rock Island, Illinois. Ken and his brother pumped gas after school, and Ken dreamed of going to college. "I'm never going to have the money to send you," his father said, "but if you can get good enough at a sport, they'll pay you to go to college."

"That made a hell of an impression on me," Bow recalled.

He concentrated on football and got good enough to draw scholarship offers from the Ivy League and the Big Ten and the Big Eight. Bow chose the University of Wisconsin, which was considered a radical outpost in the Midwest, majored in sociology, aimed for law school and thought of football not as a profession, but as a means to an end. "My father used to talk about Rick Casares and Bill George and the Chicago Bears," Bow said, "but I didn't pay much attention. I wanted to be a good football player, as good as I could possibly be, but I was more interested in getting an education."

One of Bow's Wisconsin teammates, a quarterback and defensive back named John Fabry, was a Packer fanatic who tried every Sunday to persuade Bow to watch Green Bay on television. "I didn't want to watch football," Bowman said. "I wanted to study."

Fabry dreamed of playing for the Packers. He tried out for the team, lasted long enough to play against the College All-Stars in an exhibition game, then was cut. But he never lost his enthusiasm for the team. He was, in fact, the president of the Green Bay chapter of the NFL Alumni at the time the group hosted the reunion of the first Super Bowl champions. Fabry qualified as an alumnus because of his appearance against the College All-Stars.

When the Packers drafted Bowman in the eighth round in 1964, our center was the best in the NFL, Jim Ringo, a future Hall of Famer who had been an All-Pro for seven straight seasons. Bow didn't know enough to be awed. "I was twenty-one years old," he said, "and, you know, I thought the Good Lord broke the mold after he made me. I was going to last forever. I wasn't worried about Ringo."

Bow became our starting center in his rookie season. He didn't beat out Ringo. He didn't have to. Not long before training camp began, Ringo brought an agent with him to the Packers' office to help him negotiate his contract. Lombardi had never before dealt with an agent. He wasn't about to. He traded Ringo to Philadelphia, partly to intimidate the rest of us, to keep us away from agents, partly because he felt confident Bowman could take Ringo's place. Lombardi generally tolerated players, no matter how flawed they might be in his eyes, until he could replace them satisfactorily.

Ken Bowman played for the Packers for the next ten seasons. He played with tremendous courage. His left shoulder kept popping painfully out of joint. Once he had it wired, but he delivered one crisp block, and the wires broke, and the shoulder flopped onto his chest. It looked grotesque. Even with my medical history, I didn't like looking at Bowman's shoulder. For his last seven seasons, he wore a leather harness that usually held the shoulder in place.

Bow was more than brave. He was good. "He was great," said Bill Curry, who moved into the starting lineup in 1966 only because Bow was injured. Bowman had never expected to play much in Super Bowl I. "C'mon, Bow," Max McGee called to him before the game, "stretch out and get a tan." Like Max, Bow wound up playing most of the game.

The following year, in the NFL championship game against Dallas, Bowman and I teamed up on the block that moved out Jethro Pugh and sprang Bart Starr for the winning touchdown. I must admit I didn't give Bow too much credit in my diary of the 1967 season.

> *Kenny Bowman came up to me smiling and said, "Don't take all the credit, Kramer. Don't take all the credit. I helped you with that block."*
>
> *"Shut up, Bow," I said. "You've got ten more years to play. You've got plenty of time for glory. I ain't telling anybody anything. If they think I made that block alone, I'm gonna let them think it."*
>
> —*December 31, 1967*
> Instant Replay

Even at the reunion, I still felt a little guilty. "You ought to," Bow told me. "But now you can make it right. You can tell the whole world you stood Pugh up and I pushed him back."

"I pulled you along," I said. "You were hanging onto my pants."

Bow and Fuzzy and I used to spend Tuesday mornings together, cowering in a corner of the meeting room while the world's toughest film critic, Vince Lombardi, reviewed the films of our most recent game. Bow was used to harsh reviews. "He liked to yell at me," Bow said. "He felt I had a thick enough hide." Bowman's hide wasn't *that* thick. He resented Lombardi calling him "stupid" and growling, "What are you wasting your time going to law school for?"

"I thought that was sour grapes on his part," Bowman said. "I think he really wanted to be a lawyer, but he went to law school only for one year."

Bowman went to law school for six years while he played for the Packers. He earned his law degree in 1971, played three more seasons, then set up practice in De Pere, a general practice with an emphasis on trial work. Not long before the reunion, Bow defended an accused murderer. "My client was convicted," he said, "but I'm still not convinced he was guilty."

Bow felt the conservative climate in Green Bay worked against his client, producing a widespread belief that if a man was accused of murder, he must have done something bad. Bowman himself was no conservative, neither politically nor personally. He campaigned for Senator George McGovern in 1972, and in 1984 he clearly held the team record for long hair. "I'll have to get it cut before my next trial," Bowman said.

He came to the reunion with his second wife, Rosann, and with two rings. Bow wore his Super Bowl I ring on his left hand and his Super Bowl II ring on his right.

Bill Curry was practically an aristocrat by Packer standards. His father didn't work in a factory or in a mine or on a farm. His father was the coach of a small-town high school football team in Georgia. He earned $300 a month, so Bill probably wasn't too spoiled.

Curry came to Green Bay in 1965, a twentieth-round draft choice from Georgia Tech, with great faith in God and very little in himself. "I wanted desperately to be accepted on that team," he said, "but I wasn't good enough. I didn't play well. I tried hard, but I wasn't mature."

He was too harsh on himself. He never would have started in Super Bowl I if Bow had been healthy. But Bow had missed most of the season, and Curry certainly had filled in capably. In fact, in one game against the Detroit Lions, Bill had helped me cope with Alex Karras, the actor who used to be a tackle, and after the game, I told the reporters what a terrific job I thought the kid had done. I wanted to pump him up, build his confidence. But on Tuesday, when we sat down to watch the films, Lombardi jumped on me and chewed me out. He said that in the future he would evaluate the players and I would keep my mouth shut.

On a team that had its share of sinners, Curry was a young saint, cut from the Bart Starr mold. We respected his beliefs, even if he was rather outspoken about them. "I was into talking a lot about religion then," Curry recalled. "It was sincere, but I'm more grown-up about it now."

Curry played on two NFL championship teams with us, then went to Baltimore. He and Herb Adderley and Forrest Gregg were the only players to appear in three of the first five Super Bowl games. "I started to grow up in Baltimore," Curry said. "I became a halfway good player."

Bill became a Pro Bowler with the Colts, lasted a decade in the NFL, then returned to Green Bay in 1977 to spend three seasons as an assistant coach under Bart Starr. "Bart is a great human being," Curry said.

In 1980, he became head coach at Georgia Tech. In his job, he said, he thought of Lombardi "all the time" and quoted him "constantly." Lombardi used to tell us that our priorities were our religion, then our families, then the Green Bay Packers. "I tell our players," Bill said, "that their priorities are their religion and their families first, then their education, then football, then fun. I also tell them, 'Fatigue makes cowards of us all,' and, 'Winning is a habit. Unfortunately, so is losing.'"

Curry obviously learned the lessons he once thought were so harshly taught. "They were drilled in too deeply to ever forget," he said.

Gale Gillingham's father was a trucker, "a cattle jockey," Gilly called him, off on the road much of the time, leaving Gilly and his younger brother and their mother to run a little dairy farm not far from Madison, Wisconsin.

Gilly went to the University of Minnesota as a fullback, switched to playing offensive and defensive tackle and made the switch so well that he was a first-round draft choice in 1966, one of three we had on the team, the rewards of some wise maneuvering.

At the beginning of his rookie year, I tried to help Gilly adjust to a new position, a new team, a new league. He learned so quickly and he was so talented it was clear he was going to take away somebody's job, either Fuzzy's or mine, it was just a matter of time. Fuzzy was the more likely target. He was a little older than I and just as battered. I had to back away from helping the kid when he was on the brink of breaking into the starting lineup, on the brink of displacing a veteran, one of my friends.

But I didn't have to help Gilly then. Fuzzy helped him. Fuzzy passed along the knowledge he had worked so hard to gain. Gilly was such a good kid, had such a good attitude that none of us who had been on the offensive line for so long—Fuzzy, Forrest, Ski and me—really resented his arrival. It was just the natural progression of life. Fuzzy was aging, slowing down a little bit. Gilly was young and swift and strong.

Of course we all envied him his youth and his speed and his vigor, hated him for having all the things we'd lost. Until he showed up, Forrest and I had always been the fastest offensive linemen on the team. Suddenly, we no longer were. Every time we had a forty-yard sprint, Gilly would beat Forrest and me by about three yards. Even when we anticipated the count, jumped out just a little early, he still beat us. "Look at the kid," I said.

Forrest looked at me and shook his head. "Jerry, I guess we might as well give up," he said. "We might as well stop trying to beat him 'cause we ain't going to do it."

I always used to measure guys, look in their eyes, see if they were *there*. Gilly was always there. I remember once, after I'd stopped playing, seeing the Packers play Pittsburgh and watching the way Gilly handled Mean Joe Greene. I mean he *handled* him, he dominated him, drove him right out of plays, and Greene was a hell of a player.

Several years later, in Nashville, I happened to meet Mike Reid, the former All-Pro defensive tackle for the Cincinnati Bengals who quit pro football, at his peak, to become a wonderful songwriter. (I don't think it's any accident that it's always the defensive linemen—Reid and Greene and Karras and Merlin Olsen and Bubba Smith—who become the stars of stage, screen and commercials, never the offensive linemen. Offensive linemen don't know what a spotlight is.) Mike and

I traded a few war stories, and he told me that Gilly gave him his real introduction to pro football. "He hit me so hard," Mike Reid said, "I almost couldn't fall."

Bill Bergey, Philadelphia's All-Pro linebacker, paid Gilly a similar compliment. "When you're playing football and you're concentrating and you get hit," Bergey said, "it never hurts. When Gillingham hit me, it hurt."

I really had hoped to see Gilly at the reunion. Gilly was a player.

A few months after the reunion, I decided to go up to Little Falls, Minnesota, to see Gilly. I called him, told him I wanted to visit, and he said he was awful busy, had lots of meetings and not much time. He laughed and chatted, but he sounded a little guarded, as if he resented the intrusion. I thought I detected a little bitterness.

If Gilly were bitter, I figured, he had a right to be. For one thing, even though he was All-Pro four times, he never got the kind of recognition that Fuzzy and I got, not from the public. For another, after playing on teams that won the Super Bowl his first two seasons, Gilly played on only two winning teams in his last eight seasons and never won another postseason game. That must have been frustrating for someone so talented, so dedicated to excellence, as Gilly.

He had personal frustrations, too. He used his money from Super Bowl I to buy three hundred head of black Angus cattle and a thousand-acre ranch, but in the seventies the cattle business went bad, and Gilly lost the ranch. His marriage fell apart, too. His wife left him, and their two younger children went with her, the two older stayed with him, both college basketball players. Gilly turned to selling real estate, farms and homes and waterfront lots and an occasional commercial property, to make a living.

I could understand why he might be reluctant to see me, but I decided to give it a shot, anyway. I liked Gilly too much to stay away.

On my way to Little Falls, driving from Minneapolis, I stopped in St. Cloud for a sandwich, and while I was eating, two young men, not much more than boys really, came into the place. As I was leaving, one of them turned to me and said, "Mr. Kramer?"

I was a bit surprised. I said, "Yes?"

He said, "I was a great Packer fan. I loved it when you guys were at Green Bay."

I said, "Thank you." He couldn't have been more than eight or nine years old when I played my last game.

It never ceases to amaze me, the memory and loyalty of sports fans. A couple of years ago, I was standing on a street corner in San Francisco, waiting for the light to change, when a guy, turning the corner, rolled down his car window and hollered out, "Jerry Kramer?"

I said, "Right," and he said, "Hell of a block," and drove on.

I drove on to Little Falls, a pretty little town of about seventy-five hundred people, with nice wide streets. It reminded me of towns in Idaho.

The first thing that struck me about Gilly was how good he looked. He was only forty-one, and he weighed about 275 pounds, exactly what he weighed when he stopped playing. He could still bench press more than 500 pounds, he said. A few years ago, he told me, his weight got up to 310 pounds, and one day he was watching an NBA playoff game with a few of his friends, and at halftime he said he bet he could still dunk a basketball. So Gilly went outside, and at six-foot-three and 310 pounds, stuffed the basketball four times in a row. He tried a fifth time and tore a muscle. After that, he stopped stuffing basketballs and himself. He got his weight down to 275. I guess I was still jealous of his youth and his speed and his vigor.

We went to Gilly's office and started talking like a couple of old housewives who saw each other every day. We were at ease immediately. "I was kind of a big old dumb farm kid when I got to Green Bay," Gilly said. "Many times that first year, I just wanted to take off, say the hell with this, this is too tough." I never would have suspected Gilly felt that way—except, I suppose, we all did, the first time we were exposed to large doses of Lombardi.

"I pretty much had no direction when I got to Green Bay," he said. "That was the only place that could have changed me. I didn't know much about football. I just beat up on people and that was enough. But we did things for a reason. That was the best thing. Everything was for a reason."

"What stays with you?" I said. "What do you remember best?"

"I remember losing to San Francisco my rookie year," Gilly said, "and going to the airport, and Lombardi saying, 'C'mon, I'll buy all you guys a beer.'"

I remembered that, too. We had won our first four games in 1966, and we won our next three, but in between, the 49ers beat us in San Francisco, 21–20. Lombardi felt for us. He knew how much we wanted to win. He knew how hard we'd played. I was standing next to him in the airport, and he had a rule we were not allowed to go into the bar at the airport or at any hotel we stayed in. He turned to me and said, "What do you think of everybody having a beer?"

I said, "Coach, I think it's a hell of an idea."

Gilly also remembered the time Lombardi, pumping us up to play Chicago, pumped himself up even more. "You guys whip the Bears," he said, "and I'll whip old man Halas's ass."

Gilly smiled at the memories. "Everything Lombardi did made sense," he said. "We didn't like doing some of the things, but they made sense. Everything was simple, too. I bet we had the simplest offense in football. We'd get upset if we blew three or four plays in a year."

Gilly told me he spent a couple of nights a week bowling, and he had told his bowling buddies he wished he could have taken them into the Packer locker room half an hour before a game. "That would have shown them what pro football was like," he said. "Needles going into arms, into shoulders, into knees. Some guys pacing. Some getting sick. All of us knowing it's going to be bad out there for the next three hours."

"What was the last thing you'd do?" I asked Gilly.

"I'd run the except-fors through my head," he said. "I knew what we were supposed to do most of the time, but I'd go over the except-fors."

For him, Gilly said, the best time always came a few minutes before the opening kickoff. "I love my kids dearly," he said, "but I have never been as close to people as I was every Sunday when I walked through that damn tunnel to the field. I thought so much of those guys walking with me, I didn't want to do anything to let them down. We would kill for each other. We would die for each other. We would do anything for each other."

Gilly shook his head. "I don't like what's happened to the game," he said. "The teams don't run as much. The offensive line play is just legalized holding. They stand up and they grab. They're just a bunch of steroided, milk-fed, 3.2-beer-drinking, holding sons of bitches. I liked the Super Bowl. The San Francisco 49ers had a legitimate offensive line. They had guards who could actually pull. They beat the hell out of Miami."

I chuckled, listening to Gilly get all riled up. He sounded like he was ready to go back out. He looked like he was ready, too. I went with him to a softball game that night, and he caught for his team, and every time someone hit a ground ball to the infield, he sprinted down to first base with the batter, ready to back up the throw. He moved. He got up to bat twice, and he hit a single and a home run. Gilly was still a player.

My apprehensions were wrong. Gilly wasn't bitter. He was in good spirits. "I've never been happier," he said. "I'm doing fine. I could be making more money if I were in Minneapolis, but I don't like cities, I don't like crowds. In fact, Little Falls is getting too crowded for me. I may go out West after the boys are on their own.

"I have an obligation to the children. I want them to live up to the ability they have. I want them to think for themselves. They're very intelligent kids. That must have been my wife's influence. I was hard on the kids. I didn't spare the rod. But I was fair. There was always a reason."

Gilly was very serious. "I'm going to give my two Super Bowl rings to my older sons," he said, "when they become men."

As I was driving out of Little Falls, as a big John Deere tractor rolled past me, heading in the opposite direction, I felt a real sadness. I enjoyed being with Gilly. I used to call him Angus, and he still reminded me of that. Massive shoulders and chest. A nice kid, if you can call a forty-one-year-old a kid. I'd like to see more of him. I felt the way I felt when I left Green Bay after the reunion. I knew I was leaving something good behind.

12. Three of a Kind

Ray Nitschke, Dave Robinson and Lee Roy Caffey

Vince Lombardi, who didn't like long necks, apparently did like long bodies, especially bodies seventy-five inches long. Of the forty men on the team that won the first Super Bowl game, seventeen of us used to be six-feet-three-inches tall, including all three of the starting linebackers—Ray Nitschke, Dave Robinson and Lee Roy Caffey. The trio had their height in common, and much more. All three went to the Pro Bowl in the mid-1960s, and all three came to the reunion in 1984. Robinson and Caffey, at forty-three, were content to reminisce and relax. Nitschke, at forty-eight, thought he should still be playing. Robinson and Caffey wanted to have fun. Nitschke wanted to hit people. That always was his idea of fun.

Nitsch, of course, was in very good shape, just in case. Lee Roy, a racquetball player, was in fairly good shape. Robby was a terrific ad for the Mars Distributing Company of Akron, Ohio, wholesalers of Coors and Blatz beer. Robby was the managing partner in Mars. He was managing Mars better than he was managing his waistline. "It would take an act of Congress to find out what I weigh," Robby announced. "Not even my wife knows. She just knows I'm heavy, that's all."

Robby insisted even he did not know his true weight. "Over 250," he said. "The scale in my house only goes up to 250, and I'm off the scale." He also said that every time he walked past a bar, he gained four pounds. Robby laughed louder than anybody at his own jokes. He always did enjoy poking fun at himself.

Once, during training camp, when the July sun baked the practice field, and the temperature reached ninety-two degrees, Lombardi hollered at us, "Look at the sun tans you're getting. Isn't that beautiful? Just like a health spa here."

Lombardi studied his healthy troops. "You know," he said, "a lot of people pay a lot of money to get sun tans like you've got."

"Hey, Coach," Robby yelled out. "I've had this tan of mine all my life, and I didn't spend a dime for it. But I've been paying for it ever since I got it."

Nitschke, too, could needle himself. He loved to tell the story about the time the observation tower at the practice field, a tall steel structure, fell on him, hit him in the head, flattened him. "Who is it?" Lombardi shouted. "Who got hit?" Coach was obviously worried.

"Nitschke," Bart Starr said.

Coach was obviously relieved. "Oh," he said. "Let's get back to practice."

"He knew nothing could hurt my head," Nitsch said whenever he told the story.

Lee Roy Caffey probably had the funniest story of all about Lombardi. "I always negotiated my contracts directly with him," Lee Roy said. "I'd say, 'Vince, I'm just a country boy from Texas and I'm buying land and I need all the help I can get.' And he never backed off what I asked for. He always gave it to me."

Nitschke's career lasted fifteen seasons, Robinson's twelve and Caffey's ten. Ray, the midwesterner, finished his career, fittingly, in

Green Bay; Robby, the easterner, finished in Washington; and Lee Roy, the southwesterner, finished in San Diego.

Coincidentally, when they regrouped in Green Bay in 1984, they each had three children and they each had been married for more than twenty-two years. Our linebackers certainly were a solid, stable, dependable corps.

Ray Nitschke was three years old when his father died. When Ray was ten, he washed dishes in the restaurant where his mother cooked. When he was thirteen, his mother died. An older brother became his legal guardian. The brother worked on the railroad. Ray worked the streets. He beat up other kids. "I felt I was somebody who didn't have anything," he once said, "and I took it out on everybody."

In high school, just outside Chicago, Ray channeled his anger into sports. He was a star in baseball, basketball and football. Baseball was his favorite sport. He pitched and played the outfield, and Stan Musial was his hero. He dreamed of playing in the big leagues. But football was Ray's best sport. He won a football scholarship to the University of Illinois. He played fullback and linebacker, and in 1958, when he was chosen for the College All-Star team, he and I became teammates for the first time, the beginning of a strange and sometimes strained relationship.

I started it on a sour note in the All-Star training camp. Half joking, I made some smartass remark about Ray's brain power, something about a mental giant, a genius. Ray didn't think it was funny, and it wasn't. He came out of his chair and challenged me in a loud, menacing voice. I was wrong, and I backed down, but Ray never forgot. He always looked at me like I was a dog that had bitten him once.

We had a few other confrontations during our early years in Green Bay. The last one I remember well. We were out partying, drinking more than we should have, and Ray said some things he shouldn't have said. One thing led to another, and he finally asked if I wanted to step outside. I said, "Hell, yes," and started for the door. I looked over my shoulder and Ray was right behind me. I said to myself, *Oh, self, you are in trouble!* I figured we were about to get serious and I had better get my bluff in first.

I turned and grabbed Ray around the throat and I said I was ready to tear his head off. I backed him up against a brick wall and said I was crazy enough to fight or drink, whichever way he wanted it. He looked at me and said, "No, man, you're my teammate, I don't want to fight you." And we went back inside, fortunately for me.

It was a truce, but an uneasy one. We were never that close to it again, but every time I blocked Ray in practice, for the rest of my career, I guess, I knew he'd be waiting for me—Ray and that damned forearm of his. He had one ferocious forearm, and he used it in practice the way he used it in a game, the way Dillinger used a pistol, to intimidate you, to stop you. "You want the ballcarrier to be a little shy," Nitsch said, "and a little shyer the next time." Ray held nothing back. "I came to play," he said. "I came to practice." Sometimes I thought of Ray more as an opponent than as a teammate, he inflicted so much damage in practice. He and Jimmy Taylor just didn't know what it was like to brother-in-law, to ease up.

One afternoon not long before the reunion, Fuzzy Thurston, Bob Skoronski and I were sitting around a table at Fuzzy's place, and we got to discussing how good Nitschke was, and who was better, Nitsch or Dick Butkus of the Chicago Bears, another great middle linebacker who, like Ray, wound up in beer commercials. I argued that Ray was simply the best and the toughest linebacker ever.

"We double-teamed Butkus more than any other guy we ever played against," Ski pointed out.

"Butkus was the best I ever played against," Fuzzy said, diplomatically, "but I never played against Ray."

"I think Ray was the hardest hitter the game ever had," Ski said, "but Butkus was the best defensive player."

At the reunion, the question was put to Nitschke: "Did anybody hit harder than you?"

"Yeah," Ray said. "Butkus did."

His last eight years in the National Football League, Ray competed with Butkus. His first eight years in the NFL, Ray competed with Detroit's Joe Schmidt and Chicago's Bill George. All four of them, all middle linebackers playing in the same division, were elected to the Pro Football Hall of Fame. Ray made the Hall of Fame even though he was picked for the Pro Bowl only once, which indicates how tough the competition was at middle linebacker.

When we beat the New York Giants, 16–7, for the 1962 NFL championship, Ray was named the Most Valuable Player. I actually thought he was the second most valuable. I thought the guy who kicked the three field goals that made the difference in the game should have been the MVP. But I would have been willing to share the award with Ray.

Ray mellowed during his Green Bay career. He mellowed off the field. He stopped drinking. "Hey, Ray, what's it like, not drinking?" Dan Currie once asked him. "It's quiet, man," Ray said. "Real quiet." On road trips, for excitement, Nitsch used to sit in hotel lobbies, with his horn-rimmed glasses and his bald head and his neat bridge of false teeth, looking more like a professor than a pro football player. He was the total family man. He did everything to help his wife, Jackie, raise the three children they adopted. He played with them. He built tree-houses for them. He loved those children. He loved all children. He had never had a childhood of his own. Once, when someone asked one of Dave Robinson's twin boys if he knew Ray Nitschke, Robby's boy looked puzzled, then said, "Oh, you mean John-John's daddy." Ballcarriers called Ray worse things.

On Christmas Eve in 1967, Jackie Nitschke invited the whole team to a party, then surprised Ray with a Christmas present. He looked out the window and saw a Lincoln Continental sitting on his front lawn. Ray almost cried. "When I was a little kid," he said, "someone gave me a ride in a Lincoln, and ever since then, I've dreamed of owning one. I never thought I would."

Ray didn't want to quit before his sixteenth season. He wanted to play just one more year, or two, or maybe three. "I could still play," he said at the reunion. "I could play for a quarter." Very reluctantly, Ray retired in 1972, but with his home in Green Bay, he remained close to the team and to the game. He is the publisher of and writes a column for the *Packer Report*, a newspaper that comes out weekly during the football season, and he does public relations for a few companies, most notably Miller. Besides making commercials for Miller Lite, he makes appearances and delivers speeches, opens doors and shakes hands. He plays in dozens of celebrity golf tournaments, and he plays very well, in the upper 70s, to a six-handicap. He even plays golf on occasion with his old hero, Stan Musial, who is now his good buddy.

I've played in several tournaments with Ray, and at one a couple of years ago, he and I and John David Crow, a running back who entered the NFL the same year we did, started talking about the big change in salaries in pro football. I had always been curious about Ray's salary, since we were rookies together and teammates for eleven seasons, but we were forbidden to discuss our salaries at Green Bay, and, believe it or not, we didn't. I looked at Ray and said, "Hey, Nitsch, what kind of a bonus did you get to sign with the Packers?"

He looked up, kind of grinned and said, "I got $500, man."

I said, "You SOB, you doubled me! I only got $250. I got $250 for signing and $7,750 for the season."

Nitschke said, "You got $8,000! I only got $7,700."

"You two are both pikers," Crow said. "I got $1,000 for a bonus and $15,000 for the season." Of course, John David won the Heisman Trophy and was the number-one draft choice that year. Now some players, even a few linemen, make a hundred times what I made. One hundred times! There hasn't been that much inflation.

The odds are Ray isn't a millionaire, but he has a good life that he really seems to enjoy. His boys are twenty-two and nineteen—neither played much football; "They heard too much of, 'Are you gonna play football like your daddy?'" Jackie Nitschke said—and his daughter is thirteen. The Miller commercials have made Ray more recognizable than he was when he was destroying running backs, and he seems to have developed the kind of self-confidence off the field he used to have only on the field. He can give speeches to kids or to Chrysler executives. He can talk the language of the kids, and he can use the buzz words of big business. Ray seems comfortable, and, finally, I feel comfortable with him.

At an NFL Alumni convention in Reno a few years back, Ray and I played golf together two or three days in a row, and I guess it was the most relaxed we'd ever been with each other, a really warm feeling. As we were saying our goodbyes, Ray said, "Thanks. Thanks for everything."

"What are you talking about?" I said.

Nitsch looked at me and said, "You know what I'm talking about."

Vince Lombardi rode Lee Roy Caffey hard. On the practice field, Lombardi would scream at him, "You ought to be ashamed of yourself, you big turkey!" Then, at the negotiating table, Coach would say to him, "You may wonder why I yell at you a lot. Every team has to have a whipping boy, and I use you as my whipping boy."

"I don't care how you use me," Caffey would say, "just as long as you pay me."

Lombardi rewarded Caffey well. "I was probably the highest-paid linebacker in the NFL," Lee Roy said.

Lombardi was important to Lee Roy, an important influence, but he was not a father figure. Lee Roy didn't need a father figure. He was the only one of our three linebackers whose father saw him play football, in high school, in college and in the pros. Lee Roy's father was an entrepreneur. He owned a produce business in Thorndale, Texas, a town of twelve hundred people. Lee Roy's professional football career eventually took him to Philadelphia, Chicago, Dallas and San Diego, as well as Green Bay, but at the end, he settled in Rockdale, Texas, twelve miles from Thorndale. Unlike many of his teammates, Lee Roy had roots.

Lee Roy went from Thorndale High to Texas A&M on a basketball scholarship, but he never did play basketball for the Aggies. He concentrated on football. He was a running back, not quite good enough to make Aggie fans forget John David Crow, and he was a linebacker, good enough to be drafted by the Philadelphia Eagles in the seventh round in 1963. When he was drafted, Lee Roy weighed 208 pounds. The Eagles told him to come to training camp at 240. Fortunately, steroids were not yet the diet of choice for athletes trying to bulk up. "I pumped iron," Lee Roy said, "and I filled myself up on milk shakes with eggs in them." Of course milk shakes and eggs had a side effect, too. "Everything I eat now turns to weight," said Lee Roy, who, in his forties, faced a constant struggle to keep his weight at 260, ten pounds above his playing weight.

In the summer of 1963, Lee Roy and Dave Robinson were teammates on the College All-Star team that did a terrible thing. The All-Stars beat the NFL champions, the Green Bay Packers. It was a long time till those of us who were already Packers forgave Robinson and Caffey and their All-Star teammates for the cruel and inhuman punishment their victory subjected us to.

Caffey spent one season in Philadelphia, then came to Green Bay in the trade that sent Jim Ringo and Jim Ringo's agent to the Eagles. Lee Roy played right linebacker in 1964, and in the first half of the 1965 season. Nitschke was at his peak then, coming off an All-Pro and a Pro Bowl season, but as he warmed up before a game against Detroit, Nitschke pulled a hamstring. Only a few minutes before the kickoff, Lombardi turned to Caffey and said, "Ray's hurt. You're going to have to play the middle."

Caffey had not practiced very much at middle linebacker. Nobody expected Nitschke to get hurt. He was indestructible. Lee Roy was inexperienced. "I go out there," Lee Roy recalled almost twenty years later, "and Detroit is killing me. I mean, everything I do is wrong, and they know it, and they're working on me. At the half, we're behind, 21–3. I come in and sit down at my locker, and I've got tears running out of my eyes. And I just know that all the guys are looking at me and thinking that I'm losing the ball game."

The first player who walked up to Caffey was Nitschke. "Now Lee Roy," said Nitsch, all bandaged up, "here's what you did wrong." And Ray gave Lee Roy a quick, condensed course in middle linebacking.

Then Bart Starr stopped and patted Lee Roy on the back and said, "Don't worry, we're going to win." One by one, with words or pats or glances, his teammates let Lee Roy know that they shared his agony, that they appreciated his effort, that they supported him. Then Lee Roy went out and had a super second half. "I'm blitzing, I'm making tackles, everything I do is right," he said. In the third quarter, Bart did everything right, threw three touchdown passes, *averaging* almost sixty yards, and we came back to beat the Lions, 31–21. It was probably the best half of football we ever played.

"From then on," Lee Roy said, "I realized what the Green Bay Packers were. It was all the guys, working together. We never got down on one of our teammates when he wasn't playing well."

Lee Roy played so well for the rest of the regular season that, at the end, his peers, his fellow NFL players, elected him to the Pro Bowl. The experience was an education for Lee Roy, who had always approached football with an easygoing attitude, a casual attitude compared to Nitschke's. "I found out playing middle linebacker that it's a whole different world," Lee Roy said. "After a game, you're beat up. You're sore. You almost have to be a madman. You can be a lot looser playing outside."

The following season, the season that led to Super Bowl I, Lee Roy concentrated on outside linebacker and made All-Pro. "I think the fact that I could play the middle or outside is why I got paid so much," Lee Roy said.

Caffey remained a good businessman after he stopped playing football. For eight years, he operated a successful Chevrolet and Buick dealership in Rockdale. Then he got together with a small group of people and applied for a charter to start a bank in Rockdale. The first time the group applied, it got turned down. Lee Roy was disappointed, and so were his associates. Several of them wanted to quit, to give up. "Hell, it's all politics," one of them said. "We can't get a bank in Rockdale."

Lee Roy wasn't about to give up, especially after he overheard some of the people who were blocking the charter talking over the CB radio.

155

"No way we'll let that big dummy of a jock get hold of a bank," one of them said.

"I'm going to put a bank in Rockdale, whether you're with me or not," Lee Roy told his partners. "If I quit on this charter, and Lombardi ever found out, he'd shoot me." Caffey's group stayed intact, reapplied and got the charter for the bank. "You just don't quit," Lee Roy said.

Lee Roy is still a stockholder in the bank, but his primary interest now is Caffey Real Estate, which he and his cousin operate. "I make most of my money buying land and reselling it," he said. He wasn't doing badly for a big dummy of a jock.

Lee Roy came to the reunion with his wife, Dana, whom he had married in college. They have three children, two older girls, Lee Ann and Jennifer Kay, and a fifteen-year-old son, Brad, who, at six-foot-one and 145 pounds, played tight end his freshman year in high school. "He's going to fill out and he'll have all the physical equipment," Lee Roy said. "He can be as good as he wants to be. He thinks I'm too critical. I know he does a lot of things right, but I'm always telling him about the things he does wrong."

Everybody has to have a whipping boy.

Dave Robinson was the youngest of eight children of a farm laborer in New Jersey. When Dave was barely into his teens, he worked with his father and three brothers cutting corn, and at the end of one week, they took all their wages and gave half to Dave's mother. She counted out more than $100 and said, "That was a very good week." Dave began dreaming then that somehow, someday, he would have a job at which he could earn $100 in a week.

His father died when Dave was a freshman in high school. The father's last wish was that his three youngest children, the three who were still at home, a girl and two boys, would go beyond high school, would complete their education. Dave's sister went to business school. Dave's brother went to Maryland State, to study and to play football. He had only a partial scholarship, which put a tremendous financial strain on the mother, who worked as a domestic, cleaning other people's homes. The brother, after college, had a chance to try out for the NFL as a free agent, but chose instead to become a minister.

Dave didn't want to be a financial burden to his mother. He decided he would go only to a school that offered him a full scholarship. Dave's College Board scores were around 1300. His athletic skills were equally impressive. He applied to forty-six colleges, and he was offered forty-six full scholarships. He narrowed his choice down to three schools—Columbia, Pennsylvania and Penn State—then selected Penn State. Eventually, he had to pick a field of study in which to major. He picked engineering for three reasons: The Russians had put Sputnik in orbit, creating a demand for engineers; Robby had earned a 99 in analytical geometry in his freshman year; and, most important, his mother told him that the engineers whose homes she cleaned seemed to earn a lot of money. Dave figured he could make his $100 a week as an engineer. He made All-American as a football player and was selected in the first round of the 1963 NFL draft by the Green Bay Packers. "Where's Green Bay?" he asked his wife, Elaine.

He found Green Bay, fortunately for Green Bay. He and Lee Roy and Ray were a magnificent and cohesive unit through the three straight championships in the mid-1960s. "Ray and I were as close as brothers," Robby said, "and Lee Roy was the first white guy from Texas I ever kissed."

Robby was also close to Willie Davis, off the field and on. "Willie played right in front of me," Robby said. "Later, when I was finishing my career in Washington, Deacon Jones played in front of me. Some people said Deacon was the best defensive end ever. No disrespect to him, but as far as I was concerned, nobody came close to Willie Davis. What he lacked in size, he made up for in intelligence. No one ever ran the same play against us twice successfully."

Robby didn't play too badly himself. He made All-Pro three straight years and the Pro Bowl four straight. But he never got overconfident. Once, after a game against the New York Giants, the Associated Press named Robby the defensive player of the week in the NFL. He was feeling good until he walked into the meeting Tuesday morning to watch the films. "From the way Vince said hello to me, I knew I was in trouble," Robby said. "I was scared to death to watch the films. *What does the AP know?* I said to myself."

During the first few off-seasons, Robby worked for Campbell Soup as a project engineer. He found out quickly that he didn't really want to be an engineer, and that soup wasn't his favorite liquid. He sold insurance for one year and then turned, as he put it, to "the malt beverage business." When Willie Davis retired from football and moved to California, Robby stepped into Willie's job at Schlitz in Milwaukee.

I always felt Robby had the same drive, energy, pride and intelligence that Willie had, and I wouldn't have been surprised if Robby had enjoyed the same kind of success. But few human beings, white or black or green, succeed the way Willie succeeded. Robby had more of a struggle. He always planned and hoped that someday, like Willie, he would have his own distributorship. Once, he came so close to getting a Schlitz distributorship, and lost it at the last moment. "I felt like the world was over," Robby remembered.

Then he remembered one of the lessons he had learned from Lombardi. "The greatest glory is not in never falling," Vince said, "but in rising every time we fall."

"I got up," Robby said. "I said to my wife, 'We *will* have a distributorship someday.'"

Robby got his distributorship only a few months before our reunion. He and three friends started Mars Distributing. Robby was vice president and managing partner. "We started from scratch," he said early in 1985, "and we're doing better than a million cases this year. In five years, I plan to be the number one wholesaler in Akron." Robby laughed. "Once you can accept second place," he said, quoting Lombardi, "it's too easy to accept third."

Lombardi was, in effect, the fifth partner in Mars. "Willie Davis once told me that whenever he'd go into a sales meeting, Vince would go in with him," Robby said. "Now I know what he meant. Every time

I start a sales meeting, I find Lombardi conducting it. It's eerie. I find myself spouting Lombardiisms when I least expect it."

Elaine did not come to the reunion with Robby. She made a few phone calls, found out that Ruth and Elijah Pitts were not coming, that Ann Davis was not making the trip from California, that none of the wives of the black players was attending the reunion. She decided to stay at home with the three Robinson boys, the twins, both twenty-one, both attending the University of Akron, and the seventeen-year-old, a senior in high school. All of the boys played some football, but none well enough, Robby felt, to play big-time college football. The youngest, a guard and linebacker in high school, was thinking of going to Rutgers, and even though the coach at Rutgers, Dick Anderson, was Robby's roommate at Penn State, he didn't think his son would play much football at Rutgers. Robby wasn't concerned. His only concern was that the boy get an education.

Robby took a lot of kidding about his weight at the reunion, and when he got home, he decided he had better lose a few pounds. He lost a few—ten or twelve. "My wife says that's like throwing two deck chairs off the *Titanic*," Robby announced.

13. An Unlikely Quartet

Willie Wood, Herb Adderley, Bob Jeter and Tom Brown

In 1960, Willie Wood, a 165-pound free agent, wore weights around his ankles so that when he stepped on the scale the Green Bay Packers wouldn't chase him out of training camp. In 1961, Herb Adderley, a rookie running back, ran into Bill George of the Chicago Bears and suffered a broken collarbone, a rough introduction to the National Football League. In 1962, Bob Jeter, a fugitive from the Canadian Football League, spent the season on the Green Bay taxi squad, trying, without much success, to learn to catch passes. In 1963, Tom Brown, fresh out of college, passed up a chance to sign with the Green Bay Packers and, instead, at the insistence of President John F. Kennedy, played first base for the Washington Senators.

A few years later, this unlikely quartet—Wood, Adderley, Jeter and Brown—was our starting defensive backfield in Super Bowl I and in Super Bowl II. Adderley was All-Pro the year we won the first Super

Bowl game, Jeter was All-Pro the year we won the second and Wood was All-Pro both years. Those three showed up at the reunion in 1984. Tom Brown never received an invitation. The oversight probably had nothing to do with the fact that he was white. The committee did send an invitation to Tom, but it never reached him. The invitation may have been mailed by mistake to his first wife. First wives have a tendency to forward only bills.

At the reunion, Willie Wood was no longer wearing weights. He no longer had to. He and Bob Jeter were both forty-seven years old and were both at least forty-seven pounds over their Super Bowl weights. "Hey, Willie, come over here," Willie Davis yelled to Willie Wood. "We want to take a group picture of you."

Herb Adderley, who outweighed both Wood and Jeter during their playing days, came in at least fifty pounds lighter than his former backfield mates. At forty-five, Herbie looked as if he could be comfortable in his old uniform and comfortable on the field. "I run between three and six miles three or four days a week," he said.

Herbie was elected to the Professional Football Hall of Fame in 1980. "When I was inducted with Bob Lilly, Deacon Jones and Jim Otto," he recalled, "I said, 'Well, this is it. I can't feel any better about football. There's no way.' I was wrong. To come to a gathering like this is even better. This reunion is better than being enshrined in the Hall of Fame."

Willie Wood made it to Green Bay the long way. He grew up on the East Coast, in Washington, D.C., where his mother and father both worked for the federal government, and went to college on the West Coast, first for one year at Coalinga Junior College in California's San Joaquin Valley, then for three years at the University of Southern California. He played quarterback at USC and, in those days of limited substitution, played safety only when the coach couldn't get a substitute in for him.

He also made it to Green Bay the hard way. "When I got out of SC," he said, "I had two strikes on me." He was the wrong color, a black quarterback when the NFL had no black quarterbacks, and he was the wrong size. "I was the only one who thought I had a chance," Willie said. He wrote letters to several professional teams, requesting a chance to try out, and the first one that responded was the Packers. When we went to Los Angeles to play the Rams in 1959, Lombardi invited Willie to the game and to the locker room. He met several of the guys, none of whom could have dreamed that in a few years this skinny five-foot-ten kid would be one of the leaders of our defense, frightening even Ray Nitschke with his mean looks.

Drafted by no one, Willie came to our training camp in 1960. "At the weigh-ins," he said, "I used to put a five-pound jogging weight on each ankle, and I still didn't hit 175. Lombardi knew I was small, but I had large shoulders and a seventeen-inch neck. Lombardi liked that." Lombardi certainly liked something. Willie made the team. "I don't think I could have made it with any other team, any other coach," he said. Lombardi paid Willie $6500 for his rookie season.

Willie was one of only three or four black players on the Packers in 1960. We didn't use the word "black" then; we still said "Negro." Willie roomed with Emlen Tunnell, one of the great safeties in the history of the NFL. Tunnell, a future Hall of Famer, was in his thirteenth season, his next-to-last. "Em taught me everything," Willie said. He couldn't have had a better tutor.

Tunnell retired after the 1961 season, holding the NFL career record for interceptions with seventy-nine, and the following year his protégé, his replacement, Willie Wood, led the NFL with nine. As a result, Willie was named to the first of his eight Pro Bowl teams. Then, in 1963, he made All-Pro for the first of six straight years. Willie deserved to be elected to the Pro Football Hall of Fame. His credentials were every bit as impressive as Herb Adderley's, and his reputation for ferocity, for tackling hard, was unmatched. All of our guys hit hard, but Willie hit extra hard. Pound for pound, Coach Lombardi said, Willie, who filled out to 190, was the best tackler in the game. "That was the one thing I had going for me," Willie said. "I wasn't a speed burner. My game was based on determination. I had to highlight that ability to stay on the team."

Nitschke called the signals, but Wood coordinated our defense. At safety, he had a perfect overall view, and he didn't mind intimidating teammates as well as opponents. "I hate to miss a tackle," Nitschke once said, "'cause I know if I do, I'm gonna get a dirty look from Willie. He'll kill you with that look."

Sometimes Willie did more than look. "Don't you ever let those running backs get to me again!" he would yell at Nitschke.

"Sure I yelled," Willie recalled. "I didn't see any reason why I had to be making the tackles he should have been making, when he was getting paid twice as much as me."

Willie's career lasted twelve seasons, all of them in Green Bay. He probably would have been better off if he had left after nine, if, in 1969, he had accompanied Lombardi to Washington, to his hometown. Willie knew by then he wanted to coach, and Vince had encouraged him. He would have loved to have served an apprenticeship under Lombardi. But in 1969, Willie was still skilled enough to be chosen for the Pro Bowl. The Packers were not about to let him go.

Willie played his last game in 1971, then joined the San Diego Chargers as an assistant coach. He coached the defensive backfield; Forrest Gregg coached the offensive line. In 1975, after three seasons in San Diego, Willie Wood became the first and only black head coach in the brief history of the World Football League. He coached the Philadelphia Bell. He coached the Bell until, more than halfway through the 1975 season, its second season, the WFL folded. Willie decided to go into the construction business.

But in 1979, when Forrest Gregg became head coach of the Toronto Argonauts in the Canadian Football League, he called Willie and offered him a job as an assistant. At first, Willie said no. But the construction business was shaky, and Willie still loved the idea of coaching. He changed his mind, assisted Forrest for one season, then, when Forrest left for Cincinnati, became the first black head coach to be hired in the CFL. He coached the Argonauts in 1980 and part of 1981, then became the first black head coach to be fired in the CFL. "That was it for me," Willie said. "I'd been fired too many times."

Willie went home to Washington again, to his second wife, Sheila, and to their two sòns, and started Willie Wood Mechanical, the heating and air conditioning firm he still operates. He would rather be coaching, using his expertise and experience in the NFL, but only if he owned the team. He does not want to be fired again. Once he dreamed of becoming the first black head coach in the NFL since its earliest days, but now the dream has faded. He believes the NFL will soon have a black head coach, and he suspects that Al Davis of the Los Angeles Raiders will hire the first one. Willie has a great deal of respect for Al Davis, who coached him at USC. So do several of my old teammates. They seem to think that Davis, in his commitment to excellence and to his players, is the closest thing left to Lombardi.

Herb Adderley always was a great athlete, so great that at Northeast High in Philadelphia, where he was a star in four sports, he jumped center on the basketball team even though he was barely six feet tall. Once, when Northeast played Overbrook High, Herbie had to jump against a six-foot-eleven center, who also happened to be a pretty good athlete. The first time he faced Northeast, Wilt Chamberlain scored fifty-two points. The second time, Herb held him to forty-eight.

The son of a machinist, a factory worker, Herb could have had scholarships to dozens of colleges. He chose Michigan State because he felt he could play big-time football and because he knew black athletes did well in the Big Ten and in the Pacific Coast Conference. "The Pacific Coast was too far away," he said.

At Michigan State, Herb was a running back, an honorable mention All-American, and never played defense. Lombardi picked him in the first round of the 1961 draft for his pure athletic ability, planning to develop him as a running back, behind Hornung and Taylor, or, more likely, as a wide receiver. Herb broke his collarbone during the exhibition season, then, when he returned, rejoined the offensive team.

Late in the season, when we were playing the Lions in Detroit on Thanksgiving Day, two of our starting defensive backs, Hank Gremminger and Johnny Symank, suffered injuries. We had only one spare defensive back. Lombardi turned to Herb. "You're the best athlete I've got," Coach said. "Go out and do the best you can."

Herb found himself in an unfamiliar position, but in a familiar setting, in Detroit, in front of a friendly crowd that remembered his college days, covering passes thrown to Terry Barr, who played for Michigan, by Jim Ninowski, who played for Michigan State. Ninowski and Barr tried to capitalize on Herb's inexperience, but, instead, Herb came up with the first of his forty-eight NFL interceptions and helped us preserve a close victory. He never went back to the offense. Herb was All-Pro the next season and four more times after that. He also went to the Pro Bowl five times. He roomed with Willie Wood, and often they stayed up till two or three in the morning, talking football. Willie passed Em Tunnell's lessons along to Herb.

After nine years in Green Bay, Herb was traded to Dallas and spent his last three seasons with the Cowboys. He was the only man to play in four of the first six Super Bowl games, I and II with the Pack, V and VI with Dallas. His loyalty remained with Green Bay. "As far as I'm concerned," Herb said at the reunion, "I never played for the Dallas Cowboys. I'm the only guy in the country who has a Dallas Cowboys Super Bowl ring and doesn't wear it. I don't even look at it."

He wore his Super Bowl II ring to the reunion. "I'm a Green Bay Packer fan for life," he said. "I'm committed. And the reason is these guys—and Lombardi." Herb's eyes swept the hospitality suite at the Thrifty Inn. He looked at his Green Bay teammates, at his fellow members of the Hall of Fame, at a group of men who would always be champions. "Out of all of us," he said, "Lombardi is the greatest legend of all."

Herb came to the reunion alone. He had been divorced for several

years, but he was still on good terms with his ex-wife, Barbara, and
with their daughter, who was finishing high school, looking ahead to
college. They all lived in Philadelphia, where Herb ran Adderley
Industries, a construction company specializing in the installation of
underground and aerial cable. He worked hard at the business, at least
partly because he remembered Lombardi's advice: "The harder you
work, the harder it is to surrender."

"Do you think of him often?" I asked.

"Every day," Herb said. "And I love my father, who is also deceased,
but I don't think about my father every day."

Bob Jeter grew up happily in Weirton, West Virginia, a steel-mill
town he loved so much he thought he would never live anywhere else.
"Weirton had forty thousand people," Jete said, "and just about everybody worked in the mill and knew everybody else. We never had a
house key. We never locked our door even when we went away."

In Weirton in the early 1950s, blacks and whites worked together,
played together, prayed together and went to school separately. Until
his senior year in high school, Jeter played football at a segregated
black school and was almost unnoticed outside Weirton. In his senior
year, he switched to Weirton High and, as a high-scoring running back
and defensive back on an integrated team, got so much attention he
became a high school All-American.

The oldest of six children of a steel worker—a younger brother,
Tony, later tried out for the Packers—Jeter chose Iowa University from
a flock of Big Ten offers. He and Willie Wood almost became college
teammates. Wood, whose high school also was segregated until his
final year, planned to go to Iowa until two of his high school teammates enrolled there. Then Willie decided to go farther west.

At Iowa, in his junior year, Jete played sensationally in the Rose
Bowl, racing eighty-one yards for a touchdown, rushing for close to
two hundred yards. But in his senior year, he played on a bad ankle,
less spectacularly, and didn't think he'd be selected high in the 1960
NFL draft. Before the draft, he signed a three-year contract with the

British Columbia Lions of the Canadian Football League. When the Packers selected him in the second round, Jeter was stunned. When Lombardi found out Jete had signed with British Columbia, Lombardi was stunned.

Jeter played two seasons in British Columbia, then was traded to Hamilton. He tried to renegotiate his contract, failed and left the team. He heard that the Pittsburgh Steelers were interested in him and reported to their training camp. After one week, the Steelers' coach told Jete to call Lombardi and find out whether the Packers, who still had the right to negotiate with him, wanted to exercise that right. Jeter called.

"Where are you?" Lombardi said.

"Home," Jeter said. He didn't want Lombardi to find out he had worked out with the Steelers.

"How soon can you get here?" Lombardi said.

Jeter flew to Green Bay the next day, and Willie Wood met him at the airport. "What were you doing in the Steelers' camp for a whole week?" Willie asked.

We couldn't activate Jeter in 1962 because he was still under contract in Canada. But he did practice with us, as a wide receiver. "I had trouble catching the ball," Jete said. "I had hands like boards."

Jeter spent the next couple of years working hard to improve his hands. By the time he did, he was no longer a wide receiver. In 1965, he became a cornerback. In 1966, he ran two interceptions back for touchdowns. In 1967, at the age of thirty, he made All-Pro. "He was a late bloomer," Willie Wood said. "We had a hell of a time getting him to think defensively."

Jeter spent nine years in Green Bay. "I couldn't wait to get back to training camp each year," he said. "I knew what Lombardi was going to put us through, but I still wanted to get back. I looked forward so much to the guys and the camaraderie. I couldn't wait to hear Willie Davis telling his stories, laughing so hard the tears came out of his eyes. And every year, I knew we were going to win something. Later, when I was with the Bears, I dreaded the start of training camp."

He spent three years in Chicago, matching the twelve-year careers of Wood and Adderley.

Jeter always came to our training camp in good shape. He came to the reunion in good shape—for a defensive tackle. But the extra weight didn't diminish his enthusiasm. "It feels like the clock's turned back," he said. "I feel like I want to play again." The feeling faded when his knee began acting up, the curse of old running backs, even ones who switched to defense. "It hurts when it rains or gets damp," Jete said.

His wife of more than twenty years, Gwendolyn, stayed home with their two teenaged sons, Robby and Carlton, both basketball players at Quigley High in Chicago. Gwendolyn was working as a substitute teacher and running a day-care center. Jete was looking for work. Not long after the reunion, he took a job with Foxville Products, distributing health, skin and beauty products.

"I had to come back and see the guys," he said. "Those were the best years of my life."

Tom Brown came from an athletic family. His father, once a marathon swimmer, was director of water safety for the American Red Cross and author of the book *Teaching Johnny to Swim*. His older brother, Dick, coached the runner Mary Decker in her bid to win a gold medal in the 1984 Olympic Games. His younger brother, Robert, coached the baseball team at St. Alban's School in Washington, D.C. Tom went to high school just outside Washington. He was a baseball star and played football, too, because he thought football would get him a scholarship to the University of Maryland. It did, and in his senior year, Tom intercepted twelve passes, a school record. Lombardi invited him to the NFL championship game between the Packers and the Giants in New York in 1962. Tom looked around our locker room and thought, *These guys are too big. I'm not going to play this game.* Still, Green Bay drafted him in the second round in 1963, and Lombardi tried to persuade him to play pro football. For once, Vince was overmatched. John F. Kennedy and Fidel Castro pushed Tom toward baseball.

When President Kennedy initiated the Cuban blockade, his response to the missile crisis, Fidel retaliated with a baseball blockade, barring all Cuban players from competing in the United States. Fidel's ban created a first-base crisis on the Washington Senators. They signed Tom Brown out of the University of Maryland and decided to give the local hero a shot at first base in spring training in 1963. "My first game, I got a couple of hits," Tom recalled. "The next game, I got a couple more. I worked hard. I hustled. I played well defensively."

At twenty-two, Tom needed minor-league experience. But the Senators, who were tempted to keep him anyway, made up their minds after they invited President Kennedy to attend the opening game. "I'll show up," the President replied, "but only if that Brown boy plays."

Brown played. He played for three months in the major leagues. He managed only seventeen hits in three months before he was sent down to the minors. In December 1963, Lombardi called and asked Tom if he wanted to take a chance on football. "Let me give baseball one more shot," Tom said.

He went to spring training in 1964 and still couldn't hit, not the way he wanted to. "I just didn't have any confidence," he said. He retired from baseball at the age of twenty-three and reported to St. Norbert College. One year later, he was a starting safety, and in 1966, in the game against Dallas for the NFL championship, he made two big plays in the closing minute. We were winning, 34–27. Dallas was driving toward a tying touchdown. On third down and goal to go, Tom fell on Pettis Norman a little more than a yard short of a touchdown. On fourth down, while Dave Robinson wrapped his arms around Don Meredith, the Dallas quarterback, Brown intercepted a wobbly pass Meredith intended for Bob Hayes in the end zone. The interception put us into Super Bowl I and put Tom Brown into a trivia question: Who is the only man to play in baseball's major leagues and in football's Super Bowl?

"Tom was a self-made ballplayer," Willie Wood said. "He didn't have blazing speed, but he was very astute. He was never out of position."

After five seasons in Green Bay, Tom heard that Lombardi was going to Washington. He called Vince and said he'd love to go to Washington, too, to go home. "I figured the town would go crazy for Lombardi and I'd make a lot of money," Tom said. He had dislocated his shoulder in Green Bay, so the Packers let him go. In Washington's opening game under Lombardi, Tom reinjured his shoulder and was out for the season. The following year, Lombardi was dead, and the Redskins told Tom they didn't need him. He played his final football game at twenty-eight.

Tom was forty-three at the time of the reunion, living in Salisbury, Maryland, not far from where he grew up, with his second wife, Nancy, and their two young children. Tom was a distributor for Charles Chips, the snack-food company, and in his spare time he often coached youngsters in football and baseball. "So many people have a misconception about Lombardi," he said. "They act crazy with kids and then use Lombardi as an excuse. They say winning is the only thing. If Lombardi were coaching kids, he wouldn't put the same emphasis on winning. He wouldn't be hollering and screaming. He knew how to deal with professionals, and he would know how to deal with kids. I hate it when people misuse him."

14. Red and the Rest of the Receivers

Red Mack, Carroll Dale, Boyd Dowler, Marv Fleming, Bob Long and Bill Anderson

He had a beard. He was almost bald. He looked like he didn't weigh more than 150 pounds. He was the only guy at the reunion I didn't recognize. "Who the hell is that?" I asked.

"That's Red Mack," somebody said.

Red Mack.

I had almost forgotten him. He spent only one season with the Green Bay Packers, the season we won the first Super Bowl game. It was the sixth season of his professional football career, and the last. He was only in his twenties, but the game had aged him. His nickname was "The Thousand-Year-Old Man."

The following summer, he came to training camp, and he was cut, and he packed up and went home and never played football again. He went to work for the Bendix Corporation in South Bend, Indiana, and when he came to the reunion, he'd been with Bendix for more than seventeen years. He started at the bottom and worked himself up to production control supervisor.

Red may have been the happiest guy at the reunion.

He may also have been the happiest guy at Super Bowl I.

Red Mack was a wide receiver with bad knees, a former running back at Notre Dame. He began the 1966 season with Atlanta, an expansion team. Atlanta dropped him after the first game. He figured his career was over. He went home to South Bend, then got a phone call from Green Bay. Bob Long, one of our receivers, was hurt. We needed a fourth wide receiver, behind Carroll Dale, Boyd Dowler and Max McGee. Red flew to Green Bay and worked out for three days. Then Lombardi told him he was on the team. "You're probably not going to play much," Lombardi warned him. "You'll be on the specialty teams mostly."

Red didn't catch a pass all year. But he played on the suicide teams, on kickoffs and punts. He made the tackles on two of our kickoffs in Super Bowl I. After the game, in the locker room, he had tears in his eyes. He hugged everyone. "This is the greatest moment of my life," he said. He walked up to Lombardi and said, "Thank you for letting me be part of this," and Lombardi said, "Red, if you didn't belong here, you wouldn't be here."

The next morning, when we boarded the plane to fly back to Green Bay, Red settled into his seat and buried his face in his hands. "You all right?" one of the guys said.

Red looked up, and the tears spilled down his cheeks. "I'm so happy," he said. "I've never been a part of anything like this before."

He cried at the reunion, too. "I'd lost something," he said, "and now I've regained it." He wore his ring from Super Bowl I. "A guy offered me a Porsche for it once," Red said, "and I wouldn't trade it. I wouldn't give it up for all the money in the world."

Red was choked up. The funny thing is, I'll bet he never cried when he was growing up in Pennsylvania, in the orphanage.

Red Mack spent five years in an orphanage because his parents split up and neither of them wanted him. Marv Fleming grew up without a father. Bill Anderson's parents were divorced, and his father died before he was ten. Bob Long's father worked in a steel mill, and Carroll Dale's in a coal mine. Boyd Dowler was a misfit among our receivers. Both his parents went to college, his father was a high school coach and Boyd knew, even when he was a teenager, that he wanted someday to be a coach. Boyd was the only one of our seven receivers, including McGee, who did not attend the reunion. He had to work. Boyd was the quarterback coach of the Tampa Bay Buccaneers, in the middle of his fifteenth season as an assistant coach in the National Football League.

Carroll Dale was one of our saints, a man of deep religious convictions. He was active in the Fellowship of Christian Athletes and often led our prayer meetings. I had great respect for him as a ballplayer, and I enjoyed hunting grouse and playing golf with him, but Carroll always made me a little uncomfortable. He never said anything, but I couldn't help feeling he was sitting in judgment on me and everyone else. It was probably just my imagination, more than anything, and my guilt. And I may have resented Carroll, too, because he came to us in a trade for Dan Currie, who was one of my drinking buddies. Dapper Dan never made me feel guilty. Next to him, *I* was a saint.

Carroll came from Wise, a little coal-mining town in the mountains of Virginia. He went to J. J. Kelly High School and scored close to two thousand points in basketball. But football was his game. He considered the University of Tennessee, then decided to stay closer to home, to go to VPI, Virginia Tech. He majored in education, and excelled in football, as a defensive end and a wide receiver. The Los Angeles Rams drafted him in the eighth round in 1960.

He spent five frustrating seasons in Los Angeles, five losing seasons. He didn't like the city and he hated losing. Once, when he was wide open in front of seventy-five thousand people in the Los Angeles Memorial Coliseum, Carroll dropped a pass. "Couldn't catch one in a basket for a long time after that," he said.

He wanted desperately to be traded, and one morning between the 1964 and 1965 seasons, while he was traveling around Tennessee and

Virginia selling sporting goods, he heard he'd been traded to Green Bay. Carroll was delighted. He liked small towns and hunting and fishing and winning.

The first three years Carroll played for us, we won the NFL championship each year, and he played an important part in each of those championships. He gained more yards and scored more touchdowns than any other Packer receiver in those three seasons. He was our deep threat.

Carroll roomed with Ray Nitschke, and he'll never forget what happened one night in Milwaukee, the night before a game, when we were staying in a hotel tower that had semicircular rooms. Ray went to bed early, and Carroll dozed off watching television. A knock on the door woke Carroll up. He thought it was one of the coaches checking up. He opened the door and found Nitsch standing in the hallway, stark naked.

Ray had gotten up to go to the bathroom and had thought, mistakenly, that the door to the hallway was the door to the bathroom. When he stepped out, the door slammed behind him, locked automatically.

When Carroll saw his naked roommate, he fell on the floor laughing. Ray was half blushing, half furious. "Don't tell anyone," he said.

"I didn't," Carroll recalled, "till I saw somebody."

Carroll had his own special memories of Lombardi, too. "He made everyone feel important," Carroll said, "and, unlike most coaches, who criticized you the worst when you lost, Coach Lombardi was able to control himself after a defeat. If you played hard and lost, he didn't run you into the ground. He figured you already hurt enough. But if you won, especially if you won big, he let you know every mistake you made, loud and clear. As the guys always said—after a victory, you had the feeling you were in the wrong locker room."

After eight years in Green Bay, and two Pro Bowls, Carroll played his fourteenth and final season in Minnesota. He wound up in his third Super Bowl. He liked Bud Grant, the Minnesota coach. "He was my kind of guy," Carroll said. "He loved hunting and fishing and he hated practice."

Carroll settled down in Bristol, Tennessee, right on the Virginia border. He came to our reunion at the age of forty-six, his waistline trim and his hair thinner, with his wife, Pat. They had been married for more than twenty-five years, and the oldest of their three children, Vicki, was married and a nurse. Carroll spent weekends in Bristol and weekdays in Wise, managing a surface mine for the Strouth Coal Company—CVC. Part of the mine, a twenty-man operation, was on land owned by Carroll's mother. Carroll had been underground, where his father worked for thirty-five years, enough times to know he was far better off above the ground, supervising the operation. "It's a simple life," Carroll said. "But I enjoy it."

Boyd Dowler always struck me as self-confident to the brink of cockiness, partly, I guess, because he was, at six-foot-five and 225, so tall and handsome, partly because he was, unlike so many of us, always a winner, in high school and college. Yet Boyd wasn't as con-fident as he seemed. He never thought he was going to have a career as a professional football player, and in high school in Wyoming, even though he was all-state in three sports, he insisted, "I was no phenom." Only colleges from Wyoming and the neighboring states recruited him.

He chose Colorado, majoring in physical education to prepare him-self for coaching, and in his senior year, he performed a remarkable trick. He led his team in passing and in catching passes. He was a good enough passer to be selected as the All–Big Eight quarterback, and in a versatile single-wing offense, he also served as a receiver. Green Bay chose Boyd in the third round of the 1959 draft. "It wasn't a very good draft for the Packers," Boyd said. "Of the top four players they picked, I was the only one who was still with them after one year. That was Lombardi's first season as head coach, but he had nothing to do with the draft. He didn't take over till after the draft."

As a wide receiver, Boyd was the rookie of the year in the NFL in 1959, and he led Green Bay in receptions in seven of his eleven seasons. Even though our offense stressed running over passing, he was named to the NFL All-Decade team of the 1960s. Boyd was our punter for two seasons, and in 1967, in the chilling 21–17 victory over Dallas that brought us our third straight NFL championship, Boyd scored our first two touchdowns. Two weeks later, he scored our first touchdown against Oakland in Super Bowl II. In 1968, the year Lombardi stopped coaching in Green Bay, Boyd experienced the first losing season of his life. He played one more year, then turned to coaching. "I'd always been a good listener," Boyd said. "I'd always believed my coaches."

George Allen hired Boyd to coach the Los Angeles Rams' receivers. Boyd spent one year with Los Angeles, two with Washington, three with Philadelphia, four with Cincinnati and five with Tampa Bay. Then, only a few months after our reunion, the Bucs released Boyd. He was, suddenly, unemployed.

Boyd decided not to look for a job with another team. He decided to get out of professional football. His son, Brian, was a high school football player, a starting wide receiver as a sophomore on a strong team, a candidate to be the starting quarterback as a junior. Brian was only sixteen, but he had already lived in five different cities. Boyd didn't want to move him again. Boyd took a test to be licensed to sell insurance in Florida. He had been married for twenty-four years—his wife, like Carroll Dale's, was named Pat—and every summer for twenty-four years Boyd had reported to a training camp. At forty-seven, he was ready to start real life.

Our third starting receiver, the tight end, Marv Fleming, was different from the other two. Marvin, in fact, was different from just about everyone. He came to the reunion, only forty-two, still a bachelor, with his girl friend, a German model named Karma, and with an earring in his left ear. Marvin said he started wearing the earring when he left Green Bay and joined the Miami Dolphins in 1970. The first time he met Don Shula, the coach of the Dolphins, Marvin said he kept waiting for Shula to say something about the earring. Shula didn't say a word. Finally, Marvin turned his left ear toward Shula and said, in his high-pitched voice, "Notice anything, Coach?"

Shula said, "Yeah, you lost one of your earrings."

Marvin, of course, was a Californian, raised in the Compton section of Los Angeles by his mother, who was a beautician. At Compton High, Marvin played football and basketball and high jumped six-foot-seven, then elected to attend the University of Utah. Why?

"They needed some color there," Marvin explained. "They had me and Billy McGill, a basketball player, and two other blacks on campus. Right after I started there, the dean of women called me into her office and said, 'Mr. Fleming, not only do I have a letter from one concerned parent, but I have letters from fifty concerned parents.'

"I knew what they were concerned about. A black student at Utah State had raped a white girl, and I guess they were afraid I was going to do the same thing. 'Don't worry,' I told the dean. 'In the first place, I'm here to get an education. In the second, I want to play pro football and I don't want to get in trouble. And, besides, all I'm doing is a little petting.'

"A few weeks later, halfway through the football season, I happened to pass the dean as I was walking across the campus. 'Congratulations on your playing,' she said.

"'Thank you,' I said.

"'Are you still petting?' she said.

"'Yes,' I said.

"She said, 'Keep up the good work,' and walked on."

Marvin always had stories like that, and I never could quite figure out when Marvin was telling the truth, when he was kidding and when he was fantasizing. I wasn't sure he knew which was which, either.

In 1963, Green Bay drafted Marvin in the eleventh round, which certainly made him a long shot to win a place on a team that had just won two straight NFL championships, especially since our starting tight end, Ron Kramer, was the best in the league. But Marvin was one of three rookies in 1963—Dave Robinson and Lionel Aldridge were the others—who became important members of the team. Marvin was very young when he became a Packer, only twenty-one according to his date of birth, twenty according to him. Marvin did have trouble with facts.

I don't think I ever gave Marvin the credit he deserved as a player, probably because I always measured him against Ron Kramer, the prototypical tight end, massive and menacing, and possibly because Lombardi screamed at him so much he seemed to be questioning Marvin's commitment. Once, when Marvin forgot a play, Lombardi swung a chair at his head. Another time, Lombardi said he couldn't understand why Marvin couldn't seem to remember anything. "Have you been masturbating, mister?" Lombardi demanded to know. "Is that the problem?" Lombardi was dead serious. "Your eyes are dull. Have you been masturbating, mister?" It was hard not to laugh, except for Marvin.

"Lombardi pushed me and pushed me and pushed me," Marvin said, "and then a lot of times he'd put his hand on my shoulder and say, 'Way to go there.' No one else saw him do it, but I saw it, I felt it and I said to myself, 'This man likes me, and it's okay for him to push me, it's okay.' I love it, that memory. I can still see Lombardi letting me know that I had arrived, letting me know that he knew I was a good football player. *Marvin, you're all right.*"

Marvin needed reassurance. Twenty years later, he clearly remembered Ron Kramer telling him that he was going to make it, and he remembered Ray Nitschke telling him that he had. He appreciated their encouragement. He respected his teammates. "Whenever I said a bad word in front of Carroll Dale," Marvin recalled, "I always said, 'I'm sorry.'"

He had a sly sense of humor. Marvin and I went bow-hunting once, and after he'd tested the bow a few times, he turned to me and said, "Jerry, it's all coming back to me how to do it, just like my great-great-granddaddy did." After the fiery riots and looting in Watts in 1965, he offered to sell his teammates television sets, charred but cheap, and after Cassius Clay changed his name, Marvin handed out matchbooks that said, "Muhammad Fleming."

After seven seasons in Green Bay, Marvin spent five in Miami and became the first man to play in five Super Bowl games, the first to collect four winner's shares. Marvin probably made more money from football than anybody else on our team. He started at $13,000 a year and finished, in 1974, at more than $100,000 a year. Bart Starr never made $100,000 for one season. I never made it for three. And Marvin probably kept every penny he earned. He wasn't a spender. He often happened to visit the homes of married teammates at dinnertime. He didn't drink and petting wasn't very expensive.

Marvin's habits may have changed slightly after he stopped playing football. "I work hard," he said at the reunion, "and then, at some point, I treat myself to something fine. My next treat is going to be a Submariner Rolex watch, an $11,000 watch. You can wear it underwater. It's good down to a thousand feet. If this watch goes down a thousand feet, I hope I'm not with it. I won't pay $11,000 for it. I'll pay half that. I'm going to go to Hong Kong to buy it."

Marvin was an actor, sometimes. He played small roles in several television shows, and in the movie *Heaven Can Wait* he portrayed a football player. He had one line. "Hey, Mr. Farnsworth, you ever play college football?" he said. Marvin was also an agent, representing a few little-known football players, and a skier, representing a resort in Utah. Marvin said he was one of the best black skiers in the world. He was certainly one of the best in Utah. Marvin said he was thinking about working on the other side of the camera. He was more interested in creating stars than in becoming a star. "I know the ingredients it takes," he said. Marvin dressed well, traveled frequently, kept in shape, worried about the teammates who didn't. "You only have one body," he said. "You have to take care of yourself." He had a good life, Marvin said, and, finally, he had a father.

Not long before the reunion, he received a message that the father he had never known was in the hospital, seriously ill. Marvin went to the hospital and saw his father on a respirator. "I said to myself, 'This is my father,'" Marvin said. "'If it hadn't been for him, I wouldn't have had this fantastic life I've led.' I said, 'I love you, Dad. Get well.' He started crying. He pressed my hand.

"Now I have a dad. We're getting to know each other. We're becoming friends."

When Bob Long started his junior year at Wichita State University in Kansas in 1962, the odds against him becoming a Green Bay Packer were about the same as the odds against him becoming a millionaire, a pair of million-to-one shots. He was a basketball player at Wichita State, not a football player, and for spending money, to supplement his scholarship, he worked for a few dollars an hour in a pizzeria close to the campus, spilling cheese and tomato sauce onto dough and onto himself. The pizzeria was called Pizza Hut. It was the first Pizza Hut in the United States.

Five years later, Bob Long played in Super Bowl I for the Packers and opened the first of the thirty Pizza Huts he eventually owned in Wisconsin. By the time of the reunion eighteen years later, Bob Long was the managing partner of RAL Asset Management Group, a booming investment firm that was already doing $20 million a year in sales. Bart Starr and Bob Skoronski were general partners in RAL, both, in effect, working part time for their former teammate. Starr was the quarterback and Skoronski the offensive captain when Long was a rookie, a squeaky little kid trying to learn the fundamentals of football. Now the big guns were working for the squeaky kid.

"What are you going to do when Bart comes in late one day?" I needled Bobby. "You going to scream at him? You going to chew him out?"

Bobby turned a bright embarrassed red.

Bob Long's success was as remarkable as Willie Davis's, as dramatic as Max McGee's. Bobby grew up in New Kensington, a Pennsylvania steel-mill town north of Pittsburgh, and he decided to accept a basketball scholarship to Wichita State because he wanted to get as far away from the mills as he could. He played on a Wichita State basketball team that ranked among the top ten in the country and qualified for one NCAA and two National Invitational tournaments. Two of Bob's teammates, Dave Stallworth and Nate Bowman, played for the New

York Knicks when the Knicks were the champions of the National Basketball Association.

In 1963, a handful of NFL scouts came to assess the football prospects at Wichita State. On their way to football practice, the scouts passed an intramural touch football game in which the Wichita State basketball team was playing. The scouts paused and saw Bob Long catch pass after pass after pass. He scored seven or eight touchdowns. In the early and mid-1960s, before pro football became the ultra-specialized game of the 1970s and 1980s, teams were willing to gamble occasionally on gifted athletes with minimal football experience. Dallas, for instance, signed Cornell Green, a basketball player at Utah State, and turned him into a fine defensive back. Green and Long faced each other in college on the basketball court; a few years later, they faced each other in the NFL championship game.

The scouts urged Long to try football in his senior year in college, and even though he played in only seven games, he set five Wichita State pass-catching records. Green Bay picked him in the fourth round of the 1964 draft. When he came to training camp, Bobby had plenty of raw talent, speed and moves and hands, and didn't know what the hell to do with it. But he had a good attitude and worked hard, and by his second season he was a pretty decent player.

The man he had worked for in Wichita was starting to spread Pizza Hut around the country, and he offered Bobby the exclusive right to franchises in northern Wisconsin. Bobby needed to come up with about $20,000 to get started. He thought about it for a while. He even asked me for advice. "Hell, go for it," I said. "You're young. You don't have any responsibilities. Take a shot." Bobby, who majored in business administration at Wichita State, persuaded a few banks to give him loans and tried to persuade teammates to invest. Most of us wished him luck and turned him down. I was too involved in other things. But Fuzzy and Max, the restaurateurs, put up $2000 apiece.

"In 1975," Bobby said, "when Pepsi took over Pizza Hut, Max cashed in his $2000 investment for close to a quarter of a million. He used that money to convert The Left Guard in Minneapolis to the first ChiChi's." The $2000 Max put into Pizza Hut grew into millions.

The money and effort Bob Long put into Pizza Hut grew into millions, too. Besides RAL, which acquires, syndicates and manages real estate, from trailer parks to shopping malls, Bob is deeply involved in Pizza Slices, Inc., which holds franchising rights to Rocky Rococo Pan Style Pizza restaurants. Rocky Rococo, offering pizza by the slice at drive-in windows, intends to compete with McDonald's and Burger King, not with Pizza Hut. At the time of the reunion, Bobby and Bart were planning to open Rocky Rococos in Washington, D.C., and Denver, as well as Milwaukee. "It's like winning the Super Bowl all over again," Bobby said.

"My business career reflects my sports career," he added. "The fact that I dared to take a chance as a pro football player showed a certain amount of courage—or stupidity. I always felt, nothing ventured, nothing gained. You've got to gamble." That sounded very much like the advice I gave Bobby when he was still a squeaky kid.

Bob also shared my feelings about the stereotyping of the athlete. "Sometimes it's not an advantage to be an ex-athlete," he said. "The media has the ex-athlete typed. There's so much publicity about the ones who don't make it, who can't adjust. You have to overcome the stereotype before you can prove yourself as a businessman."

Bobby's football career spanned seven seasons, the first four in Green Bay, the fifth in Atlanta. Midway through the 1968 season, he was leading Atlanta in pass receptions. Then, on Interstate Highway 75 in Georgia, a car jumped the divider and slammed into Bob's car, driving the engine into him. He broke his right foot, elbow, kneecap and hip, plus three vertebrae on the right side of his back. The doctors feared he would never run again. His football career seemed finished.

But in the summer of 1969, Vince Lombardi called him and asked him to come to Washington, to play one more season. "I wasn't one of Vince's favorites in Green Bay," Bobby said. "When I hurt my knee during a scrimmage before the 1966 season, he yelled, 'Drag him off the field and let's get on with the scrimmage.' I had torn cartilage in my knee, but for six weeks he made me keep playing. Outside of yelling at me about my knee, I don't think Vince talked to me for ten or fifteen minutes during my four years in Green Bay. But when he called me up and asked me to come back and play for him, he must've talked to me for half an hour. I was depressed, mentally and physically, and he lifted me up. He told me I'd be a starter for him.

"When Vince Lombardi asks you to come back and play for him, that has got to be the greatest compliment you can receive as a football player and as a man. He treated me beautifully in Washington. I was a part of his past. I was a reminder of his championship years. I was one of his favorites. I was only half the receiver, physically, that I'd been in Green Bay, but I worked like hell for him. I gave him everything I had."

In 1969, with the Redskins, with bad knees, Bob Long caught forty-eight passes, more than he had caught in his five previous NFL seasons combined. Then Lombardi died, and so did the incentive for Bob to keep playing. He put in half a season in Los Angeles, then retired. He came to the reunion, at the age of forty-two, with his second wife, Joan, and with strong feelings about Lombardi.

"I attribute a great deal of my success to him," Bob Long said. "He taught me discipline, and he taught me to be aggressive, to make it happen, to run to win. He taught me honesty. You knew where you stood with him. The man always walked the way he talked."

Bill Anderson, battered and beaten, almost quit football before he became a Packer. He spent six seasons with the Washington Redskins, from 1958 through 1963, and in those six seasons, the Redskins, the perfect losers, won only seventeen games. "We changed coaches every time you looked around," Anderson said. "We had only eighteen or twenty people who could play, and the others shouldn't have been there. We were whipping boys."

Anderson, one of the few people who could play, took a fierce whipping. Double-teamed every game—"pounded to death," he said—he still managed to lead the Redskins in receptions in 1959 and

1960 and to be selected for the Pro Bowl both years. But by 1964, at the age of twenty-eight, Anderson was so tired of taking beatings he took a job as an assistant coach at the University of Tennessee, his alma mater.

The next year, he decided to give pro football one last chance, but halfway through the exhibition season, when Washington traded him to Green Bay, he came very close to going home. "Lombardi wanted me as a tight end," Bill recalled. "I wasn't fast enough anymore to be a wide receiver, and I wasn't really a good enough blocker to be a tight end. *What does he want me for?* I wondered. *He must want me for some reason.* Had he not been there, I probably would have said the hell with it."

Anderson reported to Green Bay. Ron Kramer was gone, and Marv Fleming was starting at tight end. Anderson was going to back up Marvin. One evening, after Bill had been in training camp for a few days, Lombardi asked him to come to his office. "I left the office three or four hours later," Bill said. "He wanted to know everything about my life from day one."

We won our first six games, and even though Bill played only sparingly, he thoroughly enjoyed the unfamiliar taste of victory. "It was fun playing again," he said. Late in the season, he moved into the starting lineup. On the first play from scrimmage of the game against Baltimore for the Western Conference championship, Bart Starr hit Bill with a pass, and then Baltimore's Lenny Lyles hit Bill like a bomb. The football popped free, and Baltimore's Don Shinnick scooped it up and raced for a touchdown. Anderson was knocked dizzy on the play, and Starr, trying to tackle Shinnick, was knocked out of the game.

Zeke Bratkowski replaced Bart. Anderson stayed in the game and had the best day of his Packer career. He caught eight passes, matching his total for the entire regular season, and his eighth catch helped set up the field goal that beat Baltimore in sudden-death overtime. Bill Anderson was proof that every man on our roster played a role in our success.

Bill's role diminished in 1966, as Marvin began to master his position, but still, after Super Bowl I, Lombardi wanted Anderson to come back in 1967. "I was committed to getting married," Bill said, "but I told Coach Lombardi that I'd come back if he'd give me a no-cut, no-trade contract. He promised he wouldn't trade me, but he said he couldn't promise not to cut me. I decided to give up football and get married."

Anderson and his bride settled in Knoxville, Tennessee, and by the time of our reunion, he had his own insurance agency and did the commentary on the University of Tennessee football broadcasts. His marriage, however, had ended in divorce after fifteen years. "I guess if I had it all to do over again," Bill said, "I'd go back and play the 1967 season and forget about getting married."

William "Red" Mack was a tough kid, a miniature version of Ray Nitschke, furious with his father, who was an alcoholic, and furious with the world. "I had nothing as a kid," Red remembered, "except a bad temper. If somebody did something I didn't like, I beat the hell out of him."

Then, at St. Paul's Orphanage in Crafton, Pennsylvania, a man named George Palooka, crippled by polio, befriended Red Mack. He gave Red a football uniform and an outlet for his fury. "One thing I learned in the orphanage," Red said, "was that it didn't make any difference how small you were, the other guy still had to prove himself. I never felt anyone was better than me till he proved it."

Red was never big, but he was brave and he was quick. In high school, he played so well he earned an appointment to Bullis Prep, traditionally a training ground for the Naval Academy. But when he finished at Bullis, Red decided to go to Notre Dame. "It was the best decision I ever made," Red said. "If I had gone anywhere else, I never would have finished college. At Notre Dame, they make you finish. I got my degree in business."

Red was a good football player at Notre Dame, but a preseason injury wiped out most of his senior season, and as a 175-pound running back, who had already undergone knee surgery, he didn't expect to be drafted by a professional team. But the Pittsburgh Steelers chose Red in the tenth round in 1961, mostly, he felt, because he was a local boy. He went to training camp and, obviously, didn't have the size or the speed to make the team. But he had too much guts to be cut. He played on the kickoff team and, for a $25 bonus for every tackle he made inside the twenty-yard line, ran over 250-pounders.

The Steelers kept Red for three seasons, then traded him to Philadelphia for one, then took him back in 1965. In 1966, Atlanta claimed Red, but couldn't use him, and Lombardi picked him up. "I was a nobody," Red said, "but when I got to Green Bay, they made me feel like I'd been there twenty years. The guys told me where to get a haircut, where to get my car washed, where to buy groceries. They treated me with respect.

"That was what Lombardi did: He instilled in his players respect for each other. He didn't look down on anybody—he treated me the same as Bart Starr or Jimmy Taylor—and they didn't look down on one another. It was never a bitching contest. Green Bay didn't have the best talent. We had better talent in Pittsburgh in '63. But the Steelers weren't in condition. They didn't respect each other.

"The Packers were the best organization in football. I was so lucky to get with a coach who wasn't worried about winning and losing. I know that's a funny thing to say about Lombardi, but he really wasn't. He was worried about the human aspect. He knew the winning would come from that."

If we impressed Red, he impressed us, too. The thing I'll always remember about him is the time he and Ray Nitschke lined up to go one-on-one in the nutcracker drill, our supreme test of courage. Nitsch looked over at Red, whom he outweighed by sixty pounds, and said, "Oh, no, I can't go against this guy."

Red dug in, prepared to charge. "Get in here, you son of a bitch," he said, "and let's go."

They went at each other, and Ray just about killed him. Ray fired a forearm that knocked Red to his knees, and Red shrugged it off and got up and went at Ray again and got blasted again. "I never felt anyone was better than me till he proved it," Red said, "and Ray proved it. He made me look like the grass. He was the fiercest competitor I ever came across, and he was also a gentleman."

Lombardi cut Red Mack the week before we played our first exhibition game in 1967. He called Red to his office and explained that he felt he had to go with the younger players, that he appreciated what Red had done for him and that he would be happy to try to find Red a job on another NFL team or a job coaching and playing in the minor leagues. Red said thank you, but no. "My wife and I have talked it over, and I'm going to hang it up," he said.

"My knees were starting to give me problems on a daily basis," Red explained at the reunion. "Since my junior year at Notre Dame, I've had six knee operations. I've also had a dislocated shoulder twice. When you're my size, you're going to get the hell beat out of you, and I did. I've got a bad shoulder now, and bad knees, and a bad hip, and I have trouble walking, and I'd do it all over again tomorrow, I wouldn't change a thing."

Red's wife, Jean, joined him at the reunion. They had been married for twenty-two years. "She feels like she's an ordinary woman," Red said, "and she expected the wives at the reunion to be flashy, to be impressed with themselves. But they weren't. They couldn't have been nicer to her. They were just like their husbands. Green Bay had no big shots in 1966 and still had no big shots in 1984. The players still love and hug and respect each other, and some of them could buy and sell everything I've got without even thinking about it."

The Macks had three children, all sons, the youngest in high school, the middle one a sophomore at Indiana University, the oldest a senior at Notre Dame, considering a career in the diplomatic service. "He has a 3.2 average," Red said. "You have to put my four years together for 3.2."

He was obviously so proud of his sons, so proud of his wife, so proud of a life that had started so dismally. "Till the day I die," Red Mack said, "I'll remember Lombardi saying that if, after we leave football, we love our religion, we love our family and we love our job, then he'll have been a success." Red smiled and stood as tall as he could. "He was a terrific success as far as I'm concerned," he said.

15. You Gotta Have Hart and a Few Others

Zeke Bratkowski, Don Chandler, Doug Hart and Steve Wright

One of the amazing things about my Green Bay teammates is that I honestly believe a book could be written about each of them, from the brightest Starr to the lowliest substitute, and that each book would have its own plot, its distinct theme.

The Zeke Bratkowski story, for instance, is the familiar story of the understudy who takes over for the star, and triumphs, but with a twist: The understudy goes back to being an understudy, without resentment, without bitterness, with enthusiasm. He is the ultimate backup, the quintessential standby. He is the sidekick, the hero's best friend. Karl Malden can play the part.

Don Chandler's story is, basically, the rarest of success stories, of a man who knows when to quit, who gets out when he's on top, while Doug Hart's is the opposite kind of success story, of a man who doesn't know when to quit, who won't give up until he reaches the top. Steve

Wright has already written his story. He called his autobiographical book *I'd Rather Be Wright*.

As a matter of fact, we had several authors on the team that won the first Super Bowl game. Paul Hornung's book was *Football and the Single Man*, Ray Nitschke's was *Mean on Sundays*, mine was *Instant Replay*, Bill Curry's was *One More July* and Bart Starr's was *Quarterbacking*. Zeke kept threatening to write the Polish book of quarterbacking. He said it was going to be a half-page pamphlet.

The American dream shifts from generation to generation. Zeke Bratkowski's grandparents emigrated to the United States from Poland, and when their son, Zeke's father, was invited to try out for a major-league baseball team, they told him no, to forget the tryout, to go to work in the zinc plant in Danville, Illinois. A quarter of a century later, when the Brooklyn Dodgers invited Zeke to a tryout in Vero Beach, Florida, his father told him no, to forget the tryout, to stay at the University of Georgia and earn his college degree. Like his father before him, Edmund Raymond Bratkowski did what he was told.

Zeke, who was an outfielder, and his father, a pitcher and a first baseman, shared more than an unfulfilled dream. On weekends, when Zeke was growing up, the Bratkowskis fished and hunted together, putting catfish, pheasant, quail, duck and rabbit on the table, next to the fresh vegetables Zeke's mother grew in her garden. "We didn't have much money," Zeke said, "but we never went hungry."

Zeke went to Georgia on a football scholarship, majored in insurance and played baseball, too. In football, as a junior, he led the country in passing. As a senior, he led the country in punting. He put himself in the record book, though not exactly the way he would have liked to. He threw more interceptions in three seasons than any other passer in the history of major-college football. Still, the Chicago Bears made him a high draft choice and rewarded him, in 1954, with a three-year no-cut contract starting at $11,000 a season.

After his rookie season with the Bears, Zeke took a cut in pay. He went into the Air Force for two years. He served with Max McGee. He said Max was a great pilot who broke every Air Force rule and regulation. He said Max was a great gin player, too. "I still owe him fourteen million dollars," Zeke said. "I intend to pay him as soon as I get it."

Zeke rejoined the Bears in 1957, spent four seasons with them, most of the time on the bench, then two and a half with the Los Angeles Rams. At Los Angeles, he was, finally, the regular quarterback, but on a team that regularly lost. Then, midway through the 1963 season, he was traded to Green Bay, to the reigning NFL champions, to back up Bart Starr. "Bart picked me up at the airport the day I arrived and took me to his home to watch films," Zeke recalled, and that was the beginning of a professional and personal relationship that—despite the fact Bart and Brat were competing for the same position—may have been the closest on the team, the most enduring. "He's like a brother to me," said Zeke, who, like Bart, never had a real brother.

On Mondays during the season, while most of us played golf and hunted and washed down our wounds, Zeke and Bart studied game films. "He just took me under his wing," Zeke said. In 1963 and 1964, Zeke rarely played and never complained. In the second game of the 1965 season, against Baltimore, Bart got hurt in the middle of the third quarter, and Zeke stepped in. The Colts moved ahead of us, 17–13, but with less than three minutes to play, Zeke threw a perfect thirty-seven-yard touchdown pass to his old flying buddy, Max McGee, to win the game.

The following week, Bart was healthy, and Zeke was back on the bench. He didn't throw another pass for a month, and he still didn't bitch. "I've played under the two-quarterback system," Zeke said, "and I know what it is—it's impossible. Coach Lombardi has to go with one quarterback, with Bart, and I have to be ready."

Late in the season, against Minnesota, Bart injured a finger on his passing hand in the first quarter, and again Zeke stepped in. The Vikings moved ahead of us, 19–14, but late in the third quarter, Zeke again teamed up with a veteran, the tight end Bill Anderson, on a dramatic game-winning touchdown pass.

The following week, Bart was healthy, and Zeke was back on the bench. He didn't throw another pass for three weeks, till we faced Baltimore for the Western title. Then Bart got hurt on the first play, and Zeke once more stepped in. He completed twenty-two of thirty-nine passes, including two for two on the drive that won the game for us in sudden-death overtime.

The following week, of course, Bart was healthy, and as we won the first of three straight NFL titles, Zeke was back on the bench.

In 1966, Zeke—the oldest man on the team—was again a super sub. He replaced Bart in three of our last five regular-season games and passed superbly, and we won all three. In the most significant of the three games, the one against Baltimore to determine the Western Conference champion, Zeke stepped in after Bart suffered a rib injury and brought us from behind to win. By then, the Colts must have hated the sight of Zeke.

In 1967, as we earned our third title in a row, Zeke practically duplicated his 1966 performance. He replaced Bart in four regular-season games and passed superbly, and we won three out of four.

Zeke didn't play much after that. In 1968, he backed up Bart; in 1969 and 1970, while Bart played, he served as a coach; and in 1971, reactivated at the age of forty, he backed up Bart one more time, his fourteenth and final season as a player. Then, when Bart retired, Zeke rejoined the team with which he had begun his pro career, the Chicago Bears, and worked as an assistant coach for three seasons.

Naturally, when Bart became head coach of the Packers in 1975, he hired Zeke to coach the quarterbacks. They were a team, on the field and off, both family men, both committed to the work ethic. They lived across the street from each other in De Pere, and their wives, Cherry Starr and Mary Elizabeth Bratkowski, were best friends. Their children went to school together. "Bart is one of the greatest people I've ever met," Zeke said. "Our friendship is so deep, it's like gold. We've never had a fight, never a serious disagreement. Our families took half a dozen vacations together. We spent every Christmas together for twenty years."

In 1982, Brat and Bart broke up, not personally, but professionally.

Zeke received an offer he couldn't turn down, to be offensive coordinator of—of all teams—the Baltimore Colts. The Colts' new head coach, Frank Kush, was new to the National Football League, but not to Zeke. Zeke's son, Steve, played for Kush at Arizona State. He played his father's old position, backup quarterback. Kush needed Zeke's experience and intelligence more than Bart did.

Zeke put in three seasons with Kush, in Baltimore and in Indianapolis, and his job, like Dowler's and Pitts's and Curry's, kept him from attending our reunion. He still had strong ties with Green Bay. His youngest child, Kassie, was a student at the Green Bay branch of the University of Wisconsin. His oldest, Bob, once a wide receiver at Washington State, was the offensive coordinator at Weber State, and Steve, too, was picking up where his father left off. Steve Bratkowski worked with Bart Starr Jr. in the commodities business in Memphis.

Not long after the reunion, after Kush stepped down in Indianapolis, Zeke switched to the New York Jets and began to prepare for his thirtieth season in the National Football League, his sixteenth as a coach. "I'll be using Lombardi's principles," he said, "but I won't quote him too much, I won't say it's from him. A lot of people are intimidated if you talk about him too much."

Fifteen years after he died, Vince Lombardi was still intimidating players. He still moved them, too. "I saw Vince's brother Joe recently," Zeke said, "and I asked him where Coach is buried in New Jersey. I want to go out there and visit his grave."

Donny Chandler played in nine championship games in his twelve years in the National Football League. His first year, with the New York Giants, his team won the championship. His last year, with the Packers, his team won the championship. His final season was his finest season. His final game was his finest game. He quit on top.

Don was a winner, and he associated with winners. Twelve of his teammates—six Giants and six Packers—were elected to the Pro Football Hall of Fame. His first two roommates—Sam Huff and Frank

Gifford of the Giants—were elected to the Hall of Fame. I was his third roommate. Even Chandler couldn't win 'em all.

We were roommates during each of the three years Donny spent in Green Bay. Not coincidentally, we were the champions of the NFL during each of the three years Donny spent in Green Bay. He was our kicker. He was our leading scorer for three straight years.

He was solid, honest, consistent, considerate, a hell of a human being. I respected him. I admired him. I loved him. He liked me, too. He named his youngest child after me. He was the best man at my second wedding. He was my business partner. We were almost as close as Zeke and Bart.

Donny grew up in Tulsa, the son of a maintenance worker for Western Union, and played college football at the University of Florida. He was a running back, good enough to be drafted in the fifth round by the New York Giants, good enough to be named to the College All-Star team. But as a professional, with a bad shoulder, he became primarily a punter and a place-kicker. He was one of the best of both. He led the NFL in punting in 1957, and in scoring six years later. He kicked a fifty-three-yard field goal for the Giants and a ninety-yard punt for the Packers.

At the beginning of his New York career, he lived near Yankee Stadium in the Concourse Plaza Hotel, once the home of Babe Ruth and, later, Joe DiMaggio. Donny inherited his quarters from Frank Crosetti, a shortstop who played with Ruth and DiMaggio. The Giants were giants in the late fifties and early sixties; they owned the city, and even a country boy like Chandler enjoyed it. One evening, in a small night club in Greenwich Village, Donny was dazzled by the voice of an unknown singer just starting her career. Someone told him her name was Barbra Streisand. Another evening, in a saloon near Madison Square Garden, Donny was asked to pose for a photograph with the voluptuous Swedish actress Anita Ekberg. Donny said he would.

Then he was traded to Green Bay, and he found Wisconsin had

different virtues. In his last year in New York, he paid close to $500 a month for a three-room apartment; in his second year in Green Bay, he paid $105 a month for a three-bedroom two-bathroom house. In Green Bay, he found a face more familiar to him than Streisand's, a voice more familiar, too. He found Vince Lombardi. When Donny was a rookie running back in New York, Lombardi coached the Giant running backs and screamed at Donny so often he almost went home to Oklahoma. But in Green Bay, they became buddies. Don was a reminder of New York, and Vince loved New York. Often, at the end of practice, the two would share the sauna and, to Don's amazement, Lombardi would confide in him, tell him his plans, his thoughts.

In 1967, the last year Lombardi coached the Packers, Don kicked nineteen field goals in twenty-six attempts and thirty-nine extra points in thirty-nine attempts during the regular season. Then, in Super Bowl II, against Oakland, he kicked four field goals in four attempts and three extra points in three attempts, for a total of fifteen points, a Super Bowl scoring record that survived for seventeen years. When the editor of *Sport Magazine* announced at the conclusion of the second Super Bowl game that the Most Valuable Player was again Bart Starr, Pat Chandler, Don's loyal wife, threatened to strangle him. The editor, not Bart. Don capped his super year by playing in the Pro Bowl for the first time in his career. Then, at the age of thirty-three, with no more worlds to conquer, and nowhere to go but down, Chandler retired. His timing was perfect. I should have retired, too.

I was with Donny, at his home, when he made the decision. I said goodbye and went off to training camp, to a frustrating and losing season, and both of us damn near cried. "It bothered me so much," Donny said, "I took off for Idaho and went fishing. When the Packers played the College All-Stars, I deliberately was nowhere near a radio or a television set. I didn't want to know what was happening. When you give up something you've done all your life, it's got to bother you. I missed the people, not the games. Certainly not the games. The last few years, I got to the point where I hated the games. You know, you go out there three times, and you've got to perform three times, and if you don't, there's no place to hide."

Chandler never earned more than $27,000 in salary in his football career, but with performance bonuses and championship checks, he came out of the game in solid financial condition. "I didn't have any debts," he said, "and I had my house in Tulsa paid for from the day I moved in, and I had seventy or eighty thousand in the bank."

He turned his assets and his energies to the real-estate market, and for several years, he flourished. He and I invested in a couple of projects together. I even moved to Tulsa for a while, to be close to Don, to work with him. Wink and I got married in a church in Tulsa and took an apartment in one of the buildings Don and I and our partner owned. I had my usual dreams of wealth and glory, but Don was more conservative, more cautious, more sensible. He decided to pull back. He had money in the bank, and gas in the tank, and, besides, the rising mortgage rates kind of scared him. Something else scared him, too. His brother, who was twenty-one months older than Donny, suffered a heart attack on the golf course and died at the age of forty-one. "He had four kids and he'd worked hard all his life," Don said, "and he had nothing to show for it. I'd been working ten hours a day, seven days a week, and I decided life is too short. Why not enjoy it?"

Donny retired a few years later. He was comfortable. He still owned property, still had investments, still had income. He even got involved in a pizza place his older son was going to manage in Lakeland, Florida—Mazzio's Pizza. Donny just wasn't going to work hard on anything except getting his golf scores down. He didn't have any desire to go to football games, but he didn't mind settling in front of the television set Sunday afternoons and Monday nights and watching the games. "Pat gets all over me for that," he said. Donny tried to persuade me to slow down, too, but he knew I wouldn't, or couldn't. "I know it's hard not to compete," he said.

He figured he'd won. He'd married the woman he'd been in love with since high school. He'd earned more money than he'd ever dreamed of when he was majoring in education and planning on coaching. He had two sons and two daughters, one grandchild and no misgivings. "I couldn't have written a better script," he said.

I don't see Donny very much anymore, but I think about him often, and I know he thinks about me. He told me he keeps a copy of *Instant Replay* on his desk, and every now and then he'll pick it up and read about when we were young. "I get goose bumps every time," he said.

Donny and Pat and their two boys flew to the reunion in a Cessna 421, comfortably, at a nice leisurely pace. Donny said he felt a little like a man without a team, because the Giants got rid of him and the Packers only had him for three years, but he was looking forward to seeing the guys. He had seen almost no one from the team except me since Super Bowl II, but he tried to keep track, especially of Max. Donny thought a lot of Max. "I always thought he had more brains than any three of us put together," Donny said.

The thing that struck Donny at the reunion was the way everyone had been altered, physically. "Some weigh more, some weigh less and some weigh the same," Donny said. "But, outside of Herbie, nobody's got his old physique."

Doug Hart never heard of the Green Bay Packers when he was growing up. He barely heard of professional football. The only thing he knew was that Detroit had a team called the Lions, and the Lions had a big end named Leon Hart. He also heard that the Lions had a good quarterback, but he didn't know the quarterback's name. He knew it wasn't an easy name for him to remember, like Hart. He didn't have the slightest idea that the quarterback, whose name was Bobby Layne, grew up only a few miles from his own hometown of Handley, Texas, just outside Fort Worth.

Handley High wasn't very big, an AA school, only ninety-eight students in Doug's graduating class, and even though he played football, baseball and tennis and ran track, nobody outside Handley was very impressed. Except the football coach who offered Doug a scholarship to play running back and safety at Midwestern State University in Wichita Falls, Texas. But just before Doug graduated from Handley High, Midwestern State gave up football. The coach had no choice. He had to withdraw the scholarship offer. Doug, whose father was a plumber, had no choice, either. He went to work laying carpets. At night, he went to classes at a nearby college, Texas-Arlington.

After one semester of carpets and night classes, Doug got another invitation to play college football. Not from a big four-year school like Midwestern State. From Navarro Junior College in Corsicana, Texas. Doug liked the idea of going to Navarro because its football team wore plastic helmets that looked just like Notre Dame's. The football team at Handley High wore old leather helmets and envied teams that had plastic helmets. Doug enrolled at Navarro for the spring semester in 1958. But he wasn't comfortable in Corsicana, and before he ever got to wear a plastic Navarro helmet in combat, he dropped out. He went back to laying carpets and going to night classes at Texas-Arlington, studying to be an engineer.

In the spring of 1959, walking across the Arlington campus one night, Doug bumped into one of his high school football teammates. "Why don't you try out for the football team here?" the former teammate said. "They'll let anybody try out."

Doug spent three weeks at spring practice and impressed the coaches enough to be invited back to a final tryout in the fall. After the final tryout, Texas-Arlington offered Doug a football scholarship. "They gave me books, fees and tuition," Doug said, "and I became a college jock." He also became, at the age of twenty, a fulltime college freshman. He started five games as a freshman and every game for the next three years. He was a running back and a defensive back. He broke tackles and he made them. He didn't weigh 180 pounds, and he didn't attract enough attention to be drafted by any NFL team. Still, professional football knew more about him than he knew about professional football. Three teams tried to sign him as a free agent, the Dallas Texans of the young American Football League, and the Pittsburgh Steelers and St. Louis Cardinals of the National. Doug signed with St. Louis. "I thought Pittsburgh still wore leather helmets," he explained.

The Cardinals cut him after two weeks. "I went home and figured it was all over," Doug said. "That was it. Professional football was a far reach for me anyway."

Doug decided he would attend law school. First, he took a job with Bell Helicopter. Three days after he started work, he got a phone call from Pat Peppler, our personnel director, who invited Doug to try out for the Packers. We were looking for a defensive back. "I don't want to quit my job just to get cut again," Doug said. Peppler consulted with Lombardi, who suggested a three-day tryout in Dallas right before we played an exhibition game against the Cowboys. Doug agreed.

He showed up at our workouts and began trying to cover Max McGee and Boyd Dowler. He watched the way Willie Wood did it, and he tried to do it the same way. He found out Willie Wood was once, like him, a free agent. To Doug's surprise, he was able to stay close to McGee and Dowler. To Doug's amazement, the Packers offered him a job. He spent the 1963 season on the taxi squad, watching Willie Wood make All-Pro, learning the game. He spent the next eight seasons as an active player. He quickly became a regular in our poker game and on my hunting trips. Doug and I hunted bear together with bow-and-arrow. We took our wives hunting, too, with stronger weapons and weaker targets. Doug's nickname was Li'l Brother, and I often felt as if he were my little brother. He was a lot like me in many ways, only smaller.

Doug played, in his early years, at 182 pounds, even though he was one of the biggest eaters on the team. In training camp, while almost everyone else had to take tiny portions to lose weight, Doug would fill his tray with meat, bread, potatoes, dessert, milk, everything. If he ate a truly enormous meal, he would balloon up to 182½. If I looked at food, I gained weight. I hated Doug when I was hungry.

Halfway through the 1964 season, when he was a twenty-five-year-old rookie, Doug broke into our starting lineup. He was a starter for the rest of his career except, ironically, in the two Super Bowl years, when he played behind Tom Brown. While he polished his football skills, he began building the base of a successful business career.

"When you played for the Packers," Doug recalled at our reunion, "you were a part of something special. People's expectations of you were very high. And your own expectations rose. I expected much more of myself after I became a Packer."

In his last few years as a player, Doug became the host of a television show called *Packerama*. Doug said he was more intelligent, handsome and wealthy than the previous host. I should have known better than to recommend Doug to succeed me.

Doug also entered the snowmobile business toward the end of his playing days. In the early 1970s, Doug and the industry thrived. He became the president of Arctic Enterprises. But in the late 1970s, Doug and the industry suffered. Between fuel shortages and snow shortages, people felt they didn't need snowmobiles anymore. In 1979, Doug switched to Satellite Industries Incorporated, the world's largest supplier of portable restrooms. Doug figured that no matter what, people would always need toilets. His father, the plumber, probably had the same idea.

Doug became president and chief operating officer of Satellite Industries, and between 1979 and 1984, the size of the company doubled, and its operations expanded into seventeen countries. Doug kept score carefully. "I still feel like I'm on a grading system," he said. "I keep remembering Lombardi saying, 'In the final analysis, we're all judged by our performance. How do you want to be judged?'"

Satellite Industries was based in Minneapolis. So was Doug, with his wife, Marilyn, and their three children. The oldest, Tracy, entered the University of Minnesota shortly before our reunion. Their son, Doug Jr., played soccer and ran track in high school and, more important, was a computer whiz. Their youngest, Kelly, was approaching her teens. "I've lived about two-thirds of my life now," Doug said, "and the most important thing to me is for the kids to be educated and to have good principles to lead their lives by."

Doug, family-oriented, continued to think of the Packers as family. He always wore his Super Bowl II ring and he enjoyed the conversations the ring initiated. "I'm still a Packer," he said. "I'm still a member of the championship team."

When he and Marilyn arrived at the reunion, Fuzzy hugged him so hard he broke his glasses. Doug and Marilyn took the opportunity to visit their roots, their old home in Green Bay, the house they lived in when two of their three children were born. "The people who bought the house from us were still living in it," Doug said. "They gave us a quick tour. It hadn't changed that much. The trees were taller, and the grass was still high. I never did mow the lawn much when I was there."

A few months later, Doug joined us for the mini-reunion at Tommy Joe's place in Texas. Doug came in style. When we went hunting, he looked like a model for L. L. Bean. He had a beautiful gun, a side-by-side with silver inlays between the barrel and the stock. He wore a proper shooting coat and smoked a proper pipe. He was properly outfitted, and I could tell it was important to him that he look just right. I understood. I'm the same way. I have to play the role. I have to have matched clubs and matched club covers in a coordinated golf bag. I knew that if we went fishing, Doug would have a beautiful bamboo fly rod and a handsome fly case. It made me feel good seeing him look so good, so prosperous. He had time to play and time to work and time for his family. He was good people. He was living the kind of life style I always envisioned and never quite caught up to. Or slowed down for.

Doug could still eat. We went to a Mexican restaurant in Edinburg, Texas, for dinner one night. There was nothing fancy about the place except the tank of huge live lobsters that had just been flown in from Maine. We each had a big order of shrimp Mexican style, and then a four- or five-pound lobster apiece, and Doug, who was still pretty trim, was sitting next to Kos, who was almost twice his size, and, just like in training camp, Doug was outeating Kos and me. The only difference was that this time Kos and I tried to keep up.

We laughed and drank white wine and played poker and ended up in a dangerous Texas saloon. It was dangerous because of the barber chair. They didn't cut your hair. They scalped you. They put you in the barber chair and leaned it all the way back, and then the bartender stuck two funnels in your mouth, one in each corner, and poured booze into both funnels, maybe tequila in one and grain alcohol in the other, and as the mixture hit your tongue, the bartender released the chair and it sprang forward, and you gulped and swallowed hard and quick. One young woman must have repeated the ritual ten times in an hour. None of us tough old football players could stay close to her. "We'll be doing all this again in twenty-five years," Doug said. "Well, we'll be trying, anyway."

I looked at Doug and Kos and Tommy Joe and Lee Roy and I thought of all the good things that had happened to them and to me since we were brought together on a football team in Green Bay, Wisconsin. "Pro football was the greatest thing that ever happened to me," Doug said. "I'd drop everything to do it again, to play just one more season."

I think I was always prejudiced against Steve Wright because Bear Bryant, whom I admired, always had harsh things to say about Steve. Bear Bryant didn't like Steve Wright at all. Steve wasn't exactly in love with him, either.

Steve said Bear didn't know what to do with him at Alabama because Bear had never coached anyone like him. "I was the first big player he ever had," Steve said. "I was six-six, 280, when I got out of high school. Most of his players were 180, 190, 200. They were scrawny." They were hungry, too. Steve wasn't.

Steve's family was upper middle class. His parents both went to Purdue. His father was an engineer for DuPont for thirty years. More than seventy colleges tried to recruit Steve, and he probably would have gone to a Big Ten school except that scholarships in the Big Ten were based on need, and Steve's father earned too much money for him to receive a full scholarship. He chose Alabama because his high school coaches in Louisville had played for Bryant at the University of Kentucky.

"Alabama was like a Marine boot camp," Steve said. "They tore you down and then tried to build you back up in Bryant's image. An assistant coach punched me when I was a sophomore. I followed Newton's third law. You know, for every action, there's a reaction. I punched him back. You weren't supposed to do that. I never did play first string at Alabama. I was kicked off scholarship three times. They tried to run me off. I could have dropped out and gone elsewhere, but I figured if I can put up with this, I can put up with anything in life."

Steve stayed, majored in sociology and minored in English, and in his senior year, mostly because several pro teams expressed interest in him, he was promoted to the second string. We drafted him in the fifth round in 1964. The New York Jets drafted him, too, in the AFL, and offered him more money than we did. But he wanted to play in Green Bay. "It was the only way to go," Steve said.

He came to training camp as a defensive end, was converted to offensive tackle and spent four seasons with us, three of them championship years, backing up Forrest and Ski. "Coach Lombardi was exactly what everyone said he was," Steve said. "He knew I had potential. He gave me time to learn. He taught me. I was never taught football at Alabama."

Steve learned what to do and, even slimmed down to 250, had the physical equipment to do it. But I never felt he had the intensity, the burn that most of us had. Steve was just happy to be in Green Bay. "I was just happy to be there," Steve agreed. "There were so many intelligent individuals on that team. I never saw that anywhere but Green Bay. And they all got along. Everywhere else, they were fractioned and cliquish."

Steve played almost everywhere else. He played pro football for more than a decade. He went from Green Bay to the New York Giants to the Washington Redskins to the Chicago Bears to the St. Louis Cardinals to the World Football League.

Then he settled in Maitland, Florida, with his second wife, Sandy, and began selling veterinary pharmaceuticals. He had been selling them ever since, often on the road. "Lombardi time is ingrained in my mind," he said. "If I have an appointment, I will be there fifteen minutes early."

Steve hadn't changed much. He was still just happy to be there. "I'm living where I want to live," he said, "and doing what I want to do. I'm never going to get rich, but I'm happy."

He was unhappy for a while, when he stopped smoking and gained thirty-five pounds. "I felt fat and sloppy," he said. "That's the second-worst feeling in the world. The worst is cold and wet." He started smoking again and, two years later, when he came to the reunion, he was down to playing weight, 250 pounds.

He brought Sandy to the reunion, to meet the players she had heard Steve talk about for ten years. "I told her about Starr and Hornung and Nitschke," Steve said. "There were heroes in football in those days. There are no more heroes. Just millionaires."

Steve enjoyed the reunion, rubbing elbows with the heroes, and the millionaires.

16. New Faces of 1966

Donny Anderson, Bob Brown, Jim Grabowski, Dave Hathcock, Phil Vandersea and Jim Weatherwax

We had two kinds of rookies on the team that won the first Super Bowl game, those with impeccable credentials and those with none. Thanks to trades and wise planning, we had three first-round selections, including Gale Gillingham. Our other two blue-chippers, Donny Anderson of Texas Tech and Jim Grabowski of Illinois, were both All-American running backs. Anderson was the back of the year in the Southwest Conference, Grabowski broke Red Grange's rushing records at Illinois and, because Green Bay had to bid against the American Football League for their services, both received handsome bonuses and contracts that made them, in their first season, the two highest-paid players in the history of the Packers. They represented, between them, a million-dollar package.

None of our other four rookies was selected in the first ten rounds of the draft. They came from Arkansas AM&N, Los Angeles State, the

University of Massachusetts and Memphis State, not exactly tradi-
tional football powers. One of them was twenty-six years old, one had
played less than a full season of college football, one had survived three
colleges and a split kneecap and one played nine different positions
during his NFL career. None of these four was overpaid. Remarkably,
six of our seven rookies lasted for at least four seasons in Green Bay.

We forgave Donny Anderson for being rich. We teased him, of
course, but we didn't really abuse him. We knew it wasn't his fault. He
was just born at the right time to meet the dawn of the dollar explosion
in pro football. He grew up near Lubbock, Texas, on a spread that was
half ranch and half farm. His father raised cattle and crops and him.
When Donny was twelve years old, his father told him he wasn't going
to use a whip on him anymore. "He said the next time he hit me, it
would be with his fist," Donny recalled. "He was a tough old cowboy."

Donny was a tough young football player, a legend in college. He
led Texas Tech in scoring, rushing, pass receiving and punting, among
other things, and earned a nickname that had to pump up his market
value—"The Golden Palomino."

He struck gold when Green Bay and Houston of the AFL each said
it would match any offer the other made. Donny played one side
against the other, raising the ante, until, he said, "Hell, at the end, I
just couldn't think of anything else to ask for." The Packers' winning
bid came to a little more than $600,000, including bonus and salary
for three years. "To be honest," Donny said, "I wasn't worth it. Not at
the time."

To earn his pay, to live up to expectations, all Donny had to do was
make the Packer fans of Wisconsin forget Paul Hornung. He tried. He
had a decent rookie season with a couple of spectacular moments. He
also tried to make the women of Wisconsin forget Paul Hornung.
He had a decent rookie season off the field, too, with a couple of
spectacular moments. After all, Donny was a good-looking kid, young
and single, with money in his pockets. I liked him anyway. He wasn't

cocky. He had a good attitude. He fit in right away. His fellow Texan, Max McGee, showed Donny how to get around Green Bay.

"One of the first times I went out with Max," Donny said, "he told me, 'Now, remember, if I get to dancing, you make sure and tell me to go home 'cause I'll be drunk. I don't ever dance unless I'm drunk.' Max got to dancing a lot that night, and the next morning, in the locker room, he came up to me and said, 'You got my car?' I said, 'No,' and he said, 'Boy, I thought I gave it to you.' And he just shrugged and ran off to practice. Max never worried too much about anything."

Donny never quite lived up to his enormous potential. He was talented and versatile—he ran, caught passes, punted and returned punts and kickoffs—but he never became a superstar, never became a Hornung. Maybe he didn't have Paul's gifts. Maybe he didn't have Paul's blocking. He never gained a thousand yards rushing in a season, never made All-Pro. He did get to play in the Pro Bowl—once. He spent six years in Green Bay, then three in St. Louis, and most of the time he played on losing teams. Yet, because of his first two seasons, his two Super Bowl years under Lombardi, Donny said, "I always felt like a winner."

In the two seasons he played under Lombardi, Donny developed a system to anticipate Vince's actions and reactions. "All you had to do was figure out the norm," Donny decided, "and Vince would do the opposite. That's the way I've tried to be. I've told a lot of people that if I were on the highway of life, and ninety-five percent of the people were driving south, I'd want to be on the other side, driving north."

Donny drove himself hard to succeed after his football days. "I didn't want somebody to look over my shoulder," he said, "and say, 'Well, Donny Anderson sure had a good chance, and he blew it, didn't he?'" Donny didn't blow it. He started Donny Anderson Insurance Associates and Donny Anderson Investments, a real-estate firm, and by blending the mental toughness he got from his father and Lombardi with the financial counsel he got from his CPA brother, Donny came up a big winner.

He settled very comfortably in Dallas with his wife, Karen, who modeled for Neiman-Marcus, and their two children. When the older child, the boy, was eleven, shortly before our reunion, he played on a soccer team that reached the state finals. Donny put so much emphasis on winning that some of the other players' parents complained at a team meeting that he had tunnel vision. Donny was surprised. He expected the other parents to be tougher mentally.

Donny himself was still tough, still an athlete. At the reunion in Green Bay, a sturdy forty-one, Donny was probably the best golfer. Later, at the smaller get-together at Tommy Joe's place, Donny skipped the poker and the hunting and concentrated on racquetball. He played at the McAllen Athletic Club against Lee Roy Caffey, his best friend in the world. "If I were down and out," Donny said, "and I could only make one phone call, I'd go for Lee Roy."

On the racquetball court, Donny went for Lee Roy's blood. They banged into each other, swore at each other, tried to destroy each other. "And when it was over," Donny said, "we were friends again. That's what love is."

The odds were always against Bob Brown. He was one of twelve children of a Louisiana sharecropper. Only one of the twelve went to college. The odds were eleven-to-one, and Bob was the one. He went to Arkansas AM&N on a football scholarship.

When he showed up at the Green Bay training camp in the summer of 1966, he had already tried out twice for the San Francisco 49ers and had been cut twice. He had been playing minor-league football for the Wheeling Ironmen in West Virginia. He was an old rookie at twenty-six. "I was a hundred-to-one shot," Bob said, "and I made it." Once again, Lombardi saw something, saw a spark. "All he wanted was the best ballplayers," Bob said. "He threw the race thing out the window."

Bob was a defensive lineman, a huge one, at least six-foot-six and, sometimes, 275 or 285. There was nothing cute about the way he played. He was just bull strength coming straight ahead with all he had. He wasn't going to go around you. He wasn't going to lull you. He wasn't going to play games with you. He was just going to run the hell over you. I used to try to stick my helmet under his chin, into his chest. I still remember the look in his eyes the first few times we measured each other. He wasn't quitting and I wasn't quitting. We had, again, a basis for a relationship.

We called Bob "Hock" or "The Hocker"—from ham hocks—because of the size of his hands. They were enormous. His feet weren't exactly delicate, either. He wore a size-15 shoe. He made his own shower sandals from a used car tire. He really did.

Bob loved to eat, and even though Lombardi kept telling him to cut down, to lose weight, Bob kept gaining. He was hungry in more ways than one. He knew poverty. He knew deprivation. He burned to play pro football. After one game, Ray Nitschke, who'd been playing alongside him, came up to Bob and said, "I had a tough time all day, Bob. Where were you?"

"I got hurt, Ray," Bob said. "Couldn't move. Think I broke my leg."

"Why didn't you go off?" Nitsch said.

"I was afraid to," said The Hocker. It had taken Bob a few years to move into the starting lineup, and he wasn't going to move out just because he thought he had a broken leg. As it turned out, he did have a broken leg.

The Hocker did not enjoy calisthenics, especially up-downs. Up-downs were one of Lombardi's favorite forms of torture. You ran in place until he yelled, "Down!" and then you dove onto the ground and lay there till he shouted, "Up!" and then you jumped up and ran in place again. You kept doing this till Lombardi got tired. "The Hocker never hit the ground," Donny Anderson said. "Never once. He'd just kind of fall to his knees. Then he'd get up and kind of run in place. Not very fast. He'd always do two exercises to three for everyone else."

Bob seemed to grow a little each year. Once, during the off-season, the Packers sent him and Donny Anderson and Lee Roy Caffey to an air force base in San Antonio to undergo a series of special tests. One test determined body fat. Donny went first. He got strapped onto a scale and lowered into a narrow tank of water and weighed, and after he emerged, he went to Bob Brown and said, "Hock, that tank's pretty tight. I'm afraid you're so big, you'll get stuck when they submerge you, and there's no way for them to pump the water out fast enough to save you. You'll drown. I can see the headlines: 'The Green Bay Packers' Bob Brown Drowns in Test for Body Fat.'" The Hocker elected to skip the test.

He played eight seasons in Green Bay, one in San Diego and two in Cincinnati. He made the Pro Bowl at the age of thirty-two and played his last NFL game at thirty-six. Then he returned to Arkansas, to his wife and their seven children. His wife Shirley taught advanced biology at West Memphis High. Their oldest son, Bob Jr., played football for a while at Memphis State University, then dropped out. He was six-foot-three and 275 pounds. Bob arranged for him to get a tryout with the Packers in 1985. "He wants to play," Hock said, "but I don't know if he's mean enough. You got to be mean out there."

Bob Jr. was nice. "He was such a nice young man," Forrest Gregg said after the tryout. "You could tell he was Bob's son. He sounded like him, and he was overweight. He could be a football player, but first, he has to get his knee 'scoped."

The Hocker had two daughters in college, one at Spelman in Atlanta, the other at Arkansas–Pine Bluff. He had a son playing high school football who, at sixteen, was six-foot-three and 250 pounds and still growing.

Bob didn't make it to the reunion, and nobody knew for sure why. I heard rumors that he wasn't working, that he hadn't worked for a long time, and I heard rumors about his weight. The reports ran from 350 pounds up. Several of the guys were really upset when they heard that Bob didn't make it. They thought The Hocker was going to make them look thin.

I heard Bob was spending most of his time in Arkansas just fishing. That didn't sound so bad to me. I decided to go visit him.

West Memphis looked like a hard place to live. The people looked hard. The buildings looked hard.

I went to West Memphis with visions of a man who was saying the hell with the world, who had decided of his own free will not to struggle, not to make the fight. I thought it might be a way for me to go. Quit beating my head. Quit pushing. Quit shoving. Just sit by the river and fish and live off the fat of the land. I ought to learn not to have preconceived notions. It didn't look like there was any fat of the land to live off of.

Bob came and met me in a beat-up pickup truck. He was immense. "Hocker," I said, "you look like a house." He laughed, good-naturedly, and I said, "Make that an apartment house. What do you weigh? You know?"

"Not exactly, Jerry," he said.

"If you had to bet, what would you say?"

"If I had to bet? I'd say about 385. I can tell by the way my clothes feel on me. I weighed 350 last year. Clothes felt better then."

"What size jacket you wear?"

"Jacket?" Hocker said. "About a sixty."

We went fishing, for crappies and brim, at Lake Midway in Arkansas. We picked up bait and beer, and we went out in a fourteen-foot metal boat. The most exciting part of the day was when we switched ends. You could feel the boat shake, wiggle and groan.

"How do you support yourself?" I asked Bob.

"That's a good question, Jerry," he said. "I do a lot of gambling. Horses sometimes. And we got a dog track here. I'm a professional dog player. I'm pretty good friends with a lot of dog owners. They tell me things."

"Damn, Bob, you're fishing, you're gambling, you're doing all the things I'd like to be doing."

He shook his head. "Tell you, Jerry," Bob said, "I'd cherish a decent job. I don't want to do this the rest of my life. It's got to catch up with you one day. I think a job is more secure."

The Hocker talked the way he played football. No guile. No subterfuge. Just open. Straight ahead. "I'm not well off or nothing," he said, "but I'm happy. I'm not on drugs. I never spent a day in jail in my life. My mind is at rest, and I don't look hungry, do I?"

We fished for several hours, and Bob made me feel good. His life wasn't the way I'd pictured it. He wasn't rebelling. He was surviving. But there was something fundamentally decent about him. "I'm not religious," he said, "but I believe in a Supreme Being. This is a beautiful place. I had a principal in elementary school, she told me the United States was wide open. 'You can be whatever you want to be,' she said, 'but whatever you choose, if you want to be a garbage man, you be the best you can be.' I always remembered that."

On the way back to West Memphis, we stopped for a beer, and when we sat down at the bar, Bob pulled out a hundred-dollar bill with a flourish. He said he was buying. "Robert can pay his way," he said.

He wasn't wearing either of his Super Bowl rings, but he said he liked to wear the big one once in a while. "People down here don't know what it is," he said. "I've had people tell me it's a Mason ring." Bob shrugged. "You see, Jerry, all our names will be in Canton, in that Hall of Fame they have there, for winning the first Super Bowl, but there are more important things in your life. Like providing for your family. Raising your kids. You know what I do? I try to live within my means and always treat everybody decent."

"Want that on your tombstone?" I asked.

Bob laughed. "Never gave it a thought," he said. "Wasn't planning on leaving yet."

Bob drove me back to the rented car I'd parked in West Memphis. He smiled, took my gnarled old claw in his big paw and said goodbye. As I walked to my car, he called out, "I love ya, Jerry. I love ya."

I didn't know whether to laugh or cry. I was used to hearing that from my wife and kids. I never could get used to heavy old guys telling me they loved me.

Jim Grabowski always ate well. His father was a butcher on the northwest side of Chicago. Grabo went to Taft High School and, even though he was only sixteen when he started his senior season, he was the player of the year in Chicago. He chose Illinois from dozens of schools and broke Red Grange's records for yards gained rushing in a game and in a career. He was the outstanding player in the Rose Bowl and he finished third in the balloting for the Heisman Trophy. He majored in business administration and made the academic All-American team. The Miami Dolphins of the AFL wanted Grabowski just as much as the Green Bay Packers did.

The Packers sent a small private plane to Chicago to pick up Grabo and his lawyer and fly them to Green Bay to meet Lombardi. Grabo was twenty-one years old. He had never flown in a private plane. He had never met Lombardi. "No matter what he says, no matter what he offers, no matter what he promises, no matter how charming he is or how persuasive," Jim's attorney advised him, "tell him you have to have twenty-four hours to think about it. Twenty-four hours. Okay?"

Grabo agreed. Then he met Lombardi. He met Lombardi on Lombardi's turf, in a Packer meeting room, surrounded by pictures of Hornung and Taylor and Starr, surrounded by trophies and plaques. The Packers were about to play the Baltimore Colts for the 1965 Western Conference title. Lombardi sat down with Grabo and the attorney and outlined his offer, roughly $400,000 for three years, including a signing bonus. "What do you think?" Lombardi said.

"I'll take it," said Grabowski.

His attorney almost cried. "I broke every rule of smart negotiating," said Grabo, who had earned $1,000 working the whole previous summer, "and I never regretted it. The guys in Green Bay were so good. They accepted Donny and me so readily. I was the antithesis of Donny. He was dating Playmates, and I was about to get married. We were roommates." Grabo splurged on a new car, a Riviera, and put the rest of his bonus in the bank. In training camp, he had to sing like all the rookies. He stood up and sang "Do-Re-Mi," from *The Sound of Music*.

Grabo had a modest rookie season, concentrating on special teams, then got off to a great start in 1967. Halfway through the season, he had more than four hundred yards rushing, including a pair of hundred-yard games, one against his hometown team, the Chicago Bears. He was, by far, our leading rusher. Then, against Baltimore, Grabo got hit hard by a cornerback named Bob Boyd, and his right knee snapped. He could hear it go. He missed most of the rest of the season. He underwent surgery. He was never the same football player again. He had a good attitude, a great heart and a terrible knee.

He lasted five years in Green Bay, then completed his career at home, in Chicago, with the Bears. He was a nice kid, earnest, intelligent, a pleasure to be around. So was his wife Kathy. I was glad to see both of them at the reunion. Grabo had been working for ten years for a company called Motivation Merchandise in Chicago, selling items for incentive programs, everything from sweaters to television sets to Tony the Tiger dolls. "You try to increase the sale of products by offering other products as premiums," Grabo said. "It appeals to the greed factor."

Grabo had no complaints with life, only with his knees. "They're really screwed up," he said, the familiar running back's lament. Jim was the youngest guy at the reunion. He had turned forty only a few weeks earlier. "It's good to be the kid again," he said.

Dave Hathcock was a one-man track team at Memphis State University. He ran the hundred in 9.7 seconds, set school records in the high hurdles, the low hurdles and the long jump. A sturdy six-footer, Hathcock also threw the discus and put the shot and thought seriously of trying to train for the decathlon in the 1968 Olympics. He did not think seriously, or even casually, of football until his final year at Memphis State. His eligibility in track and field was used up, and neither Dave nor his father, a welder, could afford the tuition. So he asked the football coach for a scholarship—and he got it.

Dave didn't play even one full college season because his body got so banged up, adjusting from track and field to football. "I was hurting most of the year," he said, "but when I played, I did make a lot of tackles." He still had no thoughts of playing pro football. He was going to teach school and coach—until Green Bay drafted him in the seventeenth round in 1966 and told him that if he made the team, he'd receive a starting salary of $12,000 a year. "I didn't have the slightest idea how the Packers knew about me," Dave said, "but I knew that $12,000 was about three times what a teacher started at in Tennessee in those days."

He came to training camp and, despite his inexperience, won a job as our sixth defensive back, a cornerback, behind Herb Adderley and Bob Jeter. Dave didn't get to play much, except on special teams. In Super Bowl I, Hathcock, like Red Mack, made two tackles on kickoffs, one of them inside the twenty-yard line. But when he was covering a punt only two minutes from the end of the game, somebody hit Dave just right— "a little bitty guy," he said—and he felt a sudden burning sensation in his right knee. He had cartilage damage. He never played another down for the Green Bay Packers, never said a word about the injury. He was too happy with his Super Bowl share, which was $3,000 more than his salary for the season.

The following year, Dave was traded to the New York Giants during the training season, and the knee flared up midway through the regular season. He went on the injured reserve list. He needed knee surgery. His brief NFL career was over.

With his wife Cheryl, Dave went back to Tennessee and began teaching and coaching and raising a family. The Hathcocks had two boys and a girl, only one a teenager at the time of the reunion. Dave and Cheryl would have loved to have come to Green Bay, but, like Tom Brown, Dave never received an invitation. The Packer Alumni couldn't find him. They must not have tried too hard. The Memphis State athletic department knew where Dave Hathcock was, at East High in Nashville, teaching woodworking and industrial arts and coaching football.

At the age of forty-one, Dave had put on a few pounds, roughly fifty above his playing weight of 195. When he wore his Super Bowl I ring to school—he had twice replaced the diamond—the kids he coached asked him if he played defensive tackle or defensive end. They didn't believe he was a cornerback. His body had changed, and so had the times. "You know, till I got to Green Bay," Dave said, "I never played on the same team with a black. It's different now. The team I'm coaching at East High has only one white boy."

Phil Vandersea played fullback, left linebacker, middle linebacker, right linebacker, tight end, defensive end, defensive tackle, offensive tackle and center during his four seasons with the Green Bay Packers. He also played one season for the New Orleans Saints and one for the Montreal Alouettes.

After his playing days, Phil Vandersea put in time as a salesman, a high school science teacher, a college football coach, an assembly-line worker and, for the Massachusetts Department of Corrections, a counselor to adult felons.

Clearly, Phil Vandersea hated to get into a rut.

His one sign of consistency, when he arrived at the reunion, was that he had been married to the same woman, Sandra, for seventeen years. "We went downtown in Green Bay," Phil said, "and we got lost three times. The town was so different. But the players were the same. It was great to be with them again."

Phil Vandersea was another one of those obvious misfits who fit so well into the team that won Super Bowl I. He grew up in Whitinsville, Massachusetts, his father a machinist who worked his way up to foreman in a textile mill. Phil's older brother, Howard, went to Bates College and became head football coach at Bowdoin. Phil, recruited only by local schools, chose the University of Massachusetts and majored in hotel and restaurant management. He played football, but not spectacularly. When Green Bay drafted him in the sixteenth round, he seemed to have a bright future in the hotel or restaurant business.

His rookie year, during training camp, Phil played fullback until Jim Grabowski reported from the College All-Stars. Then Phil became our fifth linebacker. "I was real nervous," he said, "but the veterans went out of their way to be nice. I'll never forget Hornung giving me advice at linebacker. He didn't have to do that. He was a superstar. There were egos on that team, but no individuals. Lombardi controlled the egos."

In 1967, Phil went to New Orleans in the expansion draft, but the following year, he was traded back to Green Bay. "Lombardi liked players who could play more than one position," he said. Lombardi must have loved Phil. In 1968, he played tight end. In 1969, he played defensive end. In 1970, he played defensive tackle until he hurt his ankle and wound up on injured reserve. In 1971, fifteen pounds heavier than he'd been as a rookie, he played offensive tackle and center in training camp. "I kept eating my way closer to the ball," he said.

The Packers released him in the summer of 1971, and after he played one final season for Montreal in the Canadian League, Phil began switching jobs almost as often as he had switched positions. He did remain assistant football coach at Holy Cross for four years, from 1975 through 1978. Then he left football to his brother at Bowdoin, and to his son Scott, who became an offensive tackle and a linebacker on his high school team.

Phil did not wear his Super Bowl I ring to the reunion. "I don't like jewelry," he explained. "I keep it in a safe deposit box. But I do like talking about it." In his latest job with the Department of Corrections, working with inmates at a release center, preparing them for parole, Phil often talked football. The felons were impressed by a former Packer. At the reunion, Phil was impressed by his former teammates. "I think I'm the only one who isn't a millionaire," he said.

If Bob Brown was easily the Packer who had gained the most weight since his playing days, Jim Weatherwax was the one who had lost the most. Wax had played at 260 and higher, but when he showed up at the reunion, he weighed 225 or less. He lost the weight because he had to. His football knees couldn't carry too many pounds. Even at 225, he limped. "My knees are terrible," he said. "But I can live with them most of the time. It's just if I put in a fifteen- or twenty-hour day, they'll cry, they'll hurt."

Once, Wax was a young redwood from Redlands, California, six-foot-four when he was fifteen years old, six-foot-six-and-a-half when he was a high school senior. He was big and strong and agile. He could high jump six-foot-one. The University of Southern California recruited him, but he passed up USC for San Bernardino Junior College. "I was just seventeen," Wax explained. "I was an only child. I'd never been away from home. I wasn't very mature."

In his second year at San Bernardino, close to his Redlands home, Wax suffered a split left kneecap and dropped out of school to recuperate. West Texas State persuaded him to recuperate on its campus. But Wax wasn't happy in Texas, and after one semester, he transferred to Los Angeles State, which, in the middle 1960s, had a strong football program. Los Angeles State won the national small-college championship in 1964, Wax's first season, and lost only one game the following year. Wax was captain of the 1965 football team and, at six-foot-seven, a letterman on the basketball team, and both San Diego of the AFL and Green Bay drafted him. The Packers picked him in the eleventh round. He picked the Packers because of Lombardi. "Nothing against Sid Gillman of the Chargers—he was a great coach, too—but I wanted the chance to play for Lombardi," Wax said.

He met Lombardi for the first time in San Francisco in 1965 just before we played the 49ers. "I was scared to death," Wax remembered. "I tried to be a perfect gentleman. He was very polite. I weighed 275 pounds. He told me to lose a few. I reported at 260."

As a rookie, playing defensive tackle, Wax reminded me of Merlin Olsen. He had most of Merlin's strength and many of Merlin's moves, and he was even bigger than Merlin. I thought he was going to be a super player till his knees went to hell on him.

Jim had his best season in 1967. He replaced Lionel Aldridge at defensive end when Lionel broke his leg. But in 1968, Wax tore up his right knee, and surgery cost him part of that season and part of the next. In 1970, he was traded to the St. Louis Cardinals—Dan Devine, the new coach of the Packers, didn't seem to want too many reminders of Lombardi around—but his knee wouldn't pass the Cardinals' preseason physical. St. Louis shipped him back. Wax packed up and went home to California with bad knees and bright memories.

"I was originally going to get married on December 16, 1966," Wax said. "Then, because of the NFL championship game, we postponed it till January. Then, because of the Super Bowl, we postponed it till February. I got married on February 3, 1967. Paul Hornung and Willie Wood got married the same day."

Wax and his wife Jo Ann made their home in Dana Point, an hour's drive south of Los Angeles. They had two sons, and the older one, a good athlete, preferred volleyball, the big game locally, to football. Wax managed a restaurant, Marie Callender's, in nearby El Toro.

A few months before the reunion, Wax and his wife took a trip to the Midwest, and in their honor, Ron Kostelnik threw the first annual Roast Jim Weatherwax Party. Kos roasted a pig and invited the Skoronskis and Olive Jordan, Henry's widow, and her new husband to his place, and everyone feasted on the past and the present. Wax had such a good time he said he couldn't wait to come to the reunion. He and Jo Ann flew in from Phoenix with Bart and Cherry Starr, and Bart and Wax sat together and talked about the salaries and the steroids of football in the 1980s. "In 1966," Jim Weatherwax said, "it was still a game."

17. The Cheers Once More

The overweight sucked in their stomachs. The balding patted down stray strands. The aching flexed scarred knees. We wore green-and-gold jerseys with the familiar numbers of our youth, and as we stood in the twilight of the tunnel that led from the Packer locker room to the natural turf of Lambeau Field, we experienced the butterflies and the chills and the adrenaline rush that once signaled the start of every Sunday afternoon in the fall. We waited. We waited to hear the cheers of the crowd once more.

The stadium filled up, more than fifty-four thousand fans, drawn from every corner of Wisconsin. They came, basically, to see the 1984 Green Bay Packers play the 1984 San Diego Chargers, but they remembered us. Even the ones who weren't born when we won the first Super Bowl game still, strangely, remembered us.

Suzanne Jordan, who was three when her father played in Super

Bowl I, came to Lambeau Field to celebrate her twenty-first birthday. She was in her seat, waiting for her mother, when the voice on the public address system called not for the customary moment of silence, but for a cheer that Henry Jordan and Vince Lombardi would be able to hear wherever they were. Suzanne's mother, Olive, entering the stadium, heard the crowd's thunderous response and wondered what inspired it.

They were all in the stands, the widow, old wives, new wives, children grown and small, the girl friends of Tommy Joe Crutcher and Marv Fleming. I wished my wife were there. But she wouldn't go to Green Bay. Or she couldn't. Green Bay represented my life before our life. Even after almost two decades, Wink was wary. She stayed home, minding the nest. My older children sat in the stands.

We moved toward the mouth of the tunnel and blinked in the sudden light. Then the introductions began, each one setting off varying levels of cheers and whistles and applause. Max McGee, #85, pranced to the center of the field, head high, a thoroughbred going to the starting gate. Willie Davis, #87, lumbered, Dr. Feelgood, smiling so broadly more than fifty-four thousand people felt good. Herb Adderley, #26, sprinted out of the shadows, flying, got halfway to the fifty-yard line, spun around and back-pedaled the rest of the way, as if he were hounding a receiver once again.

Old #64 chose moderation, a gentle jog, halfway between Herbie's pace and Willie's, fast enough to prove I was alive, slow enough so that I could savor the cheers. They washed over me. They warmed me. I knew I could live without them, but I loved them. I flashed back more than nineteen years, to an exhibition game against the New York Giants, the first exhibition game in 1965. I'd missed most of the previous season, with the bleeding, the colostomy and the horror, and after the premature reports of my demise, I'd come to training camp in 1965 at 220 pounds, weak and wan. "You don't need to play," Coach Lombardi told me. "We'll give you your salary. We'll take care of everything. You don't have to worry."

"That's fine," I said, "but I'm going to play."

"Well, I can't count on you," he said. "I'm going to put you with the defense."

I practiced with the defense. I practiced gingerly. I eased myself into the routine. I skipped up-downs and the nutcracker drill. Donny Chandler, my new roommate, and I took turns doing calisthenics. If the team did forty sit-ups, we did forty between us. At first, he'd do thirty-five and I'd do five. After a couple of weeks, I could do thirty-five. I regained weight. Still, when we met the Giants in the opening exhibition, I didn't expect to play. In the second half, we were beating the Giants badly, and Lombardi turned to me and said, "You want to play?"

"Hell, yes," I said, and when I ran onto the field, when my name echoed over the PA system, the crowd began to cheer, and the cheers swelled to a roar. I'd never heard such a roar. I don't think any offensive lineman had ever heard such a roar. They were cheering me, I think, for being alive. There was some of that in the cheers in 1984, too.

Marv Fleming, #81, strutted to midfield. Willie Wood, #24, and Dave Robinson, #89, labored. Bart Starr, #15, trotted, a perfect pace, of course, measured in perfect strides. Bart and the players he'd coached had been booed on this field in recent years, but now the crowd welcomed him home, paid him back for the pleasure he provided in his playing days, for the pain he endured in his coaching days. The quarterback, as usual, got the loudest cheers of us all.

Fuzzy Thurston, #63, put on the most spectacular show. Arms churning, legs pumping, teeth gritting, he dashed to the center of the field, full speed. The hell with cancer, he said, the hell with age, and the fans Fuzzy loved so much loved him back. I was so happy for him, I clapped and smiled and cried. Suzy Thurston, watching, felt the tears filling her eyes, and turned to Barbara Gregg, next to her, and saw her tears, too. "That nut!" Suzy said, and hoped that Fuzzy wouldn't have a heart attack.

When we were all at the center of the field, waving and giggling and panting, we moved spontaneously into our offensive formation—Ken

Bowman at center, Fuzzy and I at the guards, Bob Skoronski and Steve Wright at the tackles, Marv Fleming at tight end, Max McGee and Carroll Dale the wide receivers, Jimmy Taylor and Donny Anderson the running backs, Bart the quarterback.

"Thirty-six, on two," Bart called, and Bow bent over an imaginary ball, and on Bart's second "Hut," Bow snapped the imaginary ball into Bart's hands, and Bart turned and handed the imaginary ball to Jimmy Taylor, and as I took one step forward and cut off my imaginary opponent, Jimmy drove through the hole between the left tackle and the tight end, between Ski and Marvin, and took a few quick steps, then stopped, angry, probably, because there were no real tacklers to punish. Our timing was good. Our execution was precise. We could still do it—as long as we didn't have to face large young flesh and blood.

A large young Packer, the latest #64, the right guard, Syd Kitson, from Wake Forest, came over to me and shook my hand. My hand disappeared in his. He was six-foot-four and 264 pounds and, at twenty-six, young enough to be my son. Kitson was born the month I played my first NFL game at Lambeau Field.

A large Charger, another guard, Doug Wilkerson, a veteran of fourteen seasons, scanned our ranks, looking for his friend and former San Diego teammate, Lionel Aldridge. Wilkerson was disappointed. He hadn't seen or heard from Lionel in a long time.

When the captains of the Packers and Chargers met at midfield to exchange the usual pregame pleasantries, some of our guys joined them. Ray Nitschke put on his game face. He introduced himself to Charlie Joiner, San Diego's veteran wide receiver, by slapping Joiner across the helmet with a mild forearm, a friendly gesture by Ray's standards. "Ray Nitschke, middle linebacker," he explained, as he swung.

Joiner, understandably, seemed startled. "He didn't like it," Ray said, "but I couldn't help it, I was so pumped up. Once you put on that jersey and step on the field, you're in a different world. It was 1967 again."

Reluctantly, Ray withdrew to the sidelines. Gratefully, the rest of us did, too. We posed for pictures for fans and for each other. We laughed. We kibitzed. And then we watched the game, heard plays called and saw bodies collide, and within us, past and present blurred. The game on the field dissolved into a game in each man's mind, and while some of us recaptured youth, and some regretted age, all of us remembered, and remembered, and remembered. Nitschke blitzed and buried Dan Fouts, the San Diego quarterback. Taylor took a handoff from Lynn Dickey, the Green Bay quarterback, and Skoronski opened a hole for him in San Diego's line. Each of us, at some moment, imagined himself in his prime. "I was in a little bit of a fog," Bart Starr said, and in his fog, it was third and one, his favorite time to go long, to loft a pass beyond the defenders, to drop it in the arms of Carroll Dale, who easily outraced the San Diego secondary and sprinted to a score. It was hard to believe, after all these heroics, that the scoreboard said San Diego 7, Green Bay 0.

Reality was intruding. "I felt uncomfortable," Ron Kostelnik said. "I was depressed by the knowledge that I would never again know the joy, the exhilaration, of hitting a quarterback."

Willie Davis felt another kind of discomfort. "I talked to Forrest," he said, "and there is a difference in commitment. Not a critical difference, but the game doesn't mean quite as much to them. There's not as much *gratitude* —that's the key word. For us, it was a way—the *only* way—to change our lives. I worry about the game being damaged—because I know what the game did for me."

Fuzzy and I stood together on the sidelines, just as we had twenty years earlier. But now we stood on the sidelines while both teams had the ball. Every once in a while, Fuzzy tilted his head and rested it on my shoulder. We were both jealous. We were jealous of Forrest, because he was so directly connected to the action, and we were jealous of the offensive linemen, because they could use their hands, opened, pushing and shoving. It made pass blocking so much easier, which was what it was supposed to do. We had to block with our necks and with our heads. We had to clench our fists and hold them close to our bodies. I wish I could have used my hands against Alex and Merlin. It would have made life so much easier.

Alex Karras prowled the field while the Packers played the Chargers. So did Merlin Olsen. Nobody else saw them, but I did. I saw them digging in, fire in their eyes. Whenever I look at a football field, I see Alex and Merlin. I must have faced them more than a dozen times apiece during our careers, on Sundays and on Thanksgiving Thursdays, always trying to frustrate and embarrass them, always trying to avoid being frustrated and embarrassed. They were my greatest rivals, my favorite enemies, the two most talented and memorable left tackles I ever confronted.

I still confront them—when I sit down to watch television and see them working as actors, see them displaying intelligence and charm and remarkable talent. I'm happy for them. I'm proud of them, almost as proud as I am of my teammates who've become successes. Alex and Merlin and I had a bond, too.

Alex and I once were true antagonists, a relationship that went back to the East-West Shrine Game at the end of our college careers. Alex and Lou Michaels played for the East; Wayne Walker, my Idaho teammate, and I played for the West. Once, Karras and Michaels got shoulder to shoulder facing Wayne, when he was snapping for a punt, and as he snapped, Karras pulled him forward and Michaels kicked him, viciously, in the belly, or a little lower. It was a charity game for crippled children, and Michaels just about crippled Wayne. I took a deep dislike to both Karras and Michaels. Alex and Wayne, ironically, wound up teammates and friends in Detroit. Alex and I wound up friends, too, but the process took a lot longer.

Whenever we played Detroit, whenever I faced Alex, I consciously wanted to hate him, and I did. Part of the hatred was manufactured, part real. It made me more intense, made me tougher. In *Instant Replay*, I referred to Alex, rather unkindly, as "a nearsighted hippopotamus." He took offense. The next time we encountered each other, on the field, he threw a forearm into me and said, "Stick that in your book, you _____," and he called me a lot worse than a hippopotamus.

The following winter, we spoke at the same banquet and jabbed at each other. "Jerry Kramer is one of the greatest linemen in the world," Alex said, "and if you don't believe it, just read his book." And then I got up and said, "Who read the book to you?" At the conclusion of my remarks, I said, "When it's all over, when everything is said and done, Alex is really—a son of a bitch." I thought that was pretty humorous, but nobody laughed, especially Alex.

A couple of years later, Alex and I became teammates—broadcasting Canadian football games. It was, at first, a very uneasy alliance. I was even bitchy on the air, sniping at every observation Alex made. It was hard to turn off the hate I had spent so many years building up.

Then, the day before a game we were going to broadcast, we both happened to show up at a stadium in Canada to watch the two teams practice. We were the only people in the stands. We sat together, warily, and finally Alex said, "You know, Jerry, we used to have some great games." I said, "Yeah, Alex, we did," and we began trading stories. I reminded him of the forearm he hit me with, and he reminded me of all the times I held him—actually, on my honor, I held him only once, and I got away with it—and pretty soon we were giggling, and the war was over. I went down to Detroit and appeared on Alex's television show, and I just enjoyed the hell out of being with him. Now, when I see him on the screen, I light up. I hate to miss his show. "There's Alex! There's Alex!" I'm like a little kid. I still call him a nearsighted hippopotamus, but now I do it with affection.

I always had affection for Merlin. I tried to hate him, but I couldn't. He was too nice, too much the gentleman. We had some brutal confrontations, with fierce intensity, but we were motivated by mutual respect, not by hatred. I always knew Merlin would be a big success, but I never dreamed it would be as an actor. I thought that was for the glamor boys, the quarterbacks and the running backs, the Merediths and the Giffords. Nothing against Don and Frank, but they just can't act as well as those two big old linemen. Which makes me feel good. The thing I love about Alex and Merlin is the range and the sensitivity they bring to their work. Alex, in particular, can make you laugh and can make you cry. That's beautiful. That proves you can be big without being dumb.

(I hate to see athletes doing things on television that make them look stupid. O. J. Simpson did a commercial for a soft drink several years ago, and while he was drinking from the bottle, he had to turn and talk to the camera, and, naturally, the liquid trickled out of the bottle and onto his shirt. It was supposed to be funny, but I didn't even smile. I wanted to scream at O. J., "Don't let them do that to you! Don't let them make you look like a big dumb football player!" O. J.'s too bright for that, too good a guy.)

While I tried to study the 1984 Packers, Bubba Smith joined Alex and Merlin in my mind—another tackle, another actor, another adversary. Bubba and I had only a few confrontations, but I'll never forget the first one, in the College All-Star Game in 1967. "Come See Bubba Smith Hit Bart Starr," the sponsor, the Chicago *Tribune*, advertised before the game, and then, early in the evening, Bubba beat me and got to Bart and trampled him and lay on him and said, "All night long, old man, all night long, Bubba gonna be here on top of you." Bart told me what Bubba said—neither of us was too delighted—and I said, "That son of a bitch! Give me a forty-one trap." I trapped Bubba, and the next play, we brought the center over on him, and then I drove him, and then we brought the tackle down on him, and then I drove him again, and then we trapped him again, and I think I called six or seven plays in a row, for the first and last time in my life. We worked Bubba's ass off, up one side and down the other, worked him over till, finally, he tapped himself on the helmet, signaling for a substitute, and headed for the bench. That's a memory I'll always cherish, Bubba beaten, even if only for a while.

San Diego led, 31–21, in the fourth quarter, and I tried to keep myself in the present, to appreciate the passing duel that was being waged between the Packers and the Chargers. But I kept slipping back to the past. I saw different faces. I saw specific faces. I didn't see specific plays, except, perhaps, for a moment, the block and the touchdown that beat Dallas in the 1967 championship game in the freezing cold. But the memory of that play didn't belong to me. It belonged to everyone. I concentrated on more private memories.

I laughed out loud when one picture popped into my mind, a vision of Ron Kramer, my old teammate, camped in the middle of the field, in the middle of the night, making love. I wasn't a witness, I can't swear it happened, but I heard about Ron's midnight ride, and that's probably the image of Lambeau Field I'll take to the grave with me: Ron Kramer, All-American, with a bottle of beer, a blanket and a friend. I could even imagine Lombardi yelling at them, "You don't do things right once in a while; you do them right all the time." Or: "Fatigue makes cowards of us all." Or: "Dancing is a contact sport. Football is a hitting sport."

I heard the cheers of the crowd, knew they weren't for me, or for Ron Kramer. The cheers were for James Lofton, a great athlete, who caught a touchdown pass to bring the Packers within three points of San Diego, 31–28. Lofton was ten years old when we played in Super Bowl I, and he went to the game. His father bought a pair of general admission tickets, but they ended up sitting on the fifty-yard line. Now James was in his seventh season with the Packers, and he had been in the playoffs only once, and he had never advanced even as far as a conference championship game. He had never seen a Super Bowl game from ground level.

I wanted Green Bay to win. I expected Green Bay to win. I figured any time a bunch of us got together, even if we couldn't play, we should be able to bring them enough luck to win. I was wrong. San Diego won, 34–28. I felt bad for Forrest. His team's record was one-and-five after five straight defeats. The losing streak would stretch to seven games until the team suddenly reversed itself and won seven of its last eight games. "These kids have their own lives to live, their own niche to carve out," Forrest said. "On game day, they're concerned with the game. The reunion didn't have any impact on them winning or losing."

Most of the new Packers agreed. "Having those players here today had no effect on me," said Paul Coffman, the tight end. "I was eight years old when the Packers won that first Super Bowl," said Greg Koch, an offensive tackle. "I lived in Texas. I was a Cowboys fan."

But some of the new players said that if they never heard again of the Packers of the 1960s, it would be too soon. They were tired of tradition. They were tired of us. And they were tired. They were licking their wounds, and we were having a party, a dinner to celebrate an ancient victory.

18. We'll Do It Again

The price we paid for the privilege of coming to-
gether again was a loss of privacy. We were relics on display, and for
too much of the too little time we had in Green Bay, we had to share
each other with well-meaning strangers who were contributing to a
good cause. We needed to be alone, to recapture the sanctuary of the
locker room, the place where we stood naked, stripped of our clothes
and our façades. We needed less time to be heroes, and more to be
human.

But Sunday night, after the game, and Monday night, after a golf
tournament, we attended banquets, and we were scattered about, like
centerpieces, one or two of us to decorate each table. We performed.
We gave familiar answers to familiar questions. We told Lombardi
stories, and Hornung and McGee stories, banquet stories that had
always earned us laughter and appreciation and free meals. The older

wives were saints, tolerating stories and sentiments they had heard so many times. The younger wives felt younger still.

We were surrounded by an appreciative audience of doctors, lawyers and businessmen who recalled our numbers and our nicknames as if they were their own, who took as much pride in our achievements as we did. They were still grateful for the special identity we gave their city. They were the main bidders for the Packer memorabilia that was auctioned off at both banquets to benefit the Boys and Girls Club of Green Bay.

They bid for team photographs and individual portraits, for old jerseys and autographed posters, for signed footballs and scarred cleats, for tangible proof that once a team from Green Bay ruled professional football. Some of us bid, too. They auctioned off a pair of shoes that Coach Lombardi once wore, and to me it smacked of grave-robbing, but Willie Davis wanted the shoes, wanted them badly, a reminder of the man and the game that changed his life, and he went to $250, outbidding Dave Robinson, to get them. Willie would display them in his apartment in Marina del Rey so that almost every day he could walk past them and think of the man who had filled the shoes.

Willie paid another $250 for a pair of portraits, one of himself, in battle gear, the other of Forrest Gregg. He would hang the two portraits in his apartment, facing each other, just as he and Forrest had faced each other on the practice field for ten seasons, had forced each other to be strong and quick and brave and inventive. Willie, in so many ways, had come the farthest of any of us, and yet, in so many ways, he was the one still tied most closely to Lombardi and to the past.

Bart Starr's jersey, #15, went up for sale, and the high bid was $500. Then, when Forrest Gregg's jersey was offered, the Texas crowd, led by Lee Roy and Tommy Joe and Donny Anderson, decided that a Texan's jersey had to bring top dollar. Caffey closed the bidding at $1,200, then donated the jersey back to the Alumni. When it was reoffered, Caffey again put in the winning bid, $500 more.

The auctioneer hawked a photograph of Max McGee in action, in football action, and from the back of the dining room, Max bid briskly for his own picture. He won at $1,000, and when he walked up to collect his prize, he looked at the photo and said, "Hell, I just paid $1,000 for a picture of mc *dropping* a pass." Max was kidding, of course. In the picture, he was making one of his lucky catches.

On Monday, in the mist at the Oneida Golf and Riding Club, where Lombardi so often played, I encountered Max on the putting green, and he suggested that we make a small side bet on the golf tournament, his team's score against mine. I was about to propose $20 when Max said, "Two hundred," and I said, "You're on."

We had 180 players, thirty-six teams, five golfers to a team, one so-called celebrity and four contributors to the Boys and Girls Club of Green Bay. The celebrities included, besides the men who played in Super Bowl I, Phil Bengtson, who succeeded Lombardi as coach of the team; Tony Canadeo, the former running back who was one of the early Packers in the Pro Football Hall of Fame; and Frank Howard, the former major-league home run hitter and manager, who had settled in the Green Bay area. We played only for team score, not for individual, a shotgun format, and first prize was, in addition to a monstrous green-and-gold golf bag you could spot a county away, a trip for the five winners to the NFL Alumni championships in Florida.

Some of the golf swings were grotesque. A few of the guys *admitted* they hadn't played golf in ten years. A few others, looking for an edge, *insisted* they hadn't played golf in ten years. Dave Robinson hit one tee shot straight up in the air and let out a laugh so loud he shook the course. Marv Fleming played out of a tattered old bag that looked as if it went with him through five Super Bowls. Ray Nitschke played for blood.

So did I. I wanted to beat Max. He and Zeke Bratkowski, the pilots, used to whip me and Donny Chandler regularly. I hate to lose. I played my ass off, and when I found out at the end that my team was low team, that we were going to represent the Green Bay chapter in the NFL Alumni championships in Florida, I didn't care. All I cared was that I had beaten Max, that I had taken $200 out of his pants. I didn't even have to worry that he might miss the money.

We stayed up late Monday night. We closed the Oneida Golf and Riding Club and then we closed Shenanigans. I didn't want the reunion to end. I felt so close to everyone. I had gone to my high school reunion in Sandpoint, Idaho, a few months earlier, and it had been a totally different feeling, a mixture of curiosity and surprise and affection, but nothing more. We had grown up. We had grown apart. I didn't recognize one old classmate at all. I would have sworn I'd never seen him before in my life. "Who's that?" I asked, and somebody said, "That's so-and-so. He's with the CIA. He's been in the Middle East the past ten years." And I said, "Well, he's perfect for that job 'cause he's invisible. He always was invisible."

I was sorry Goldilocks and Gilly and The Hocker weren't with us in Green Bay. I could understand Boyd and Elijah and Zeke having to coach, and I hadn't thought much recently about Dave Hathcock and Bill Curry and Tom Brown, but the reunion seemed to be incomplete without Hornung, Gillingham and Bob Brown. Especially Paul. He was our symbol, maybe not of the Super Bowl I team, but of earlier teams. He was our glamor, our excitement, our hero. He belonged with us. I cursed him a little for not being there. He had no right to stay away.

I drank too much. I laughed too loud. I hugged too hard. I knew we weren't just the champions of Super Bowl I. We were champions forever. Why? Why? What was the special mix? I thought of all the guys who used football to escape from the mills and the mines and the tenant farms that shaped their childhoods, all the guys who found in Lombardi the father figure they had never known at home, all the guys who learned to win in Green Bay after too many losing seasons in too many towns. That tough little man who coached us knew something, knew how to look inside people, to see strengths people never knew they had, to draw out those strengths and blend them and refine them. God, I was proud, and happy, and lucky to have been a part of it.

I thought of how lucky all of us were, and how talented, and I thought again of my one regret in life, that I didn't meet Wink earlier, that I didn't avoid the pain I endured and inflicted during my divorce. When I was growing up in Idaho, I thought women like Wink existed only in fantasies, tall and beautiful and strong and bright and exciting. I dreamed of her long before I ever met her. I wished she were at the reunion. Wink and Paul. I wanted them both there to share the moment.

"This is what life is all about," Fuzzy said.

We knew, before we parted, that we would get together again, now that we had tasted the sweet pleasure of a reunion, now that we knew for certain the memories we had nursed through so many years were not false memories, were not tricks of the mind. We really did love each other. We really did learn together. We really did grow together. We still could pick each other up, support each other, inspire each other. Sure, we had our skeletons in our closets, but it wasn't the sham of the play and film *The Championship Season.* It wasn't false camaraderie, altered memories. We hadn't been living a lie.

Were we entitled to Super Bowls for the rest of our lives? Of course not. No one was. But we were entitled to super moments, to memories and feelings no one could ever take from us, and we were entitled—we were *obligated*—to strive for Super Bowls. Deep into the Wisconsin night, as the reunion flickered and died out, Herb Adderley put his arm around me and put his face close to mine and said, "I love you, J. K. I love you. Forever." He paused. "And after."

Postscript: People Need People

The reunion wasn't quite over. Six months later, we found Lionel Aldridge. Ron Kostelnik heard that Lionel was back in Milwaukee, working in the post office. Kos set aside his $18-million-a-year business and drove to Milwaukee and waited around the post office until he spotted Lionel. Then Kos said hello, and Lionel beamed. Kos told me Lionel was back.

A couple of weeks later, I went to see Lionel. I flew to Milwaukee from Lexington, Kentucky. In Lexington, I had dinner with my partner Art Preston and Larry Richardson, the man who managed Bunker Hunt's stable. I left that world of Hunts and Firestones and immense wealth, where horses live like kings, to visit an old friend who hadn't been living like a king. Lionel was living in the YMCA.

I wondered if he'd be glad to see me, or angry, or embarrassed. I wondered if I were an intruder, if I were interfering. The last time I'd seen Lionel, he was a successful television personality. He had energy, family, clothes, a fancy car, all the trappings of success. But now Lionel was in a rough position. I worried about his reaction to me. I wasn't certain I would be comfortable if I were he. And I questioned my own motives. Do I care about the guy? Or about the book I'm writing? Would I go to see him on my own, if I weren't writing a book? I wanted to think I would. I prayed I would.

I missed Lionel at the YMCA. I had a cup of coffee there. The Y was next door to a mission, and as I drank my coffee, I watched the guys coming out of the mission. They were all sizes, all shapes. They were guys down on their luck, draped in old clothes. It made me appreciate my life a little more.

Then I went to the post office, and Lionel's supervisor told me Lionel wouldn't be in for a few hours. We chatted a while. He told me how well Lionel was doing, how much he had improved from the day he arrived, how his eyes were bright and clear and he was starting to smile now and then, to twinkle. The supervisor was pleased with Lionel's work and proud to be associated with him. "He comes in here like a regular Joe," the supervisor said. "He doesn't ask for anything special."

A *regular Joe*. That set me thinking. We were all regular Joes. We worked. We were familiar with work. We came up the hard way. Like regular Joes. And yet, after being a world champion, a Super Bowl champion, it was hard to go back to being a regular Joe. It was hard to think of yourself as a regular Joe. Like Paul, we had all been on scholarship so long. I could understand if Lionel didn't want to visit with me.

He wanted to. He came walking down a hallway, and when he saw me, he broke into a smile. "Hold on," he said, "let me get a cup of coffee and we'll have a visit." He got his, and I got mine, and we sat down, and I was glad to see him. No pity, no sorrow, just *happy* to see him. He said he was doing fine. "I was sick," Lionel said. "I was crazy. I hitchhiked. I had nothing. I slept in the streets." One night, he told me, he went to sleep in the street, and when he woke up in the

235

morning, his ring was gone, his Super Bowl II ring stripped from his finger. "I'd love to get my ring back," he said.

Lionel told me he'd heard about the reunion in Green Bay. "I wasn't ready then," he said. He looked good. A little heavy. Maybe 250, a few pounds above playing weight, redistributed. He had no visible problems, physical or mental. I told him how good it was to see him. I told him that we all worried about him, all cared about him. "I was never down so far I couldn't get back up," he said.

"You need anything?" I said.

"I don't need money," Lionel said. "I need people. I'm lonely. I need friends. I need family." He said he was hoping he might get transferred to California, to be close to his former wife and their children. "People need people," Lionel said.

He was on the clock. I told him I knew he had to get back to work. He walked me to the elevator, told me he hoped he'd see me again soon. He shook my hand and half-hugged me with his left arm. The elevator opened, and I stepped on, and just as the door was about to close, he said, "Love ya."

The door closed. "I love you, too, Lionel," I said.

I hope he heard me.